Test 1 The Writing Skills Test

GED

How to Prepare for the High School Equivalency Examination

TEST 1 The Writing Skills Test

Kathryn Fiddler

Contemporary Books, Inc.
180 North Michigan Avenue, Chicago, Illinois 60601

Published by Contemporary Books, Inc.
180 North Michigan Avenue, Chicago, Illinois 60601
Manufactured in the United States of America

Library of Congress Catalog Card Number: 77-90079
International Standard Book Number: 0–8092–8111–2

Published simultaneously in Canada by
Beaverbooks, Ltd.
150 Lesmill Road
Don Mills, Ontario M3B 2T5
Canada

CONTENTS

INTRODUCTION

This book is designed to help prepare you for the first of the five tests that make up the new GED examination. *Test 1: The Writing Skills Test* covers a range of topics. These include grammar and usage, spelling, punctuation, capitalization, sentence structure, diction and style, and logic and organization.

This introduction will answer some basic questions about the GED Test and give you an overview of Contemporary's GED Program.

THE GED TEST

WHAT IS IT?

The General Educational Development (GED) Test is a battery of five comprehensive examinations in the areas of writing skills, social studies, science, reading skills, and mathematics. First developed in 1942 during World War II, the testing program was first used to help returning servicemen complete their high school education. Since then, millions of people have taken advantage of the opportunity. The GED diploma is recognized as a valid way to complete high school; go on to college or business or trade schools; satisfy educational qualifications for government employment; or fulfill requirements for state or local licensing boards. In other words, the purpose of the GED Test is to measure the educational development of adults who have not completed their formal high school education.

The GED Test provides a means of comparing the performance of people who completed high school in the traditional way with the performance of people who take the equivalency examination. The test itself is based on the idea that many of the skills taught in high school can be acquired through life experience. The GED Tests are based on skills rather than on the mere recall of facts from various subjects. They attempt to test learning and skill development that occur from experience, from living, from reading, and from other non-traditional means. The skills emphasized are those that traditional high school graduates seem to retain long after graduation.

The tests focus on the major generalizations, concepts, ideas, and intellectual skills that are the desirable long-term objectives of a traditional high school education.

WHO DESIGNS IT?

The guidelines for the design of the GED Tests are developed by the General Educational Development Testing Service (located at One Dupont Circle, Washington, D.C. 20036) under the direction and supervision of the Commission on Accreditation of the American Council on Education. The actual test was developed and is updated by the Educational Testing Service (ETS), located in Princeton, N.J. ETS develops at least one new form of the GED test battery every year for use at the official GED testing centers. As new forms become available, the oldest forms are retired, so that in a given number of years all the old forms will have been replaced by new forms.

WHO ADMINISTERS IT?

Each state sets its own policies and procedures for administering the GED Tests. The State Department of Education sets the name and format for high school equivalency certificates and establishes the minimum test scores required for passing. In addition, it fixes age, residency, and previous high school enrollment requirements for admission to testing. The states also set fees for administration of the tests, locations of official GED testing centers, and methods of applying for the high school equivalency diploma.

HOW IS IT SCORED?

Your score on the GED Test is compared with a selected sampling of the scores of a group of graduating high school seniors chosen from all over the country. This comparison permits keeping the difficulty of all test items and written matter on the GED Test at a satisfactory level. Your performance on the GED Test is compared with the performance of students involved in regular high school programs.

Each part of the GED Test yields three scores: the **raw score,** the **percentile rank,** and the **standard score.**

1. The **raw score** is simply the number of correct answers.

   EXAMPLE: If the math section of the GED Test has 50 test items and you answer 25 questions correctly, your raw score is 25.

   Taken alone, the raw score doesn't have much meaning because it does not show how your performance compares with that of high school graduates. Therefore, it is necessary to convert the raw score into percentile rank.

2. **Percentile rank** is derived from the raw score. It compares your performance on the GED Test with the performance of a sample group of high school seniors who were given the test.

EXAMPLE: A percentile rank of 10 means that you scored equal to or better than 10 percent of the high school seniors in the sample group. In other words, about 90 percent of them did better than you. At the other end of the scale, if you had a percentile rank of 90 percent, you did as well as or better than 90 percent of the high school seniors in the sample group.

Although your percentile rank permits you to know where you stand in a particular group, the percentile ranks cannot be averaged. For that purpose another conversion score—the standard score—is used.

3. The **standard score** is the one that is reported to you. The standard scores are the means of comparing raw scores. Standard scores make it possible to compare your performance on one part of the test to your performance on another part and also allow each score to be averaged.

The following chart shows a sampling of GED standard scores and the percentile ranks associated with them.

Percentile Ranks Corresponding to GED Test Standard Scores for Public High School Seniors Tested at Time of Graduation from High School

Percentile Ranks	*Standard Scores*
99	80
99	75
98	70
93	65
84	60
69	55
50	50
31	45
16	40
7	35
2	30
1	25
1	20

WHAT IS A PASSING SCORE?

Most states require a minimum standard score of 35 on each test *and* an average score of 45 for all five tests. In order to earn the average score of 45, a person's total score for all five tests must reach 225. Below are two examples of GED score results. Example 1 shows scores of a person who did not pass the GED. Example 2 shows how a set of passing scores might look.

EXAMPLE 1:			EXAMPLE 2:		
Test 1.	*The Writing Skills Test*	35	Test 1.	*The Writing Skills Test*	35
Test 2.	*The Social Studies Test*	35	Test 2.	*The Social Studies Test*	51
Test 3.	*The Science Test*	35	Test 3.	*The Science Test*	47
Test 4.	*The Reading Skills Test*	35	Test 4.	*The Reading Skills Test*	49
Test 5.	*The Mathematics Test*	35	Test 5.	*The Mathematics Test*	43
		175			225

In Example 1, the person earned a standard score of 35 on each area of the GED exam. This shows that it is possible to pass each of the five tests and still not earn the required *total* passing score of 225.

In Example 2, the person also earned at least a passing score of 35 in each area. In addition, however, the scores are high enough so that the *total* score comes to 225.

On the average, approximately half of the questions on each test must be answered correctly in order to give a total passing score. The following table lists the average number of questions which need to be answered correctly on each of the five tests in order to get a standard score of 45 points on that test. This average is what is necessary to earn a total score of 225 points. (As Example 2 shows, however, actual scores on the five tests may range above and below the 45-point average.)

GED TEST	TOTAL NUMBER OF QUESTIONS	AVERAGE NUMBER OF QUESTIONS NEEDED TO SCORE 45
1. WRITING SKILLS	80	40
2. SOCIAL STUDIES	60	30
3. SCIENCE	60	26
4. READING SKILLS	40	22
5. MATHEMATICS	50	24

WHAT'S ON IT?

The following pages show a breakdown of the content of *Test 1: The Writing Skills Test* with examples of the types of questions asked. Correct answers are indicated on the answer grid in the margin next to each question. The table below summarizes the information.

TEST 1: THE WRITING SKILLS TEST
80 ITEMS
75 MINUTES

CONTENT AREA	PERCENTAGE OF ITEMS
Spelling, Punctuation, and Capitalization	25%
Grammar and Usage	30%
Diction and Style	15%
Sentence Structure	15%
Logic and Organization	15%

TEST 1: THE WRITING SKILLS TEST

Spelling, Punctuation, and Capitalization (25%)

Spelling words are selected from lists of commonly used yet commonly misspelled words. The emphasis is placed on typical kinds of spelling errors.

EXAMPLE

Directions: In the following group of words, one word is misspelled. Blacken the space in the answer grid under the number that corresponds to the misspelled word.

1. 1 2 3 4 5 (answer grid: 3 blackened)

1. (1) community (2) believe (3) intrested (4) occurred (5) fever

Conventional uses of the period, comma, question mark, apostrophe, semicolon, parentheses, quotation marks, and exclamation mark.

EXAMPLE

Directions: In the following sentence, four possible places for punctuation have been underlined. If there is an error in punctuation at an underlined place in the sentence, blacken the space in the answer grid under the number corresponding to it. If there is no error, blacken the space numbered (5).

2. 1 2 3 4 5 (answer grid: 1 blackened)

2. "How"(1), Mr. Johnson asked,(2) "(3)do you expect to finish everything before tomorrow?(4)" No error(5)

Conventional uses of capitalization in quotations, beginnings of sentences, proper names, titles of books, articles, days of the week, months, holidays, and in letter writing.

EXAMPLE

Directions: In the following sentence, four letters have been underlined. If one of these letters represents a capitalization error, blacken the space in the answer grid under the number that corresponds to it. If there is no error, blacken the space numbered (5).

3. 1 2 3 4 5 (answer grid: 2 blackened)

3. The Hudson(1) river(2) runs through Manhattan(3) and continues to upstate(4) New York. No error(5)

Grammar and Usage (30%)

Questions include errors in subject-verb agreement; proper sequence of verb tenses; nouns; agreement of pronouns with their antecedents (both number and person); adjectives; adverbs; prepositions; and conjunctions. Usage questions emphasize problems in standard written communication.

EXAMPLE

Directions: In the following sentence, four words have been underlined. If one of these words represents an error in grammar or usage, blacken the space in the answer grid under the number corresponding to it. If there is no error, blacken the space numbered (5).

---

4. The Perez children, Mario, Louisa, and Clara, wasn't able
                                                                  1   2

to be at the party. No error
   3   4   5

4. 1 2 3 4 5

Diction and Style (15%)

Questions cover elements of precise and economical writing; functions of simple and commonly used phrases (both figurative and literal) within a passage; techniques used to produce a given effect; vocabulary; shades of meaning among alternative expressions in relation to context; and reductive and additive devices for clear and concise writing.

EXAMPLE

Directions: If one of the answers corrects or improves the style or word choice of the underlined segment, blacken the space under the number corresponding to it. If no answer improves the underlined part, blacken the space numbered (5).

---

5. Stan was as upset as Susan was when he heard the news.

   (1) Stan became as upset as Susan was
   (2) Stan's upset was like Susan's
   (3) Stan's upset was as much as Susan's
   (4) Stan had an upset as great as Susan
   (5) No change

5. 1 2 3 4 5

Sentence Structure (15%)

Questions examine relationships between and among clauses; dangling or otherwise misplaced modifiers; awkward clauses, phrases, or appositives; conversion of short sentences into complex sentences; periodic sentences; parallel structure.

EXAMPLE

Directions: If a sentence has faulty structure, blacken the space under the number corresponding to the corrected version of it. If the sentence is correct, blacken the space numbered (5).

6. 1 2 3 4 5 (answer marked: 1)

6. Rosa was trying to get a new job, bought new clothes, and has started to look for a new apartment.

(1) Rosa was trying to get a new job, buying new clothes, and starting to look for a new apartment.
(2) Rosa tried to get a new job, buying new clothes, and has started to look for a new apartment.
(3) Rosa was trying to get a new job, bought new clothes, and starts to look for a new apartment.
(4) Rosa tries to get a new job, bought new clothes, and starting to look for a new apartment.
(5) No change

Logic and Organization (15%)

This section of the test focuses on pattern and structure of paragraphs; extracting and categorizing ideas; interrelationships among ideas in a passage; relationship between topic sentence and other sentences in a paragraph; transitional words and sentences; relevance of ideas; effective use of comparison-contrast; cause-effect; time and space flow.

EXAMPLE

Directions: Read the following paragraph and then answer the question about the paragraph's logic and organization. Blacken the space in the answer grid under the number that corresponds to the answer choice that will improve the logic and organization of the paragraph.

[1]Many people are not as physically fit as they should be. [2]Every day they go from chairs in their offices to chairs in front of their television sets without getting any exercise. [3]These people, at the end of the day, their bodies need more than sitting in chairs turning knobs.

7. 1 2 3 4 5 (answer marked: 4)

7. Sentence 3 would be best if it were

(1) left as is.
(2) changed to: *These people at the end of the day, their bodies need more than sitting in a chair or turning knobs on a television set.*

(3) changed to: *At the end of the day, these people need more than sitting in chairs turning knobs.*
(4) changed to: *At the end of the day, these people need more exercise than they can get by sitting in chairs turning knobs.*
(5) moved to the beginning of the paragraph.

CONTEMPORARY'S GED PROGRAM

Contemporary's GED Program is based on these guidelines:

(1) that all materials presented teach the student to apply the skills needed to pass the GED Test.

(2) that these skills be presented developmentally, progressing from the less difficult to the GED Test level.

(3) that all skills be identified in all exercises with explanatory answers for reinforced learning.

(4) that a sufficient number of progress assessments be included to measure learning in all skill areas.

Contemporary's GED books include the following features:

INTRODUCTION	Information on the scoring, content, skills, and question format of the GED Test.
SKILLS INVENTORY	A self-administered Skills Inventory designed to reflect the format of the actual GED.
PRESCRIPTION	A breakdown of the Skills Inventory enabling you to pinpoint those skills on which you need the greatest work.
INSTRUCTIONAL MATERIAL	Concise and clear skill instruction presented in the context of the adult language experience.
SKILL ACTIVITIES	Developmental skill activities designed to give you immediate feedback on your progress.
REVIEW ACTIVITIES	General reviews covering the material in each unit and assessment charts to measure progress.
EXPLANATORY ANSWERS	Answers that guide you through the thought processes involved in determining the correct answers and show precisely where an error might have been made.
FINAL SKILLS INVENTORY	A simulated GED Test followed by a skills assessment chart to indicate readiness to take the actual test.

If you fully utilize all the elements of Contemporary's GED Program, you will be ready to pass the GED Test. We at Contemporary Books, Inc., sincerely hope that our program will be of value to you, and we would appreciate your comments about this book.

Test 1 The Writing Skills Test

WRITING SKILLS INVENTORY

The questions on the Writing Skills Inventory are like those on the actual GED Test. You should take about forty-five minutes to complete this Inventory, although there is no time limit. Work steadily because that is good practice for taking the GED. If any questions seem to be very difficult, leave those questions for last. Don't be concerned if you are not sure of all the answers. Guess at an answer when you are not positive about the right one. You should never leave a question unanswered, because a guess is a possible right answer.

After you have finished the Writing Skills Inventory, check your answers in the Answers and Explanations section that follows the Inventory. Find out what types of questions are difficult for you by referring to the Writing Skills Chart that comes after the Answers and Explanations.

SPELLING

Directions: In each of the following groups of words, one word is misspelled. Blacken the space in the answer grid under the number that corresponds to the misspelled word.

1. (1) activate (2) relax (3) guiding (4) genorous (5) hostile — **1.** 1 2 3 4 5

2. (1) halfs (2) receive (3) legal (4) miserable (5) judgment — **2.** 1 2 3 4 5

3. (1) disatisfied (2) purpose (3) transmitter (4) frustrated (5) really — **3.** 1 2 3 4 5

4. (1) uninterested (2) proceed (3) succede (4) temperament (5) saliva — **4.** 1 2 3 4 5

5. (1) communist (2) separate (3) slaping (4) deceive (5) conception — **5.** 1 2 3 4 5

6. (1) siege (2) wierd (3) knowledge (4) idolize (5) medium — **6.** 1 2 3 4 5

7. 1 2 3 4 5

7. (1) review (2) metallic (3) refrigerator (4) writting (5) stole

8. 1 2 3 4 5

8. (1) enthusastic (2) supersede (3) submarine (4) volume (5) neighbor

9. 1 2 3 4 5

9. (1) twelfths (2) version (3) pencel (4) genius (5) soldier

10. 1 2 3 4 5

10. (1) electricity (2) enviroment (3) computer (4) abolish (5) human

CAPITALIZATION

Directions: In each of the following sentences, four letters have been underlined. If one of these letters represents a capitalization error, blacken the space in the answer grid under the number that corresponds to it. If there is no error, blacken the space numbered (5).

11. 1 2 3 4 5

11. In the State (1) of Massachusetts (2) lives an old veterinarian (3) named Dr. (4) Quack. No error (5)

12. 1 2 3 4 5

12. His article (1) on soul (2) music appeared in *the* (3) *Running Rock* magazine last Tuesday (4). No error (5)

13. 1 2 3 4 5

13. The (1) Rock river (2) runs through Beloit (3), Wisconsin, near Highway (4) 51. No error (5)

14. 1 2 3 4 5

14. "Don't (1) leave early," her boss (2) said, "because (3) I (4) still have a lot of work for you to do." No error (5)

PUNCTUATION

Directions: In each of the following sentences, four possible places for punctuation have been underlined. If there is an error in punctuation at this place in the sentence, blacken the space in the answer grid under the number corresponding to it. If there is no error, blacken the space numbered (5).

15. She's (1) got a box large enough for everything; (2) tools, (3) nails, (4) and six cans of paint. No error (5)

15. 1 2 3 4 5

16. "How," (1) Rev. (2) Carter asked, (3) "do you manage to get everything done"? (4) No error (5)

16. 1 2 3 4 5

17. The baby birds' (1) mother screamed at John's (2) friend, (3) who was approaching the nest. (4) No error (5)

17. 1 2 3 4 5

18. Mrs. (1) Jefferson started squirming in her wool shirt (wool irritates her skin) (2) but continued her speech on peoples' (3) rights. (4) No error (5)

18. 1 2 3 4 5

19. The author wrote, (1) "(2) Five years after the war, the general's (3) hearing failed him. (4) No error (5)

19. 1 2 3 4 5

GRAMMAR AND USAGE

Directions: In each of the following sentences, four words have been underlined. If one of these words represents an error in grammar or usage, blacken the space in the answer grid under the number corresponding to it. If there is no error, blacken the space numbered (5).

20. 1 2 3 4 5 — 20. Patients[1] usually appreciates[2] a doctor who[3] answers their[4] questions. No error[5]

21. 1 2 3 4 5 — 21. Hear[1] are two[2] coats[3] that[4] no one will buy. No error[5]

22. 1 2 3 4 5 — 22. This[1] kind of[2] book is neither[3] exciting nor[4] useful. No error[5]

23. 1 2 3 4 5 — 23. Mr. Jones wished[1] he has[2] more money so that he could[3] buy this[4] house. No error[5]

24. 1 2 3 4 5 — 24. The book us[1] students like more[2] than[3] the others is[4] not sold anymore. No error[5]

25. 1 2 3 4 5 — 25. The Herrick brothers, Fred, Gus, and[1] Tony, insist[2] that they were[3] on[4] time. No error[5]

26. 1 2 3 4 5 — 26. Everyone that takes[1] his[2] coat off[3] will be real[4] cold. No error[5]

27. 1 2 3 4 5 — 27. The people[1] was[2] laughing and singing[3] happily[4]. No error[5]

28. 1 2 3 4 5 — 28. The dog stuck[1] it's[2] head in the door and barked[3] loudly[4]. No error[5]

29. 1 2 3 4 5 — 29. Sarah bought[1] two lemon cakes[2] and a[3] orange one[4]. No error[5]

30. 1 2 3 4 5 — 30. By[1] the time help arrived[2], the young[3] man had fallen[4] from the building. No error[5]

31. "Hal and I been there earlier," said Mary. No error
   1 2 3 4 5
31. 1 2 3 4 5

32. The singer in the blue shirt sings more beautifuller than the others. No error
   1 2 3 4 5
32. 1 2 3 4 5

33. Either their wives or them wish to go. No error
   1 2 3 4 5
33. 1 2 3 4 5

34. Both of the photographs on the wall were took by my sister. No error
   1 2 3 4 5
34. 1 2 3 4 5

35. He said he had returned the bed because he wasn't satisfied of it. No error
   1 2 3 4 5
35. 1 2 3 4 5

36. The apartment rents for one hundred and fifty dollars, what seems expensive for that small space. No error
   1 2 3 4 5
36. 1 2 3 4 5

37. In television tonight there are several great programs. No error
   1 2 3 4 5
37. 1 2 3 4 5

38. Champagne is often drunk at weddings and other special occasions. No error
   1 2 3 4 5
38. 1 2 3 4 5

39. Not only did he dance, but also he sang. No error
   1 2 3 4 5
39. 1 2 3 4 5

STYLE AND DICTION

Directions: If one of the answers corrects or improves the style or word choice of the underlined segment, blacken the space under the number corresponding to it. If no answer improves the underlined part, blacken the space numbered (5).

40. 1 2 3 4 5

40. Her younger sister seemed deeply and persistently troubled by what she had seen.

(1) upset
(2) tormented
(3) to have been made very unhappy
(4) tired
(5) No change

41. 1 2 3 4 5

41. A cold shower makes a person feel awake and energetic; a warm bath makes a person feel relaxed and calm.

(1) When a person takes a cold shower he feels awake and energetic, but when he takes a warm bath he feels relaxed and calm.
(2) In contrast to a cold shower, which makes a person feel awake and energetic, a warm bath makes a person feel relaxed and calm.
(3) A cold shower makes a person feel awake and energetic; a warm bath, relaxed and calm.
(4) A cold shower makes one feel awake and energetic; a warm makes one feel relaxed and calm.
(5) No change

42. 1 2 3 4 5

42. The bolt of lightning cut through the still night air like fire.

(1) like a knife
(2) as though it were fire
(3) in a fire-like way
(4) very loudly
(5) No change

43. 1 2 3 4 5

43. Doctor, I'd like to engage in conversation with you if you have time.

(1) exchange ideas orally
(2) broach a topic
(3) talk something over
(4) shoot the breeze
(5) No change

44. It is often possible for you to learn from mistakes that you make. 44. 1 2 3 4 5

(1) When you make a mistake, you are given an opportunity very often to learn from it.
(2) To learn lessons, it is essential that you make mistakes that you can learn from.
(3) You can often learn from your mistakes.
(4) Making mistakes, often considered a bad thing to do, can actually be a positive experience in providing learning opportunities.
(5) No change

SENTENCE STRUCTURE

Directions. If a sentence has faulty structure, blacken the space under the number corresponding to the corrected version of it. If the sentence is correct, blacken the space numbered (5).

45. Ed was interested in good food, wanted to know interesting people, and in buying fancy clothes. 45. 1 2 3 4 5

(1) Ed was interested in eating good food, knowing interesting people, and fancy clothes.
(2) Ed was interested in eating good food, knowing interesting people, and buying fancy clothes.
(3) Ed was interested in good food, interesting people, and buying fancy clothes.
(4) Ed was interested in good food, wanted to know interesting people, and to buy fancy clothes.
(5) No change

46. At the farm the man smiled at the puppy smoking a cigar. 46. 1 2 3 4 5

(1) The man at the farm smiled at the puppy smoking a cigar.
(2) The man smiled at the puppy at the farm smoking a cigar.
(3) The man smiled at the puppy smoking a cigar at the farm.
(4) At the farm, the man smoking a cigar smiled at the puppy.
(5) No change

47. 1 2 3 4 5

47. Having roasted for ten minutes, Fred took the hot dogs out of the fire.
    (1) Fred took the hot dogs out of the fire after they had roasted for ten minutes.
    (2) After having roasted for ten minutes, Fred took the hot dogs out of the fire.
    (3) Fred, having roasted for ten minutes, took the hot dogs out of the fire.
    (4) Fred took the hot dogs out of the fire, having roasted for ten minutes.
    (5) No change

48. 1 2 3 4 5

48. Because it had rained for several days, the car was on sale.
    (1) Having rained for several days, the car was on sale.
    (2) The car was on sale because it had rained for several days.
    (3) Because its owner needed money, the car was on sale.
    (4) Because it was beautiful, the car was on sale.
    (5) No change

49. 1 2 3 4 5

49. Although Sam likes Sally, he likes Susan better.
    (1) Because Sam likes Sally, he likes Susan better.
    (2) Before Sam likes Sally, he likes Susan better.
    (3) After Sam likes Sally, he likes Susan better.
    (4) Since Sam likes Sally, he likes Susan better.
    (5) No change

50. 1 2 3 4 5

50. The pill, that he took for his headache, was an aspirin.
    (1) The pill that he took for his headache, was an aspirin.
    (2) The pill that he took for his headache was an aspirin.
    (3) The pill, that he took, for his headache, was an aspirin.
    (4) The pill, that he took for his headache was an aspirin.
    (5) No change

51. 1 2 3 4 5

51. The leader, a famous trumpet player gave the signal, and the band began to play.
    (1) The leader a famous trumpet player, gave the signal and the band began to play.
    (2) The leader a famous trumpet player gave the signal and the band began to play.
    (3) The leader, a famous trumpet player, gave the signal and the band began to play.
    (4) The leader, a famous trumpet player, gave the signal, and the band began to play.
    (5) No change

52. Wishing you the very best of luck.

(1) Wishing you and all who are going with you the very best of luck.
(2) We are wishing you the very best of luck.
(3) Our wishing you the very best of luck.
(4) Wishing you the very best of luck and a wonderful trip.
(5) No change

52. 1 2 3 4 5

53. After a long, hard day of work in the garage.

(1) After Gary's long, hard day of work in the garage.
(2) After Gary had finished a long, hard day of work in the garage.
(3) Gary, after a long, hard day of work in the garage, went home.
(4) Gary's long, hard day of work in the garage.
(5) No change

53. 1 2 3 4 5

54. Dogs bark.

(1) Dogs bark, and they bite people.
(2) Dogs bark and bite people.
(3) Dogs, barking, bite people.
(4) Dogs bark; they also bite people.
(5) No change

54. 1 2 3 4 5

LOGIC AND ORGANIZATION

Directions: Read each of the following paragraphs and then answer the questions about the paragraph's logic and organization. Blacken the space in the answer grid under the number that corresponds to the answer choice that will improve the logic and organization of the paragraph.

[1]Women as well as men study car manuals in order to avoid paying high mechanics' fees. [2]The money-saving technique of sewing clothes for each and every member of the family at home has also become more popular. [3]In hard economic times, people save money by doing things themselves that they would otherwise have someone else do for them. [4]There are some things that very few people can do for themselves, such as raising their own food. [5]However, home-cooked meals are often more nutritious than restaurant food.

55. 1 2 3 4 5

55. In sentence 2, *for each and every member of the family* is best

(1) left as it is.
(2) changed to *for each member of the family*
(3) changed to *for every member of the family*
(4) changed to *for the whole family*
(5) omitted entirely.

56. 1 2 3 4 5

56. What should be done with sentence 3?

(1) It should be left as it is.
(2) It should be omitted.
(3) It should be moved to the end.
(4) It should begin the paragraph.
(5) It should follow sentence 1, but come before sentence 2.

57. 1 2 3 4 5

57. Sentence 4 should begin

(1) the way it begins now.
(2) with *However, there are*
(3) with *Moreover, there are*
(4) with *Therefore, there are*
(5) with *Although there are*

58. 1 2 3 4 5

58. Sentence 5 would be most improved if

(1) the sentence were omitted entirely.
(2) it began with *You can also save money by cooking for yourself, and, too, home-cooked meals*
(3) it ended with *and, besides they are less expensive.*
(4) the entire sentence were joined to the end of sentence 4 with a semicolon.
(5) the sentence were shortened to *however, home-cooked meals are often more nutritious* and joined to sentence 4 with a comma.

[1]Fear is a strange emotion. [2]For example, a person who is afraid of high places probably had a bad experience trying to get down from someplace as a child. [3]Fear of a certain animal can usually be traced to a frightening childhood experience with a member of that species. [4]And the feeling of being helpless and frightened in bathwater as a baby has been found to result in an irrational fear of water in many adults.

59. Sentence 1 would be most improved if

(1) it were joined to sentence 2 with a semicolon
(2) it were changed to read: *Fear is a childish emotion.*
(3) it were changed to read: *Fear may be a result of bad childhood experiences.*
(4) it were changed to read: *Fear may be a result of experience.*
(5) it were changed to read: *Fear is the emotion of children.*

59. 1 2 3 4 5

60. In sentence 3, *with a member of that species* is best

(1) left as it is.
(2) changed to *with animals.*
(3) changed to *with some other member of that same species.*
(4) changed to *with the same kind of animal.*
(5) changed to *with the species.*

60. 1 2 3 4 5

ANSWERS AND EXPLANATIONS—WRITING SKILLS INVENTORY

SPELLING

1. **(4)** The correct spelling is *generous.*
2. **(1)** Many nouns ending in *f* form the plural by changing the *f* to *v* and adding *es.* The correct spelling is *halves.*
3. **(1)** Add a prefix or suffix (beginning or ending) to the entire word: *Dis* + *satisfied* = *dissatisfied.*
4. **(3)** The correct spelling is *succeed.*
5. **(3)** When the vowel sound before a final consonant is not that of the name of the vowel, as is the *a* sound in *wait,* double the final consonant before the addition of a suffix. The correct spelling is *slapping.*
6. **(2)** This word is an exception to the *i* and *e* combination rule. The correct spelling is *weird.*
7. **(4)** The correct spelling is *writing.*
8. **(1)** The correct spelling is *enthusiastic.*
9. **(3)** The correct spelling is *pencil.*
10. **(2)** The correct spelling is *environment.*

CAPITALIZATION

11. **(1)** In this case, *state* is not part of a specific name, so it should not be capitalized.
12. **(3)** The first word in a title of a publication is capitalized.
13. **(2)** *River* is part of a name, so it should be capitalized.
14. **(5)** No error

PUNCTUATION

15. **(2)** A colon (:) is used before a list of items.
16. **(4)** The question mark should be inside the quotation marks at the end of the question.
17. **(5)** No error
18. **(3)** Since *people* is a plural noun that does not end in *s,* the possessive is formed by adding *'s, people's.*
19. **(4)** End quotation marks are missing.

GRAMMAR AND USAGE

20. **(2)** The plural verb *appreciate* is needed because the subject, *patients,* is plural.

21. **(1)** *Here,* indicating a place, is correct in this sentence.

22. **(5)** No error

23. **(2)** The past tense *had* is needed because the verb *wished* is in the past tense.

24. **(1)** The subjective pronoun *we* is needed in this sentence.

25. **(5)** No error

26. **(4)** The adverb *really* is needed since it modifies the adjective *cold.*

27. **(2)** The plural verb *were* is required because the subject, *people,* is plural.

28. **(2)** The correct possessive pronoun is *its. It's* means *it is* or *it has.*

29. **(3)** Before a noun beginning with a vowel (except *u* when it sounds like *you*), *an,* not *a,* is used.

30. **(5)** No error

31. **(2)** *Been* is a past participle of the verb *to be.* The correct past form is *were.*

32. **(2)** The form of an adverb used for an unequal comparison between two members is *more beautifully.*

33. **(3)** The subjective pronoun *they* is correct in this sentence.

34. **(3)** The past participle of the verb, *taken,* must be used in this sentence.

35. **(4)** The preposition that follows *satisfied* is *with.*

36. **(2)** *What* is never used to refer back to something previously mentioned in a sentence. *Which* would be correct.

37. **(1)** The correct preposition would be *on.*

38. **(5)** No error

39. **(3)** *Also* should be next to the word it modifies, *sang.*

STYLE AND DICTION

40. **(2)** *Tormented* expresses more clearly and concisely the meaning of the underlined group.

41. **(3)** This sentence avoids the needless repetition of words.

42. **(1)** In order to continue the comparison begun with the verb *cut, like a knife* would be the only possible choice.

43. **(3)** This has the casual but not "slangy" style that the situation calls for.

44. **(3)** This sentence is the most concise and direct; therefore, it is the most effective.

SENTENCE STRUCTURE

45. **(2)** The items in the series are all in the same form, in other words, parallel. The original sentence does not have parallel structure.

46. **(4)** The group *smoking a cigar* should be next to *man,* which it describes. In the original sentence it appears as if the puppy is smoking a cigar.

47. **(1)** The hot dogs, not Fred, had roasted for ten minutes. The original sentence makes it appear as if Fred had been roasting for ten minutes.

48. **(3)** This sentence is the only one with parts that are logically connected to each other.

49. **(5)** No change

50. **(2)** Since all of the words are necessary for the meaning of the sentence, no commas should be used.

51. **(4)** The words *a famous trumpet player* add extra information to identify *the leader* and should be set off by commas. The two parts of the compound sentence should also be separated with a comma.

52. **(2)** Only this answer has a subject and a predicate, the basic requirements of a sentence.

53. **(3)** Only this answer has a subject and a predicate.

54. **(5)** No change

LOGIC AND ORGANIZATION

55. **(5)** The sentence is clear without these words.

56. **(4)** This is the topic sentence of the paragraph; it states the main idea.

57. **(2)** Since this sentence states an exception to the statement made in sentence 3, the word *however* should be used to make this connection between the sentences clear.

58. **(1)** This paragraph is not about nutrition; it is about doing things for oneself to save money. This sentence is irrelevant and should be omitted.

59. **(3)** Since all of the other sentences are about the childhood origins of adult fears, sentence 1 would be a better topic sentence if it stated the whole general idea of the paragraph.

60. **(4)** These words make the same statement, but they fit the style of the paragraph much better than using the scientific word *species.*

WRITING SKILLS EVALUATION CHART

Below is a list of the general subject areas covered in the Writing Skills Inventory and the total number of questions in each area. The percentage of questions in each subject area reflects the format of the actual GED test.

Enter the number of questions you got right on the chart below.

Subject Area	*Question Total*	*Number Right*
Spelling	10	____
Capitalization	4	____
Punctuation	5	____
Grammar and Usage	20	____
Style and Diction	5	____
Sentence Structure	10	____
Logic and Organization	6	____

PASSING SCORE: 40 right out of 60.

YOUR SCORE: _____ right out of 60.

It is important to study the entire book since new writing skills build upon previously developed ones; however, by seeing how many questions you got right in each area, you can determine the areas in which you need the most work.

GRAMMAR AND USAGE

WHAT IS A SENTENCE?

In the beginning, man discovered the word. By putting sounds together and using that same group of sounds to stand for the same thing, the word took on a meaning. But with the birth of the word, man's efforts to communicate were only slightly improved.

Take the case of Ur, an ancient man who woke up one morning feeling hungry. Ur looked around his cave but found nothing to eat. He went out to see if any of his friends had anything to eat, but he didn't see any food anywhere. Walking over to a group of people, Ur clutched his stomach and said quite plainly, "Food!" The other people, who were just as hungry as Ur, began looking around to see the food that Ur had spotted. But that was not what Ur meant. He hadn't *seen* any food; he *wanted* food. His simple word had failed to mean what he had meant it to mean. "Want food," Ur exclaimed. All the others began nodding; yes, they wanted food. They stretched out their hands to receive the food Ur was offering them.

The two words together still did not mean what Ur wanted them to mean. "I want food," Ur screamed in desperation. One of the group went off to his cave and returned a few minutes later carrying food for Ur to eat. At last Ur had been able to say what he was thinking; Ur had communicated.

The point of this story is that words can be grouped together to form the basic unit of communication, the sentence. However, not every combination of words is a sentence. *"Want food"* is not a sentence; it does not give all the information needed to communicate exactly what Ur is thinking. *"I want food"* is a sentence; Ur has used all the words necessary to communicate his complete thought. A sentence, then, is a group of words that communicates a complete thought.

Ur might have been able to get his meaning across by saying, "Want food," and pointing to himself. However, he could do this only if he were speaking face to face with someone else. If he were forced to leave a note for one of his neighbors, he would have to make sure that his message was complete and meant what he wanted it to mean. By leaving a note that simply said, "Want food—Ur," his neighbor might think that the note was an invitation to dinner. Only part of what Ur means has been written down. The question the reader asks is, "Who or what *wants food?"* Ur must write, "I want food—Ur," to answer his neighbor's question.

That part of a sentence that tells who or what the sentence is about is called the **subject** of the sentence. The problem with *"Want food"* is that it does not have a subject. In written communication, all sentences must have a subject.

The subject of a sentence cannot stand alone. Since sentences communicate complete thoughts, some information about the subject must be given. The words that give this information are called the **predicate** of the sentence. In the sentence *"I want food,"* the words *want food* tell something about the subject, *I*. The words *want food* are the predicate of the sentence.

We can now write a definition of a sentence:

A sentence consists of a subject and a predicate that communicate a complete thought.

Look at the following examples of sentences:

1. *Fish swim. Fish* is the subject; it tells what the sentence is about. *Swim* is the predicate; it tells something about the subject. Notice that the subject and the predicate can each be a single word.
2. *Louise asked her friends to come to her house at eight o'clock for a party. Louise* is the subject of the sentence; the sentence is about Louise. The rest of the sentence is the predicate; it tells what Louise did. Notice that sometimes the predicate is much longer than the subject.
3. *The most furious battle of the war ended. The most furious battle of the war* is the subject of the sentence; that is what the sentence is about. *Ended* is the predicate; it tells something about the subject. Notice that the subject can be much longer than the predicate in some sentences.

GRAMMAR AND USAGE: EXERCISE 1 (SUBJECTS)

Underline the subject in each of the following sentences.

1. Murray didn't come to work today.
2. The phone company wants you to call them immediately.
3. Do you understand this problem?
4. Freedom means different things to different people.
5. While walking through the park today, I spotted an old friend.
6. My boss asked me to have lunch with him today.

Answers and explanations are on page 111.

SENTENCE DETECTION

A group of words that does not have both a subject and a predicate, and does not communicate a complete thought, is called a **sentence fragment.** In other words, the group of words could be a fragment, or part, of a sentence; if something were added to the fragment, it could be made into a complete sentence.

"I took" has a subject, but it does not have a complete predicate; it also doesn't communicate a complete thought. *"I took"* is a sentence fragment. The fragment could be made into a complete sentence with the addition of a few more words. *"I took an aspirin for my headache"* is a complete sentence.

You can test any combination of words to see if it is a complete sentence by asking yourself three questions:

(1) *Who or what is this about?* This is the subject of the sentence.

(2) *What about that?* This is the predicate of the sentence.

(3) *What does this group of words say?* The answer to this question will tell you whether or not the group of words communicates a complete thought.

EXAMPLE 1. Eating popcorn at the movies.

(1) *Who or what is this about?* It is about eating popcorn at the movies.

(2) *What about that?* Nothing is said about it.

(3) *What does this group of words say?* There is no way to tell what the writer had in mind. Obviously, he wanted to say something about eating popcorn at the movies, but there is no way to tell what.

"Eating popcorn at the movies" is not a sentence; it is a sentence fragment.

EXAMPLE 2. Jim enjoys eating popcorn at the movies.

(1) *Who or what is this about?* It is about Jim.

(2) *What about Jim?* He enjoys eating popcorn at the movies.

(3) *What does this group of words say?* The words tell one thing Jim enjoys.

"Jim enjoys eating popcorn at the movies" is a complete sentence.

Apply this three-question test to the following groups of words. Write *S* in the blank next to the group of words if it is a complete sentence; write *F* if it is a sentence fragment.

_____ (1) Living in Chicago for seven years.

_____ (2) Because they wanted to see the President.

_____ (3) Seems like a lot of fun.

_____ (4) The woman that I met at the party last weekend.

_____ (5) The baby looked happy.

Only the last group of words passes the test; it is the only complete sentence. All the others are sentence fragments. Don't be fooled by (2) and (4); you might be able to find something that looks like a subject and a predicate, but you cannot answer the last two questions of the test. Something happened "because they wanted to see the President," but we do not know what. The words in group (4) are about *the woman;* the other words in this group only tell *which* woman, but they do not tell us anything *about* her. You could make this fragment into a sentence by making the subject of the sentence *I,* but then you would have to write: "I met that woman at the party last weekend."

There are three types of sentences that are a little more difficult to test for completeness: the command, the question, and the exclamation.

The Command

In a command, the subject of the sentence is understood without being written. If someone hands you a note that reads, "Get lost," you understand that *you* are the subject of the command. "Get lost" is a complete sentence even though the subject is not written down.

EXAMPLE. Get out of my way!

The Question

A question with a subject and a predicate is a complete sentence if it contains all the words necessary to communicate the questioner's complete thought. It may be more difficult to pick out the subject and the predicate since the order of words in a question is different from the order of words in a direct statement. You can overcome this difficulty by putting the words in a different order to form a direct statement.

EXAMPLE 1. Where is the nearest bus stop?

subject	*predicate*
The nearest bus stop	is where.

Where stands for the place that will be named in the answer.

You can now use the three-question test to find that this question is a complete sentence.

The Exclamation

An exclamation is a special kind of sentence that can be formed in one of two ways: with an understood subject, as in a command; or with a twisted word order, as in a question. Depending on the form of the exclamation, you can test for completeness by using one of the methods discussed on page 22.

EXAMPLE 1. How stupid of me!

subject	*predicate*
(It)	(is) *how* stupid of me.

In exclamations like this, the subject and part of the predicate are understood. If the words *it is, he is, she is, that is,* or *you are* can be added to give the exclamation a subject and complete predicate, the exclamation is a complete sentence. These words have been dropped to give extra force to the exclamation.

Words like *how* are used in exclamations for extra emphasis.

EXAMPLE 2. What a wonderful person he is!

subject	*predicate*
He	is *what* a wonderful person.

What is another common word used in exclamations for extra emphasis.

Sentence fragments are common in spoken English and in advertising. The situation and the clues you can pick up from the speaker's voice and gestures will help you fill in the missing parts of the sentence. In a coffee commercial on television, someone could drink from a coffee cup, smack his lips, and say, "Best you'll ever taste." We know that the person is really saying, "This brand is the best coffee you'll ever taste." You may even find sentence fragments in some of the things you read. These fragments make sense because the sentences that come before them help you fill in the missing parts of the sentence fragment. However, you are taking a risk every time you use a sentence fragment in your writing. Your reader or listener may not understand what you are thinking if you use sentence fragments, but he will always understand if you write in complete sentences.

GRAMMAR AND USAGE: EXERCISE 2 (SENTENCE FRAGMENTS)

Directions: If there is a sentence fragment in the following groups, blacken the space under the number corresponding to it. If all of the choices are complete sentences, blacken the space numbered (5).

1. 1 2 3 4 5

1. (1) Cats love to chase flies.
(2) When are you going to leave?
(3) Closing the store early on holidays.
(4) He is alive!
(5) All are complete sentences

2. 1 2 3 4 5

2. (1) The next person who comes in here to talk to me.
(2) Susan is not home.
(3) Please give me a discount.
(4) In spite of the fact that she is ill, she will not go to the doctor.
(5) All are complete sentences

3. 1 2 3 4 5

3. (1) A storm seems to be brewing.
(2) Dieters often sneak snacks.
(3) Because John doesn't want to go to the movies.
(4) Whenever it snows, Oscar stays home from work.
(5) All are complete sentences

4. 1 2 3 4 5

4. (1) Color television sets cost more than black-and-white sets.
(2) Ten exits more on the thruway, then six miles on the side road.
(3) Is he really going to swallow that goldfish?
(4) Check the speedometer on your car.
(5) All are complete sentences

5. 1 2 3 4 5

5. (1) Those five sisters sing with a rock band.
(2) The family meets every year around Christmastime.
(3) Cars that use less gas are more popular now.
(4) No one would work if he didn't have to work.
(5) All are complete sentences

Answers and explanations are on page 111.

Writing in complete sentences is only one step in getting your writing into shape. The next step is to examine the kinds of words that make up a sentence. Each kind of word—nouns, verbs, pronouns, adjectives, and adverbs (prepositions and conjunctions will be discussed in a later section)—presents a different set of problems. In the following pages, you will learn to recognize each of these kinds of words as well as how to avoid the errors you can make when using them. On the GED test, you will be expected to recognize these errors.

NOUNS
(WORDS THAT NAME)

Read the following story paying particular attention to the underlined words.

Sam was going to be late for work again today. Mr. Charm, the personnel director, would have something to say about this. Sam finished his morning coffee and ran to the bus stop. After what seemed like hours, a bus pulled up to the stop. It was empty. All the way to work, Sam was the only passenger. The peace and quiet gave him a chance to think. This time, Sam would have to give Mr. Charm a good excuse. He had already used the heavy traffic on Broadway as an excuse too many times.

When he finally got to work, he used a side entrance, hoping that no one would notice his late arrival. No one was in sight. In fact, the building looked deserted. Was everyone on a coffee break? Was it really that late? Suddenly, Sam found himself face to face with the one person he had hoped to avoid—Mr. Charm.

"Sam, you idiot, what am I going to do with you?" Mr. Charm growled. "You could give a person a nervous breakdown. After weeks of being late, you show up for work on a holiday! Well, I'm sure I can find some work for you to do. You may have just saved your job today."

"I am an idiot," Sam thought to himself. Somehow, saving his job didn't mean nearly as much as the missed holiday. Happiness is not working on a holiday!

All of the underlined words are nouns. Notice that nouns can be a specific name (Sam, Mr. Charm), a general name (work, coffee, bus), or a name of an idea (peace, happiness). Nouns can name a person (Sam), a place (Broadway), a thing (coffee), or an idea (peace).

We can write the following definition of a noun:

A noun is a word that names a person, place, thing, or idea.

You can often test a word to see if it is a noun by replacing that word with *he, she, it, one, they, her, him, them, hers, his, its, theirs, that, those,* or *these.* (NOTE: None of these words are nouns; only words that can be *replaced* by one of these words are nouns.)

EXAMPLE.

> This time *Sam* would have to give *Mr. Charm* a good *excuse.*
> This time *he* would have to give *him* a good *one.*
>
> *Sam, Mr. Charm,* and *excuse* are nouns.

GRAMMAR AND USAGE: EXERCISE 3 (IDENTIFYING NOUNS)

Directions: In each of the following sentences, four words have been underlined. If one of the four words is a noun, blacken the space under the number corresponding to it. If none of the four words is a noun, blacken the space under number (5).

---

1. 1 2 3 4 5

1. We thought (1) that the picnic (2) would be rained (3) out for the second (4) weekend in a row. None are nouns. (5)

2. 1 2 3 4 5

2. I ran (1) as fast (2) as I could, but I still (3) missed the bus (4). None are nouns. (5)

3. 1 2 3 4 5

3. The doctor told me that (1) my upset (2) stomach may (3) be the beginnings of an ulcer (4). None are nouns. (5)

4. 1 2 3 4 5

4. By the time I make (1) the last (2) payment (3) on my car, it will be time to buy a new (4) one. None are nouns. (5)

5. 1 2 3 4 5

5. Money may be the root of all evil, but evil spelled (1) backwards (2) is live; one does need (3) money to live (4). None are nouns. (5)

Answers and explanations are on pages 111–112.

USES OF NOUNS

A noun can have several uses in a sentence. Using the nouns in the story on page 25, we can make up a list of six separate uses of nouns.

1. A noun can name the **subject** of the sentence.

    Sam (line 1)
    Mr. Charm (line 1)
    bus (line 4)
    peace (line 6)
    building (line 11)
    happiness (lines 21–22)

2. A noun can explain or identify the subject, renaming the subject in a new way in the predicate. (In traditional grammar books, this use of the noun is called a **predicate nominative.**)

    passenger (line 5)
    idiot (line 20)

3. A noun can immediately follow another noun, giving additional information about the first noun or labeling it in some way. (In traditional grammar books, this use of the noun is called an **appositive.**)

    personnel director (line 2)
    idiot (line 15)

4. A noun can follow a connecting word like *for, to, on, up, in, at, under, through,* and *of* to give additional information about another word in the sentence; the connecting word tells you what kind of information is being given. (In traditional grammar books, this use of the noun is called an **object of a preposition;** the preposition is the connecting word.)

    work (line 1)
    bus stop (line 3)
    Broadway (line 8)
    coffee break (line 12)
    holiday (line 18)

    NOTE: *Work* in line 1 tells you what Sam is late for; *bus stop* in line 3 tells you where Sam ran to; and so on. A noun used as an object of a preposition can also show relationship between that noun and another. *The plate on the table* shows the relationship between the plate and the table; *the plate under the table* shows a different relationship between the same two nouns.

5. A noun can be the person, place, or thing that receives the action of the sentence. (In traditional grammar books, this use of the noun is called a **direct object.**)

coffee (line 3)
excuse (line 7)
side entrance (line 9)
arrival (line 10)
nervous breakdown (lines 16–17)
work (line 18)
job (line 19)

NOTE: *Coffee* receives the action of *finished; side entrance* receives the action of *used;* and so on.

6. A noun can name the person, place, or thing *to* whom or what or *for* whom or what the action of the sentence is done. (In traditional grammar books, this use of the noun is called an **indirect object.**)

Mr. Charm (line 7)
person (line 16)

NOTE: *Mr. Charm* tells to whom Sam would have to give an excuse; *person* tells to whom Sam could give a nervous breakdown.

GRAMMAR AND USAGE: EXERCISE 4 (USES OF NOUNS)

Directions: The underlined word in each sentence is a noun. Identify the use of that noun in the sentence by writing an X next to the correct description.

1. The woman you spoke to is Abby's best <u>friend</u>.

____ (1) names subject
____ (2) renames subject in the predicate
____ (3) follows another noun, giving additional information
____ (4) follows connecting word to give additional information
____ (5) names receiver of action
____ (6) names to whom or what or for whom or what the action is done

2. A person with good <u>health</u> is lucky.

____ (1) names subject
____ (2) renames subject in the predicate
____ (3) follows another noun, giving additional information
____ (4) follows connecting word to give additional information
____ (5) names receiver of action
____ (6) names to whom or what or for whom or what the action is done

3. Gordon told <u>Susan</u> not to call him again.

____ (1) names subject
____ (2) renames subject in the predicate
____ (3) follows another noun, giving additional information
____ (4) follows connecting word to give additional information
____ (5) names receiver of action
____ (6) names to whom or what or for whom or what the action is done

4. <u>Love</u> is too precious to be wasted on the young.

____ (1) names subject
____ (2) renames subject in the predicate
____ (3) follows another noun, giving additional information
____ (4) follows connecting word to give additional information
____ (5) names receiver of action
____ (6) names to whom or what or for whom or what the action is done

5. Henry, our <u>supervisor</u>, is a great storyteller.

____ (1) names subject
____ (2) renames subject in the predicate
____ (3) follows another noun, giving additional information
____ (4) follows connecting word to give additional information
____ (5) names receiver of action
____ (6) names to whom or what or for whom or what the action is done

6. I'll pay the <u>bill</u> in person because I don't trust the mails.

____ (1) names subject
____ (2) renames subject in the predicate
____ (3) follows another noun, giving additional information
____ (4) follows connecting word to give additional information
____ (5) names receiver of action
____ (6) names to whom or what or for whom or what the action is done

Answers and explanations are on page 112.

PROBLEMS WITH NOUNS

In the following reading passage, many of the problems writers have with nouns have been pointed out by underlining the words that often are used incorrectly. All of these words are correctly used and spelled in this passage. Try to figure out why these particular words might present a problem.

Mondays are awful days. On Monday, people's lives seem to change. Families that usually get along can't live together in peace on Monday. With the beginning of another week's work, the looks on men's and women's faces suddenly turn sad and sour. As they begin another week of classes and homework, noisy children become quiet. Even the leaves on the trees and the bushes in the parks seem to have less life on Monday.

A weekend's dream may be about faraway places where there are herds of deer and antelope at play, where there are unpolluted blue skies, or where there are wide sandy beaches. But on Monday, there are no dreams; there is only the steel gray world of work.

By Monday evening, the spirit of the weekend's parties has died, and people settle for life as it is. They look forward to the next weekend—or, better yet, the two weeks' vacationtime yet to come—to bring the joys of life back into their tired bodies. But a weekend, only two days' time, is too small an amount of time in which to live one's entire life. To live only on the weekends is like taking two spoonfuls of life-giving medicine to prepare yourself for a disease that you know is coming.

By the time Tuesday morning's alarm radios go off, the spirit of life has begun to stir again. Mondays, then, are like mothers-in-law—life always begins again once they're gone.

We can place almost all noun problems in one of the following five areas:

(1) naming more than one of a person, place, thing, or idea (forming the plural)
(2) showing ownership or showing the relationship between two nouns (forming the possessive)
(3) expressing quantities (amounts) of nouns that do not have a plural form (uncountable nouns)
(4) using the expressions *sort of, kind of,* and *type of* with a noun
(5) using action words (verbs) as nouns (gerunds)

Why, for example, can you write *Mondays* (line 1) and *joys* (line 16), but you must write *families* (line 2), *skies* (line 10), *parties* (line 13), and *bodies* (line 16)? Why is it *another week's work* (line 3) and *two weeks' vacationtime* (line 15)? If you can write *too many hours,* why must you write *too much time* and not *too many time?*

In the following pages, you will learn how to handle problems with nouns. After you have studied these pages and worked through the exercises, you will be able to come back to this page and answer these questions.

Forming the Plural

1. The plural of most nouns is formed by simply adding *s*.

   face, faces (line 4)
   tree, trees (line 6)
   park, parks (line 7)
   place, places (line 8)
   dream, dreams (line 11)

2. The plural of nouns ending with an *s, sh, ch, x,* or *z* is formed by adding *es.*

   class, classes (line 5)
   bush, bushes (line 7)
   beach, beaches (line 10)
   ax, axes
   buzz, buzzes

3. The plural of hyphenated nouns is formed by adding *s* to the main noun.

   mother-in-law, mothers-in-law (line 23)
   half-sister, half-sisters

4. The plural of nouns ending with *ful* is formed by adding *s* at the end of the word.

   spoonful, spoonfuls (line 19)
   handful, handfuls

It is not always correct to form the plural by adding *s* or *es* to the end of a noun. However, in the next four groups, you can find the correct plural form by taking a close look at the spelling.

5. The plural of nouns that end with a *y* is formed by adding *s* if the *y* follows a vowel (*a, e, i, o, u*).

   Monday, Mondays (line 1)
   key, keys
   joy, joys (line 16)
   guy, guys

6. The plural of nouns that end with a *y* is formed by changing the *y* to an *i* and adding *es* if the *y* follows a consonant (any other letter but *a, e, i, o,* or *u*).

   family, families (line 2)
   sky, skies (line 10)
   city, cities
   party, parties (line 13)
   body, bodies (line 16)

7. The plural of nouns that end with an *o* is formed by adding *s* if the *o* follows another vowel.

   radio, radios (line 21)
   boo, boos

8. The plural of nouns that end with an *o* is usually formed by adding *es* if the *o* follows a consonant.

   potato, potatoes
   hero, heroes

Many nouns do not follow hard-and-fast rules. When you form the plural of a noun in one of the following groups, you may need to check your spelling in a dictionary until you have memorized the correct plural form.

9. The plural of nouns ending with an *f* or *fe* is sometimes formed by adding *s*; sometimes it is formed by changed the *f* or *fe* to *v* and adding *es*.

roof, roofs		leaf, leaves (line 6)
chief, chiefs	BUT	life, lives (line 1)
oaf, oafs		half, halves

10. The plural of some nouns is exactly the same as the singular.

   one deer, six deer — one fish, four fish
   one sheep, two sheep

11. Some nouns can be used only in the plural form.

scissors	eyeglasses
news	clothes
trousers	mathematics

12. The plural of some nouns is formed by changing the spelling.

man, men	foot, feet
woman, women	tooth, teeth
child, children	mouse, mice

13. The plural of nouns ending with *man* or *woman* is formed by making the same spelling change you would make if you were forming the plural of *man* or *woman* alone.

   fireman, firemen
   policewoman, policewomen

14. The plural of some nouns ending with *is* is formed by changing the *is* to *es*.

parenthesis, parentheses	basis, bases
thesis, theses	crisis, crises

15. Many nouns have been borrowed from other languages. The plural of these nouns is formed according to the rules of the language from which they were borrowed. If you use any of these words, you will have to memorize the correct plural form.

memorandum, memoranda	alumna, alumnae
datum, data	alumnus, alumni
criterion, criteria	dictum, dicta

GRAMMAR AND USAGE: EXERCISE 5 (PLURALS OF NOUNS)

Directions: If there is an incorrect plural form in the following groups of nouns, blacken the space under the number corresponding to it. If all of the plurals are correct, blacken the space numbered (5).

---

1. (1) witches (2) lockes (3) tomatoes (4) feet (5) no error — **1.** 1 2 3 4 5

2. (1) days (2) cupfuls (3) mouses (4) jellies (5) no error — **2.** 1 2 3 4 5

3. (1) spokeswomen (2) rodeos (3) keys (4) sheep (5) no error — **3.** 1 2 3 4 5

4. (1) crises (2) step-brothers (3) churches (4) halfs (5) no error — **4.** 1 2 3 4 5

5. (1) heros (2) deer (3) wishes (4) tests (5) no error — **5.** 1 2 3 4 5

Answers and explanations are on page 112.

Forming the Possessive

The possessive marker ('), called an apostrophe, is used to show ownership or relationship. Before you make a noun possessive, make sure that a possessive is needed. Look at the following sentences:

(1) *John's* jacket is green.
(2) All four *boys'* jackets are green.
(3) All four *boys* have green jackets.

In sentence (1), the possessive is used to show the relationship between the two nouns *John* and *jacket*. Without using the possessive, you could show the relationship by writing, "John has a green jacket." The information given in sentences (2) and (3) is exactly the same. However, you must use the possessive in sentence (2) to show the relationship between *boys* and *jackets;* in sentence (3) the relationship is already shown by the word *have.* Notice that the subject of sentence (2) is *jackets,* and the subject of sentence (3) is *boys. Boys'* in sentence (2) only gives additional information about the subject; it names the *owners* of the subject.

The possessive form is also used with expressions of quantity when the noun that expresses the quantity and the noun that is being described are not connected by using the word *of.* Compare the following groups of words:

another week of work
another week's work

two weeks of vacation
two weeks' vacation

an hour of time
an hour's time

In the examples above, the possessive is used to make the relationship between words clear when the word *of* is not used.

Once you know that you must use the possessive form of a noun, decide which of the following three rules you should use.

1. The possessive of singular nouns (nouns that name *only one* person, place, thing, or idea) is formed by adding *'s.*

   Jerry's birthday — the dog's tail
   Chicago's mayor — freedom's true meaning

   Even when a singular noun ends with an *s,* you must still add *'s* to form the possessive.

   the class's work period
   Mr. Jones's new job

2. The possessive of plural nouns ending with an *s* is formed by adding only the apostrophe (').

   the two boys' mother
   the Twin Cities' school system
   (Minneapolis and St. Paul are known as the Twin Cities)
   fourteen students' shadows
   twenty-dancers' feet

3. The possessive of plural nouns that do not end with an *s* is formed by adding *'s.*

   the three women's faces — ten sheep's wool
   six people's dreams — the four children's mother

SPECIAL NOTE. When there are two possessives in the same sentence and the thing or person "owned" is the same, the second noun is usually left out.

John's hair is longer than Jane's.

The word *hair* is not repeated because it is understood that Jane's hair is being compared to John's hair.

GRAMMAR AND USAGE: EXERCISE 6 (POSSESSIVE NOUNS)

Directions: Each underlined noun in the following sentences has been made possessive. If the possessive is used and spelled correctly, write "correct" in the space provided. If the underlined word is not correctly used or spelled, write the corrected sentence in the space provided.

1. The boss's secretary just left her desk.

   ____

2. All four sisters' have blond hair.

   ____

3. Men's shoes as well as women's were on sale.

   ____

4. Two week's vacation every year is not enough.

   ____

5. Put this on the newest students' desk.

   ____

Answers and explanations are on pages 112–113.

Uncountable Nouns

The following words are examples of uncountable nouns:

advice information
cash machinery
equipment merchandise
furniture rice

These words have three things in common:

(1) they name a general class of things of which there are many specific types (*furniture* is a general name for such specific things as chairs, tables, and beds)
(2) they do not have a plural form
(3) they cannot be counted (*six sentences*, but not *six informations*)

Words that describe an uncountable noun must identify the quantity without using specific numbers. Look at the following sentence:

A large amount of time and money has been wasted.

The words *time* and *money* are uncountable nouns; the writer must write *a large amount* rather than *a large number* in order to show quantity.

The following is a list of other words and word groups that can be used with uncountable nouns:

a little	much
a bit of	a great deal of
some	a lot of
a piece of (used with some but not all uncountables)	

GRAMMAR AND USAGE: EXERCISE 7 (UNCOUNTABLE NOUNS)

Directions: If there is an error in one of the following sentences, write the corrected sentence in the space provided. If there is no error in a sentence, write "correct" in the space provided.

1. Jack can drink an amazing amount of alcohol.

____

2. There were much monkeys at the zoo.

____

3. His favorite meal is rice and porks.

____

4. All the new equipments used today mean new jobs for many people.

____

5. Drugstores sell many kinds of merchandise besides drugs.

____

Answers and explanations are on page 113.

Using kind of, type of, *and* sort of *with a Noun*

When you use *kind of, type of,* or *sort of* (meaning a category or class) with a noun, you do not use the word *a* or *an* before the noun.

WRONG:	That kind of a person
RIGHT:	That kind of person
WRONG:	That type of a book
RIGHT:	That type of book
WRONG:	This sort of an apple
RIGHT:	This sort of apple

Another difficulty in using these expressions is illustrated in the following examples:

(1) John is a complainer. I can't stand that kind of person.
(2) There are two kinds of people I can't stand—complainers and liars.

In the first example, the writer is talking about only one kind of person; therefore, both *kind* and *person* must be singular. In the second example, the writer is talking about two different kinds of people; therefore, both *kinds* and *people* must be plural. It is important to use the plural only when you are naming more than one kind of person, place, thing, or idea.

A Special Kind of Noun: The Gerund

Look carefully at the following four sentences, paying special attention to the underlined words.

(1) He is sleeping.
(2) Sam and Ray are walking to the party.
(3) Sleeping is Paul's favorite hobby.
(4) Walking is the cheapest way to travel.

In sentences (1) and (2), *sleeping* and *walking* are not nouns; in sentences (3) and (4), these same words are used as nouns. In traditional grammar books, this kind of noun is called a **gerund.** All the nouns in this group end with *ing*.

These nouns can cause problems. Look at the next two sentences and see if you can tell why one of them is wrong.

WRONG: *Paul* sleeping 14 hours a day made his mother nervous.
RIGHT: *Paul's* sleeping 14 hours a day made his mother nervous.

Since *sleeping* is used as a noun, the possessive must be used to express the relationship between the two nouns *Paul* and *sleeping*. Be on the lookout for this special kind of noun, and remember to use the possessive in sentences like the following.

> That *secretary's typing* is very fast.
> Martha is worried about her *husband's drinking* too much.
> Don't worry about *Ed's leaving* town; he'll be back.

GRAMMAR AND USAGE: EXERCISE 8 (NOUN REVIEW)

Directions: In each of the following sentences, four words have been underlined. If one of these words is an error in the sentence, blacken the space under the number corresponding to it. If there is no error in the sentence, blacken the space under number (5).

1. 1 2 3 4 5

1. We saw a large amount [1] of deer [2] along the highway [3] on our vacation [4] last year. No error [5]

2. 1 2 3 4 5

2. Skyscrapers' [1] outlines [2] against the sky look pretty [3] to a sightseer's [4] eye. No error [5]

3. 1 2 3 4 5

3. Cities' [1] are often filled with tourists [2] in summertime [3] because of vacations. [4] No error [5]

4. 1 2 3 4 5

4. Our friends [1] told us about that kind [2] of a fish [3] before we jumped into the lake. [4] No error [5]

5. 1 2 3 4 5

5. Sarah's [1] parents [2] were worried about Jimmy [3] walking through the park at midnight. [4] No error [5]

6. That young man's (1) honesty (2) was proven when the boss (3) left him alone with the cashes. (4) No error (5)

6. 1 2 3 4 5

7. Both John's (1) and Jane's mother-in-laws (2) are going to be in town (3) next weekend. (4) No error (5)

7. 1 2 3 4 5

8. "These shoes (1) are my foots' (2) best friends!" (3) exclaimed the shoestore's (4) owner. No error (5)

8. 1 2 3 4 5

9. The band's (1) lead singer (2) has the perfect voice (3) to sing the blues. (4) No error (5)

9. 1 2 3 4 5

10. The lawyer's (1) eyeglass (2) were found next to two handfuls (3) of bullets from a revolver. (4) No error (5)

10. 1 2 3 4 5

Answers and explanations are on pages 113–114.

VERBS
(WORDS THAT SHOW ACTION OR HELP TO MAKE A STATEMENT)

All of the underlined words in the following sentences are verbs. As you read each sentence, try to make up a definition of a verb.

(1) George drinks at least ten cups of coffee a day.
(2) Al ran to the store for more beer.
(3) If you open your mouth, I will close it for you.
(4) Susan thinks about her own problems too much.
(5) Do you remember the day Martin Luther King was shot?
(6) Ann is always on time, but I am always late for work.
(7) Donna became very upset when John asked her for a divorce.
(8) The weather seems better today than it was yesterday.

All of these words can be placed in one of the following groups:

SHOWS PHYSICAL ACTION: drinks, ran, open, will close, was shot, asked

SHOWS MENTAL ACTION: thinks, remember

LINKS SUBJECT TO A WORD OR IDEA THAT DESCRIBES THE SUBJECT: is, am, became, seems, was

In addition, these words set the sentence in a time period:

IN THE PRESENT: drinks, open, thinks, remember, is, am, seems

IN THE PAST: ran, was shot, became, asked, was

IN THE FUTURE: will close

Notice that a verb is not always a single word. The time period of the action or the idea of the sentence sometimes makes it necessary to use more than one word. *Was shot* and *will close* are examples taken from the sentences above. Sometimes the verb is even more complicated, as in the following sentence:

Paul *would have had to come* to the meeting if he *had wanted to vote*.

We can now make up a definition of a verb:

A verb is a word or group of words that shows action, either physical or mental, or helps to make a sentence by linking the subject to a word or idea that describes the subject in the predicate and also sets the sentence in a time period.

GRAMMAR AND USAGE: EXERCISE 9 (IDENTIFYING VERBS)

Directions: Read each of the following sentences carefully. Select the verb or verbs in each sentence and write them on the line below the sentence.

---

1. If he had married her, he would have been very unhappy.

    ____

2. Mark became upset because his telephone was ringing constantly.

    ____

3. Traffic is a major problem in cities because it creates noise, pollutes the environment, and wastes energy.

    ____

4. Gary can throw a baseball so hard and so fast that it is in the catcher's mitt before you can see it.

    ____

5. Marion thinks she knows what she wants, but she has been wrong before.

    ____

Answers and explanations are on page 114.

PROBLEMS WITH VERBS

The underlined words in the following passage point out some of the problems writers have with verbs.

Whether I am in love now, remembering some happy time in the past when I was in love, or am looking forward to some time in the future when I will be in love again, I know that I can find a song to fit my mood somewhere on the current list of best-selling records.

When I first realize that I love someone, there are songs filled with sunshine and happiness that tell me how beautiful life and love are. After I have loved that person for a long time, I search out more quiet, tender love songs.

When I find myself listening seriously to songs about jealous lovers, I know without much thought that, even though I loved that person at one time, that special feeling is gone. That person fades from my life, but songs of long lost loves, of loneliness, of emptiness bring my thoughts back to all those other people I had loved and lost before. Then, into my sad thoughts come songs of hope that tell me that I will love again.

I am sure that I will have loved many times by the end of my life, and I am just as certain that there will have been songs to see me through it all. If I were loved by the same person throughout my life, I would need only happy and tender love songs. The songwriters seem to know better.

As we discovered when we defined a verb, a verb sets a sentence in three basic time periods:

IN THE PRESENT: I *am* in love (line 1)
IN THE PAST: I *was* in love (line 2)
IN THE FUTURE: I *will be* in love (line 3)

By studying the underlined words in the last three paragraphs of the passage, you will notice that verbs sometimes have to indicate a more complicated time period:

(1) I love — in the present, right now
(2) I have loved — starting in the past and continuing in the present
(3) I loved — in the past
(4) I had loved — in the past, but in a more distant past than in line 11
(5) I will love — in the future
(6) I will have loved — in the future, but looking back at what will then be past
(7) If I were loved — at no place in time; the situation does not really exist

Almost every verb can take one of these seven forms. Each form is called a **tense.** Using the right tense and knowing how to form that tense are the chief problems that writers have with verbs. In the following pages, you will learn how to form verb tenses and how to deal with each of the seven tenses. It is not important to remember the names of the verb tenses. The errors you will be expected to recognize on the GED test will involve (1) using the wrong tense or (2) incorrectly forming the tense of the verb.

Forming Verb Tenses

Each verb tense is based on one of three main forms of the verb. These three forms are called the **principal parts** of the verb. Look at the following diagram of the verb *to love:*

love	loved	have loved
will love		had loved
		will have loved
		were loved

There is a form for the present and future, a form for the past, and a form of the past used in combination with another word or words for all other tenses. Although the third principal part of *to love* is the same as the second, many verbs have three completely different principal parts.

eat	ate	have eaten
will eat		had eaten
		will have eaten
		were eaten

The third principal part of a verb is called **the past participle.**

For verbs like *to love,* the past and the past participle are formed by adding *ed* to the end of the present (the *e* is added only if there isn't already an *e* at the end of the verb):

present	*past*	*past participle*
walk	walked	walked
listen	listened	listened
smoke	smoked	smoked

For verbs like *to eat,* you will have to memorize the irregular forms for the past and past participle. Until you have memorized the correct forms, check your dictionary. Look up the verb under the form you would use with the word *to* (as in *to love, to eat, to drink,* etc.); this form is called the **infinitive.** Immediately following the pronunciation of the infinitive, the dictionary will list the correct form for the past and the past participle if they are irregular.

To help you get started, study the following list of the principal parts of the most common irregular verbs. If you have been using a form of a verb that is different from the one given in this list (for example, suppose you use *teached* for the past of *teach* instead of the correct form, *taught*), write your form next to the correct form and circle it. From time to time, come back to this list and review these circled words until you have committed the correct form to memory.

present	*past*	*past participle*
arise	arose	arisen
awake	awoke, awaked	awaked, awoke, awoken
be (am, is, are)	was, were	been
beat	beat	beaten
become	became	become
begin	began	begun
bet	bet	bet
bite	bit	bitten
blow	blew	blown
break	broke	broken
bring	brought	brought
build	built	built
buy	bought	bought
catch	caught	caught
choose	chose	chosen
come	came	come
cut	cut	cut
dive	dived, dove	dived
do	did	done
dream	dreamed, dreamt	dreamed, dreamt
drink	drank	drunk
drive	drove	driven
eat	ate	eaten
feel	felt	felt
fight	fought	fought
find	found	found
flee	fled	fled
fly	flew	flown
freeze	froze	frozen
get	got	got, gotten
give	gave	given
go	went	gone
grow	grew	grown
have, has	had	had
hear	heard	heard
hold	held	held
hurt	hurt	hurt

present	*past*	*past participle*
keep	kept	kept
lay (put or place)	laid	laid
lead	led	led
leave	left	left
lie (recline)	lay	lain
lie (say something untrue)	lied	lied
lose	lost	lost
make	made	made
meet	met	met
pay	paid	paid
prove	proved	proved, proven
put	put	put
read	read	read
ride	rode	ridden
ring	rang	rung
run	ran	run
say	said	said
see	saw	seen
sell	sold	sold
send	sent	sent
set	set	set
shake	shook	shaken
shoot	shot	shot
shrink	shrank	shrunk
sing	sang	sung
sit	sat	sat
sleep	slept	slept
speak	spoke	spoken
spin	spun	spun
steal	stole	stolen
swim	swam	swum
take	took	taken
teach	taught	taught
tell	told	told
think	thought	thought
throw	threw	thrown
understand	understood	understood
wear	wore	worn
wring	wrung	wrung
write	wrote	written

When the dictionary lists more than one form for the past or for the past participle, the first form given is the preferred form; the other forms are acceptable though not preferred.

GRAMMAR AND USAGE: EXERCISE 10 (IRREGULAR VERB FORMS)

Directions: Underline the correct past tense form of each verb in parentheses.

1. Hank (brung, brought) home presents for the whole family.
2. The artist (drew, drawed) a picture of the historic street.
3. The money (lay, laid) on the sidewalk for two hours.
4. They (set, sat) there a long time without speaking.
5. Although prices (rose, raised), salaries didn't.
6. A former student (teached, taught) math to all the new students.
7. Alice (catched, caught) a cold last week when she went walking in the rain without a hat or coat.
8. Bob (choose, chose) a small black car rather than the big red one his wife wanted to buy.
9. The postman (lay, laid) the mail on top of the mailbox.
10. Alan (rose, raised) his hand and (rose, raised) to speak.

Answers and explanations are on pages 114–115.

The Present Tense

The present tense of almost all verbs is formed as follows:

singular	*plural*
I love	we love
you love	you love
he, she, it loves	they love

Notice that the form changes only when the subject is *he, she,* or *it* (or a noun that could be replaced by *he, she,* or *it*). Verbs that do not follow this form must be memorized. The two main exceptions are the verbs *to have* and *to be. Have* changes to *has* for the subjects *he, she,* or *it*. The verb *to be* is more irregular:

singular	*plural*
I am	we are
you are	you are
he, she, it is	they are

The present tense is used for actions that are performed in the present; this includes statements that are always true (since they are just as true in the present as they were in the past) and actions that are performed regularly.

She *is* not ready.

He *has* the flu again.
The sun *rises* in the east.
They *go* grocery shopping every Saturday.

The present tense can also be formed as shown in the following sentences:

(1) I *am working* too hard.
(2) Mary is too busy to talk to you now; she *is watching* a new television program.
(3) Although it often surprises my guests, my dog *does eat* at the table with everyone else.
(4) I'm surprised to hear that George can't stand Gary; after all, they *do live* together.

Each of these sentences concerns something that is true now, in the present. The verbs in sentences (1) and (2) are formed by combining the present tense of the verb *to be* with the *ing* form of the main verb to express an action that is going on now and will continue to go on until some time in the future. The verbs in sentences (3) and (4) are formed by combining the present tense of the verb *to do* with the present tense of the main verb to add extra force to the verb.

The Present Perfect Tense

The present perfect tense of almost all verbs is formed as follows:

singular	*plural*
I have loved	we have loved
you have loved	you have loved
he, she, it has loved	they have loved

Even the irregular verbs can be correctly put in the present perfect tense if you remember that this tense is formed by combining the present tense of the verb *to have* with the past participle of the main verb:

present tense of to have	+	*past participle*
I have		eaten
she has		gone

The present perfect tense is used to show that the action of the sentence started in the past and continues or has just ended in the present. It can also be used to show that something happened at an unknown time in the past.

John *has lived* there for seven years. (He still lives there.)
He *has driven* a Cadillac. (We don't know when.)

When you use the present perfect tense, make sure that you use the past participle and not the simple past form of the main verb.

> WRONG: She has already came.
> RIGHT: She has already come.
> WRONG: They have just ate dinner.
> RIGHT: They have just eaten dinner.

The Past Tense

The past tense of almost all verbs is formed by using the second of the three principal parts for all subjects.

The past tense is used to express completed action, action that is no longer taking place.

> Sue and Tom *danced* every dance at last night's party.
> The president *lived* there as a boy.

Be careful to use the simple past and not the past participle when you use the past tense.

> WRONG: I done it.
> RIGHT: I did it.
> WRONG: We seen the accident.
> RIGHT: We saw the accident.

The Past Perfect Tense

The past perfect tense of all verbs is formed by combining the past tense of the verb *to have* with the past participle of the main verb:

past tense of to have	+	*past participle*
she had		written
they had		gone
I had		loved

Notice that the past tense of the verb *to have* is always *had*.

Look at the following sentences in which the past perfect tense is used correctly:

> By the time Ralph *arrived,* they *had celebrated* already. They *had drunk* the champagne and *had sung* "Happy Birthday, Ralph!"

The verb *arrived* is in the past tense because the event took place at some time in the past. But, at an earlier time in the past, three other actions took place. To show that these actions took place at a more distant time in the past, it is necessary to use the past perfect tense. Whenever you wish to show the earlier of two past actions, use the past perfect tense.

Remember to use the past participle of the main verb when you use the past perfect tense:

WRONG: He had already ate before we got there.
RIGHT: He had already eaten before we got there.

The Future Tense

The future tense of all verbs is formed by combining the verb *will* with the present tense of the main verb:

will	+	*present tense*
you will		love
they will		go
she will		write

The future tense is used to indicate an action that will take place at some time in the future.

NOTE: It is no longer necessary to use the form *shall* with the future tense. You may simply use *will* in all cases.

The Future Perfect Tense

The future perfect tense of all verbs is formed by combining the verb phrase *will have* with the past participle of the main verb:

will have	+	*past participle*
they will have		driven
I will have		loved
she will have		sung

Look at the following sentences in which the future perfect tense is used correctly:

(1) By this time tomorrow, we *will have driven* more than halfway across the state.
(2) She will arrive at eight o'clock, and by that time we *will have cleaned* the entire house.

As these sentences demonstrate, the future perfect tense is used in one of two ways:

(1) to place the sentence in the future, but looking back at what will then be past
(2) to indicate the earlier of two future actions

When you use the future perfect tense, be sure to use the past participle of the main verb:

WRONG: If I take two more aspirin, I will have took more than six in one day.
RIGHT: If I take two more aspirin, I will have taken more than six in one day.

The Subjunctive

The subjunctive can be formed in one of two ways:

(1) by using the form of the present tense without *s* or the verb *be*

It is important that he *be* notified immediately.
I insist that she *finish* the work before she leaves.
It is urgent that he *see* her right away.

(2) by using *were* + some other form of the main verb (past participle, infinitive, or the *ing* form)

If he *were elected* president, there wouldn't be any economy.
If he *were to die* tomorrow, I don't know what I would do.
If I *were living* in the nineteenth century, I could live on my salary.

A verb is correctly used in the first of these two ways in situations of urgency, in commands, or in sentences that use such word groups as *it is essential that, it is urgent that, it is important that, it is imperative that,* or *it is necessary that.* Look at the underlined subjunctive verbs in the following paragraph:

> Signs really affect a person's life. Square ones in the park demand that one not <u>drink</u> alcoholic beverages, <u>walk</u> on the grass, or <u>feed</u> the animals. The triangular ones by the side of the road advise that one <u>be</u> careful crossing the street. Diamond-shaped signs insist that one <u>slow</u> down for school children. It's no wonder that Joe has a sign on his wall urging that he <u>relax</u> and <u>do</u> whatever he wants.

Notice the difference between the subjunctive and the present tense:

SUBJUNCTIVE: The supervisor demanded that Joe write to his cousin in Washington.

PRESENT: Joe writes to his cousin in Washington once a month.

The subjunctive form is the same no matter what the subject—always use the form of the present tense you would use with the subject *I* or the verb *be*.

The subjunctive is also used in situations that are only wished or that are contrary to fact. Although there are many such situations, the most common error is illustrated in the following sentences:

WRONG: If I was the king of the world, things would be a lot different.

RIGHT: If I were the king of the world, things would be a lot different.

WRONG: If George was here, I'm sure he would know what to do.

RIGHT: If George were here, I'm sure he would know what to do.

Summary of Verb Problems

A great deal of information about the tenses of verbs has been given to you in the preceding pages. To help you review for the GED exam, we can make up a list of important things for you to remember. Errors in one of these areas are the most likely to show up on the test.

(1) With all the compound verb tenses (present perfect, past perfect, future perfect, subjunctive, as well as more complicated tenses) use the past participle of the main verb:

John *has* just *eaten* three pieces of cake. (present perfect)

Marion *had written* twelve letters of complaint before she finally discovered that the problem was all her fault. (past perfect)

By the time you get here, *I will have spoken* to my brother about your problem. (future perfect)

If this book *were stolen,* I don't know what I would do. (subjunctive)

I *would have written* earlier, but I just couldn't find the time.

(2) Do not use the past participle when the sentence calls for a simple past tense:

WRONG: I *seen* a good movie last night.

RIGHT: I *saw* a good movie last night.

(3) Use the subjunctive *were* in sentences that do not take place at any point in time, such as situations that are only wished or that are contrary to fact:

> I wish I *were* home in bed.
> If George Washington *were* still alive, I wonder what he would think of the American government.

There are two other verb problems that should be mentioned at this point:

(1) it is incorrect to use the word *ain't*
(2) in sentences in which the subject of the verb is not the performer of the action of the sentence, you must use the past participle of the main verb

Although many people use *ain't* in informal spoken English, it is considered incorrect in written English and on the GED test.

WRONG: I ain't worried.
RIGHT: I'm not worried.
WRONG: She's right, ain't she?
RIGHT: She's right, isn't she?

In your reading, you may find sentences constructed like one of the following six sentences:

(1) All of the work *is done* by computer.
(2) All of the work *has been done* by computer.
(3) All of the work *was done* by computer.
(4) All of the work *had been done* by computer.
(5) All of the work *will be done* by computer.
(6) All of the work *will have been done* by computer.

Although *All of the work* is the subject of the verb, *All of the work* is not the performer of the action of the sentence. The *computer* is the performer of the action. Sentences like these are said to be written in the **passive voice.** The most important thing for you to remember about this kind of sentence is that you must always use the past participle of the main verb.

WRONG: The cash was took.
RIGHT: The cash was taken.
WRONG: The bell was rang early.
RIGHT: The bell was rung early.

GRAMMAR AND USAGE: EXERCISE 11 (PROBLEMS WITH VERBS)

Directions: In each of the following sentences, four verbs have been underlined. If one of the verbs is used or formed incorrectly, blacken the space under the number corresponding to it. If all of the verbs are correct, blacken the space numbered (5).

1. When the horse saw (1) the rattlesnake, it kicked (2) and almost threw (3) its rider, who wished he was driving (4) his car instead. No error (5)

   1. 1 2 3 4 5

2. The fans will scream (1) with excitement when the Olympic swimmer comes (2) out of the locker room and says (3) to the timer either, "I ain't (4) ready yet," or, "O.K. Let's go." No error (5)

   2. 1 2 3 4 5

3. Award winners always thank (1) their parents, who teached (2) them what is important in life; their neighbors and friends, who were (3) understanding and interested; and their fellow workers, without whose hard work it all would have been (4) impossible. No error (5)

   3. 1 2 3 4 5

4. A monument was dedicated (1) by the mayor with these words: "I have made (2) progress in this city. I have learned (3) how to deal with the problems. I have saw (4) what must be done." No error (5)

   4. 1 2 3 4 5

5. Many laws are being changed (1) now. Many states no longer require (2) that a person is (3) twenty-one to drink liquor, and the national voting age has been lowered (4) to eighteen. No error (5)

   5. 1 2 3 4 5

6. 1 2 3 4 5

6. If Paul and Linda were (1) twenty-one, they could get married, (2) but they are (3) only fifteen and will have (4) to wait six more years. No error (5)

7. 1 2 3 4 5

7. Her grandfather was (1) healthy before he had (2) a heart attack last year. So far this year he has felt (3) quite good, but he watches (4) his diet very carefully. No error (5)

8. 1 2 3 4 5

8. Everyone laughed (1) when the ugly old man on the television show sang, (2) "I wish I were (3) ten years younger. Then I would marry (4) a go-go dancer." No error (5)

9. 1 2 3 4 5

9. We know that people have used (1) old sayings since the time that history begun (2) to record them. Who could better express (3) the thought contained in the saying: "The road to hell is paved (4) with good intentions." No error (5)

10. 1 2 3 4 5

10. John reported (1) that he had finished (2) his chores. "I fed (3) the dog and done (4) the laundry," he said. No error (5)

11. 1 2 3 4 5

11. After the foreman had rang (1) the bell, the workers came (2) back and took (3) their places, which they had left (4) for lunch. No error (5)

12. As newspapers are read (1), they usually are being carried (2) to work or are resting on a kitchen table. When they have been finished (3), they are dumped (4) in the garbage. No error (5)

12. 1 2 3 4 5

13. Farmer Dell lied (1) when he said (2) his chicken laid (3) golden eggs. So far she has lain (4) only white and brown ones. No error (5)

13. 1 2 3 4 5

14. "He has taken (1) two hours to get the mail," Mrs. Jones complained (2). "Maybe they caught (3) him and made (4) him confess." No error (5)

14. 1 2 3 4 5

15. Mike did (1) what he had to do and found (2) the person that had stole (3) the money, but the jury let (4) the guilty man go. No error (5)

15. 1 2 3 4 5

Answers and explanations are on page 116.

SUBJECT AND VERB AGREEMENT

The following two sentences are almost the same, but there are two very important differences:

(1) I love to dance.
(2) George loves to dance.

The subjects of the two sentences are different. Although both sentences are in the present tense, the form of the verb is different in each sentence. When we examined the present tense of verbs, we noted that a verb changes its form for the subjects *he, she, it,* and nouns that can be replaced by *he, she,* and *it*. In every sentence that you write, you must (1) determine the subject of the sentence and (2) use the correct form of the verb for that subject. Each time you go through this two-step process, you are making the verb *agree* with the subject.

The following two paragraphs illustrate the principle of subject and verb agreement.

> If you believe what you read, rock stars are glamorous people who lead exciting, fun-filled lives. They drive flashy, expensive cars, and they can meet anyone who turns them on. Rock stars have been pictured in the newspapers and on television as evil in their influence on their fans and possessed by the demons of fame and fortune. From the stories that are told, one can only conclude that rock stars must be heartless, reckless, cruel people.

> Harold Crigsby is a rock musician who plays with the band "Starstreak Survivors." He drives a 1967 Ford with a bad oil leak. Harold can make barely enough to support himself and his widowed mother and to take his girlfriend Mary Jane to the movies on Wednesday night. Harold has been featured in the newspapers twice: once for rescuing a drowning puppy and once for speaking to the local Boy Scout troop about the dangers of drugs. Everyone who meets him says, "What a nice person he must be!"

Examine the underlined subjects and verbs in these two paragraphs. What conclusions can you draw from the following lists:

rock stars (they)	*Harold Crigsby (he)*
are	is
drive	drives
can meet	can make
have been pictured	has been featured
must be	must be

The subject of a sentence can name one person, place, thing, or idea, in which case the subject is *singular* (Harold, he). The subject can also name more than one person, place, thing, or idea, in which case it is *plural* (rock stars, they). Singular subjects require singular verbs (he is); plural subjects require plural verbs (they are). Notice that some verbs are the same for both singular and plural subjects (can, must).

In addition, the subject of a sentence can be described as being one of three *persons:*

(1) the person or persons speaking
I am a star.
We are the stars in this show.
(2) the person or persons being spoken to
Harold, *you* are a star.
Harold and Maude, *you* are stars.
(3) the person or persons being spoken about
He is a star.
They are stars.

The idea of *person* also holds true for places, things, or ideas. Notice that the form of the verb is different for different persons. Look at the diagram below for the verb *to be:*

	first person	*second person*	*third person*
PRESENT			
singular	I am	you are	he, she, it is
plural	we are	you are	they are
PAST			
singular	I was	you were	he, she, it was
plural	we were	you were	they were

The form of the verb changes for different subjects. The correct form is determined by two things:

(1) the number of the subject, either singular or plural
(2) the person of the subject, either first, second, or third

All verbs must agree with the subject of the sentence in number and in person.

This rule is easy enough to apply when the subject of the sentence is clear and simple.

WRONG: Harold are a star.
RIGHT: Harold is a star.

Harold is a singular subject (Harold is only one person), and Harold is the person being spoken about (third person); therefore, the form of the verb must be the third person singular, *is.*

Do not be confused by the short forms *don't,* meaning *do not,* and *doesn't,* meaning *does not. Don't* is used only for plural subjects; *doesn't* is used only for singular subjects.

WRONG: Harold don't like reporters.
RIGHT: Harold doesn't like reporters.

However, sometimes it is more difficult to find the true subject of the sentence. When we discussed the subjects of sentences, we discovered that we could determine the subject by asking the question, "*Who or what is this about?*" Asking this question will help you solve the problems of subject and verb agreement illustrated in the following examples.

EXAMPLE 1. Mrs. Kretch, as well as her five sons, (go, goes) to the Starlight Lounge every day after work.

The sentence is about Mrs. Kretch. The words *as well as her five sons* only give additional information. Since the subject of the sentence, *Mrs. Kretch,* is a third person singular noun, the verb that agrees with the subject is *goes.*

Do not make the mistake of using the plural *go* to agree with the noun *sons. Sons* is not the subject of the sentence.

EXAMPLE 2. Two new singers, together with rock star Mick Swagger, (was, were) on television last night.

The sentence is about two new singers. The words *together with rock star Mick Swagger* only give additional information. Since the subject of the sentence, *two new singers,* is plural and in the third person, the verb that agrees with the subject is *were* (a third person plural verb).

Do not make the mistake of using the singular verb *was* to agree with the noun *Mick Swagger. Mick Swagger* is not the subject of the sentence.

EXAMPLE 3. The effect of films about crime, violence, and sex on children with impressionable minds (is, are) hard to determine.

The sentence is about the effect of films about crime, violence, and sex on children with impressionable minds. Notice that there are both plural and singular nouns in the complete subject. However, as we learned when we examined the uses of nouns, a noun used as the object of a preposition (of, about, on, with) gives additional information about another word in the sentence. In the sentence above, we can break the complete subject into the following parts:

the effect
of films — gives information about *effect;* the effect of what
about crime, violence, and sex — gives information about *films;* films about what
on children — gives information about *effect;* effect on whom
with impressionable minds — gives information about *children;* what kind of children

The word *effect* is called the **simple subject** of the sentence. All the other words in the complete subject only give additional information to make it clear what effect is being discussed. To solve the problem of subject and verb agreement, you must clear away the words that only give additional information.

The effect ______ (is, are) hard to determine.

Since *effect* is a third person singular noun, you must use the third person singular verb *is.*

In all sentences, the verb agrees with the simple subject.

EXAMPLE 4. Martha (is, are) one of those people who (is, are) concerned about the inhumane treatment of animals.

The sentence is about Martha. Since the subject of the sentence, *Martha,* is a third person singular noun, the verb that agrees with the subject is *is.* However, you would be wrong if you used the form *is* for both verbs in this sentence. The subject of the second verb is not *Martha.* To understand the problem of agreement in this sentence, you must take the sentence apart:

Martha is one of those people.
What people are you talking about?
I am talking about those people who (is, are) concerned about the inhumane treatment of animals.

The words *who (is, are) concerned about the inhumane treatment of animals* give additional information about the word *people.* This part of the sentence is about *people,* not *Martha.* The word *who* is used to replace the word *people* so that the additional information can be attached to the sentence. The word *who* is the subject of the verb in this part of the sentence. Since *who* stands for *people,* a third person plural noun, the verb that agrees with the subject is the third plural *are*. Thus, the sentence should read:

> Martha *is* one of those people who *are* concerned about the inhumane treatment of animals.

It is correct to use the singular verb in both parts of the following sentence:

> Martha, who *is* concerned about the inhumane treatment of animals, *is* a member of the ASPCA.

In this sentence, the group of words set off by commas gives additional information about Martha. The subject of this group of words is *who,* but in this case, *who* stands for the third person singular noun *Martha.* Thus, you must use the third person singular verb *is.*

This problem of agreement will occur whenever you see a group of words attached to a sentence by the words *who, which,* or *that.* (You will learn more about these word groups in the next chapter.)

WRONG: George is one of those men who *is* fascinated by machines.

RIGHT: George is one of those men who *are* fascinated by machines.

WRONG: The solution to these problems, which *is* caused by human neglect, *have* not been found.

RIGHT: The solution to these problems, which *are* caused by human neglect, *has* not been found.

WRONG: One of the desks that *was* ordered for the office has a defective lock.

RIGHT: One of the desks that *were* ordered for the office has a defective lock.

In the first sentence, *who* stands for the plural noun *men;* thus, you must use the plural verb. In the next sentence, *which* stands for the plural noun *problems;* thus, you must use the plural verb. Notice that the singular verb *has* is used to agree with the singular subject *solution*. In the last sentence, *that* stands for the plural noun *desks;* thus, you must use the plural verb. The singular verb *has* agrees with the singular subject *one.*

EXAMPLE 5. Right in the middle of the street (was, were) the two lost boys.

The sentence is about two lost boys. The words *right in the middle of the street* tell something about the boys; they tell where the boys were. These words are part of the predicate of the sentence. The writer has turned the sentence around to have a certain dramatic effect on the reader. However, the subject of the sentence is still *two lost boys,* a plural subject that requires the plural verb *were.*

Whenever you find a sentence like this, it may help to think of the sentence in a subject-predicate form:

> The two lost boys (was, were) right in the middle of the street.

Finding the subject of a sentence is only part of the process of finding a solution to the problem of subject and verb agreement. It is often difficult to remember that, although the *plural* form of most *nouns* ends with an *s*, it is the *singular* form of most *verbs* that ends with an *s.* Look at the following two sentences:

(1) The two boys walk to school every day.
(2) That little boy walks to school every day.

The noun *boys* is plural, and the verb *walk* is also plural. The noun *boy* is singular, and the verb *walks* is also singular.

When the subject of the sentence is *I, we, you, he, she, it,* or *they,* it is fairly easy to remember the correct form of the verb. For this reason, you might find it easier to replace the subject of a sentence with one of these words before you choose the form of the verb that agrees with the subject. For the two sentences above:

(1)	The two boys	walk to school every day.
	They	walk to school every day.
(2)	That little boy	walks to school every day.
	He	walks to school every day.

Although you can solve many of your problems in this way, some kinds of subjects present special problems in agreement. In the following pages, these troublesome kinds of subjects will be discussed.

GRAMMAR AND USAGE: EXERCISE 12 (SUBJECT-VERB AGREEMENT)

Directions: In each of the following sentences, two forms of the verb are given in parentheses. Underline the form of the verb that agrees in number and person with the subject.

1. A common cure for aches and pains (is, are) aspirin.
2. Mr. Johnson together with his brother (own, owns) a garage.
3. One of the secretaries (make, makes) coffee every morning.
4. Not one of the typewriters that (was, were) stolen (have, has) been found.

5. Susan as well as her sister and brother (have, has) decided to leave Chicago.
6. Sam (is, are) one of those people who (is, are) always late for work.
7. The use of television to educate as well as entertain and inform people (have, has) been very successful.
8. Waiting in line for unemployment checks (was, were) the employees who had been laid off.

Answers and explanations are on pages 116–117.

(1) When the subject is a noun that names a number of people or things collectively (collective nouns), you must use a singular verb when the subject is thought of as a single unit.

The following nouns are used in this way:

audience	family
class	group
club	jury
collection	orchestra
corporation	staff
crowd	team

EXAMPLES

(1) The whole *group is* out to lunch.
(2) My *family is* going on vacation tomorrow.

BUT

(3) The *members* of my family *are* going on vacation tomorrow.

In the last example, the subject of the sentence is the plural noun *members;* therefore, the verb must also be plural.

(4) The *family are* occupied with their individual problems.

In this sentence, the noun *family* is not thought of as a single unit; the members of the family are thought of as individuals with separate and distinct problems. Since the meaning behind *family* in this sentence is plural, you must use a plural verb.

(2) As you learned when you studied nouns, some nouns are always plural in form (they always end in *s*). Most of these nouns are

like collective nouns; when they are singular in meaning (naming a whole class of things as a single unit), they require a singular verb. Some other nouns that are plural in form but singular in meaning also require singular verbs.

The following nouns are used in this way:

data	news
economics	physics
mathematics	tactics

EXAMPLES

(1) *Mathematics is* a very useful subject to study.
(2) No *news is* good news.
(3) The *data* compiled by our computer *is* top secret.
BUT
(4) The *data* on welfare, education, and population *are* collected by different agencies of the federal government.

In the third sentence, the word *data* is used to describe many bits of information as one unit. Although the form of the word is plural, the meaning is singular; therefore, a singular verb is required. In the fourth sentence, three kinds of data are described. Since the word *data* is used with a plural meaning (three separate kinds), the plural verb is required.

Some nouns that are always plural in form require a plural verb:

eyeglasses
scissors
pants

EXAMPLES

(1) The *scissors are* on the table.
(2) George's best *pants were* completely covered with mud.
(3) The *pair* of scissors *is* on the table.
(4) George's best *pair* of pants *is* at the cleaner's.

Although these words require a plural verb when used alone, a singular verb is used when the word is connected to the expression *pair of.*

(3) Some subjects always take a singular verb even though the meaning may seem plural:

each	someone
either	anyone
neither	nobody
one	somebody
no one	anybody
everyone	everybody

EXAMPLES

(1) I don't think *everybody is* here yet.
(2) *Anyone* who wants to come *is* welcome.
(3) *Each student* in the class *is* responsible for his own work.
(4) *Neither* of these books *is* any good.

One way to remember that these subjects take a singular verb is to think of the meaning behind the subject. The group of people described as every*body* or every*one* is thought of as being composed of *single,* individual bodies. Since the word *body* and the word *one* are singular, you must use a singular verb for correct agreement.

In some sentences, you can substitute a collective noun for the subject to help solve the problem of agreement:

I don't think *everyone* is here yet.
I don't think *the group* is here yet.

(4) Some subjects take either a singular or plural verb depending on the meaning they get from another word in the sentence.

The following words are used in this way:

all	part
some	half (and other fractions)
none	most
	number

EXAMPLES

(1) *All* of the *cake is* left.
(2) *Some* of that *pizza was* for you.
BUT
(3) *All* of the *boys are* here.
(4) *Some* of the *people have* gone home.

In the first two sentences, the words *all* and *some* refer to the singular nouns *cake* and *pizza;* therefore, the singular form of the verb is required. In sentences (3) and (4), the words *all* and *some* refer to the plural nouns *boys* and *people;* therefore, the plural form of the verb is required.

The form of the noun will not always tell you whether the meaning is plural:

(5) A *number* of problems *are* difficult to solve.
(6) The *number* of problems on the test *is* up to the teacher.

In sentence (5), *a number of problems* means that there are *many* problems; since the meaning is plural, the plural form of the verb is used. In sentence (6), *the number of problems* means the *specific* number; since the meaning is singular, the singular form of the verb is used.

(5) For sentences that begin with *here* or *there,* you must look for the true subject of the sentence to determine the form of the verb. The subject is found after the verb, as in Example 5 on page 60.

EXAMPLES

(1) Here *are* the two *boys* now.
(2) Here *is* the *boy* I wanted to see.

Be especially careful with the forms *here's* (meaning *here is*) and *there's* (meaning *there is*):

WRONG: There's the *books* on cars I wanted.
RIGHT: There *are* the *books* on cars I wanted.

Although this rule applies to sentences that begin with *here* or *there,* do not use this rule for sentences that begin with *it.* These sentences may seem to be formed in the same way, but *it* always requires a singular verb.

EXAMPLES

(1) Here *are* the verbs that confuse me.
(2) It *is* the verbs that confuse me.

The two sentences may look the same in form, but their meanings are different. Sentence (1) could be the answer to the question, "Which verbs confuse you?" The answer is about many specific verbs; the meaning is plural. Sentence (2) could be the answer to the question, "Of all the various kinds of words, which kind confuses you the most?" The answer is about the general class of words called *verbs;* the meaning is singular. In sentence (2) *verbs* is used as a collective noun.

(6) Amounts and measurements used as subjects usually require singular verbs.

EXAMPLES

(1) Two miles *is* a long distance to run.
(2) Ten dollars *lasts* a very short time nowadays.

In both of these sentences, the subjects can be thought of as a single unit. Since the meaning is singular, the verb is also singular.

(3) Ten new one-dollar bills *were* neatly stacked on the counter.

In this sentence, the subject is composed of ten separate and distinct units. Since the meaning is plural, the verb is also plural.

GRAMMAR AND USAGE: EXERCISE 13 (SUBJECT-VERB AGREEMENT)

Directions: In each of the following sentences, two forms of the verb are given in parentheses. Underline the form of the verb that agrees in number and person with the subject.

1. There (is, are) about twenty chairs in the room.
2. Seventy tons of paper (are, is) needed to print 12,000 copies of this book.
3. Our basketball team always (lose, loses) the first game of the season.
4. Each of these questions (is, are) explained at the end of the section.
5. Every pair of scissors (are, is) broken.
6. All of the paychecks (have, has) arrived, but some of them (is, are) wrong.
7. None of these coats (look, looks) good on me.
8. Neither of the movies on television tonight (are, is) good.

Answers and explanations are on pages 117–118.

In the preceding examples of troublesome subjects, the key to subject and verb agreement was found by looking at the meaning of the subject. However, all of the subjects we have discussed so far have been only one word (once the complete subject was reduced to the simple subject). In many sentences, the subject is composed of two or more nouns connected by *and, or, neither . . . nor, either . . . or,* or *not only . . . but also.* These subjects are called **compound subjects.**

When all of the nouns in a compound subject are singular, or when they are all plural, the problem of agreement is fairly easy to solve. In the following pages, we will examine the various kinds of compound subjects, paying special attention to the more difficult problems of agreement.

(1) A compound subject joined together by *and* almost always takes a plural verb.

EXAMPLES

(1) Sam and Joe *make* a lot of money.
(2) Wood and steel *are* building materials.
(3) George and his two sons *have* gone on a fishing trip. (Note that it doesn't make any difference that part of the compound subject is singular and part of it is plural.)

BUT

(4) The secretary and treasurer of the club *is* not present tonight. (This sentence is correct if, and only if, the same person is both the secretary and the treasurer.)

(2) A compound subject joined together by *or, nor, either . . . or, neither . . . nor,* or *not only . . . but also* takes either a singular or a plural verb depending on the part of the subject nearest to the verb. The verb agrees both in number and in person with the part of the subject nearest to it.

EXAMPLES

(1) The father or his *sons are* going to be proved right.
(2) Neither Mamie nor *Mimi wants* to go.
(3) Neither Mamie nor her two *sisters want* to go.
(4) Not only the players but also the *coach is* disappointed.
(5) Either you or *I am* going to have to leave.

Look at the following analysis of these five sentences:

	first part of subject	*second part of subject*	*verb*
(1)	father (singular, 3rd person)	sons (plural, 3rd person)	are (plural, 3rd person)
(2)	Mamie (singular, 3rd person)	Mimi (singular, 3rd person)	wants (singular, 3rd person)
(3)	Mamie (singular, 3rd person)	sisters (plural, 3rd person)	want (plural, 3rd person)
(4)	players (plural, 3rd person)	coach (singular, 3rd person)	is (singular, 3rd person)
(5)	you (singular?, 2nd person)	I (singular, 1st person)	am (singular, 1st person)

The same rule applies to sentences with three or more parts to the compound subject:

> Paul or Helen or their miserable *children are* bound to show up.

Since the noun *children* is plural and in the third person, the correct form of the verb is *are* (the third person plural form of *to be*).

(3) Be careful of sentences that have a predicate nominative (see page 27). The verb always agrees with the subject, not the predicate nominative.

EXAMPLES

(1) George and Martha *are* Sam's favorite married couple.
BUT
(2) Sam's favorite married couple *is* George and Martha.

In sentence (1), the verb agrees with the compound subject *George and Martha.* In sentence (2), the verb agrees with the collective noun *married couple.*

GRAMMAR AND USAGE: EXERCISE 14 (SUBJECT-VERB AGREEMENT)

Directions: In each of the following sentences, two forms of the verb are given in parentheses. Underline the form of the verb that agrees in number and person with the subject.

1. Jim and Alice (don't, doesn't) have the money to take a vacation.
2. Neither Jim nor Alice (have, has) the money to take a vacation.
3. A bracelet or a few records (is, are) a good gift for her.
4. The biggest bargain in the store (are, is) the shoes.
5. Not only New York but also Chicago and Washington (have, has) financial problems.

Answers and explanations are on page 118.

GRAMMAR AND USAGE: EXERCISE 15 (SUBJECT-VERB AGREEMENT REVIEW)

Directions: In each of the following sentences, two forms of the verb are given in parentheses. Choose the form of the verb that agrees with the subject, and write the correct form on the line below the sentence.

---

1. Everybody here (is, are) waiting for you, but no one (expect, expects) you to show up.

____

2. Four hours (is, are) too much time to take on this test; most students (finishes, finish) in less than an hour.

____

3. Billy Graham, together with his faithful followers, (is, are) going to offer a special service this Sunday.

____

4. Either Susan or one of her sisters (is, are) going to pick you up for the party; neither of us (has, have) the time.

____

5. Everyone who (look, looks) suspicious will be stopped by the guards, who (is, are) going to be posted at every door.

____

6. All of the audience (is, are) asleep now, although some of the people (was, were) excited when the show started.

____

7. The crowd (is, are) cheering, but our group (is, are) not impressed by the convention.

____

8. The use of drugs in the school's buildings and on the school's grounds (is, are) forbidden.

____

9. Mystery novels and collections of horror stories (is, are) Fred's idea of exciting reading. His idea of dull reading (is, are) historical novels and love stories.

____

10. A thorough knowledge of mathematics (is, are) necessary if economics (is, are) your chosen field of study.

____

11. Neither mathematics nor physics (interests, interest) him; in fact, both sciences (bores, bore) him.

____

12. Behind those two-way mirrors (stand, stands) a guard ready to arrest anyone who (is, are) foolish enough to try shoplifting.

____

13. One of your friends (has, have) just told me that there (is, are) beer and sandwiches in the next room.

____

14. Your father and brother (is, are) waiting for you in the car, but neither of them (is, are) in a hurry.

____

15. George was just fired but he (don't, doesn't) care because he and his wife (has, have) saved a lot of money this year.

____

Answers and explanations are on pages 118–121.

PRONOUNS (WORDS THAT REPLACE NOUNS)

Read the following story, paying special attention to the underlined nouns.

Rose is worried about Rose's age. "Rose is not getting any younger," Rose often says to Rose. Rose feels that at Rose's age a woman should have solved all of life's problems. Other women seem to have solved life's problems. Other women have a husband or a career; Rose does not. Rose has been waiting for Mr. Right, but Mr. Right hasn't found Rose yet. Rose looks for Mr. Right every day of Rose's life. Every time Rose meets a man, Rose examines the man to see if the man has any of Mr. Right's qualifications. George has Mr. Right's money, but George's personality is all wrong. Paul has Mr. Right's personality, but Paul has no money. Together, Paul's and George's qualifications make one Mr. Right, but George and Paul are two different people. Paul would be Mr. Right if only George would give Paul George's money. Perhaps, one day as Rose turns a corner, a man will leap out and announce, "It is the person Rose has been waiting for, Mr. Right." But just between the reader and the writer, with Rose's luck, the man will be a mugger!

Very few writers would actually write this story in this way. The nouns are repeated so many times that the writing seems stiff and formal. However, the nouns must be repeated often enough to make the writer's meaning clear. The underlined nouns could be replaced with a special kind of word called a pronoun. In the following rewrite of this story, each of the underlined nouns has been replaced by a pronoun. Notice the form of each pronoun.

Rose is worried about her age. "I am not getting any younger," she often says to herself. Rose feels that at her age a woman should have solved all of life's problems. Other women seem to have solved them. They have a husband or a career; Rose does not. Rose has been waiting for Mr. Right, but he hasn't found her yet. She looks for him every day of her life. Every time she meets a man, she examines him to see if he has any of Mr. Right's qualifications. George has Mr. Right's money, but his personality is all wrong. Paul has Mr. Right's personality, but he has no money. Together, their qualifications make one Mr. Right, but they are two different people. Paul would be Mr. Right if only George would give him his money. Perhaps, one day as Rose turns a corner, a man will leap out and announce, "It is I, Mr. Right." But, just between you and me, with Rose's luck, the man will be a mugger!

For every use of the noun, there is a pronoun that can be used in the same way:

(1) Pronouns can replace nouns used as *subjects.*

I (line 1)	he (line 5)
they (line 4)	she (line 6)

(2) Pronouns can replace nouns used as *predicate nominatives* (see page 27 for a discussion of this term).

I (line 14)

(3) Pronouns can replace nouns used as *appositives* (see page 27 for a discussion of this term).

Just between *us, you* and *me,* Rose will never find Mr. Right.

We, he and *I,* know that Rose is a fool.

(4) Pronouns can replace nouns used as *objects of prepositions.*

him (line 6)
you (line 14)
me (line 14)

(5) Pronouns can replace nouns used as *direct objects* (see pages 27–28 for a discussion of this term).

them (line 4)
her (line 6)
him (line 7)

(6) Pronouns can replace nouns used as *indirect objects* (see page 28 for a discussion of this term).

him (line 12)

In addition, there are special forms of pronouns that replace possessive nouns (*Rose's age* becomes *her age* in line 1). There is even a form of pronoun that can be used when the action of the sentence is done on or to the same person as the subject (*herself,* line 2).

We can now write a definition of a pronoun:

A pronoun is a word that can replace any noun and can be used in the same way as the noun it replaces.

Although any noun can be replaced by a pronoun, there are many different pronouns from which to choose. Notice that the noun *Rose* is not always replaced by the same pronoun:

(1) *Rose* looks for Mr. Right every day of *Rose's* life.
She looks for Mr. Right every day of *her* life.
(2) Mr. Right hasn't found *Rose* yet.
Mr. Right hasn't found *her* yet.

In sentence (1), *Rose* is the subject of the sentence; in sentence (2) *Rose* names the receiver of the action of the sentence (the direct object). Since the use of the noun is different, so is the form of the pronoun.

However, determining the use of a pronoun is only part of the process of choosing which pronoun to use. As we discovered in the study of subject and verb agreement, every noun can be described in terms of person (person speaking, person spoken to, or person spoken about) and number (singular or plural). Since pronouns replace nouns, they must describe the person and number of the nouns they are replacing. They must also describe the sex (male, female, or neuter, meaning no sex at all) of the nouns they are replacing.

Whenever you use a pronoun, then, you must ask yourself:

(1) How is the pronoun used in the sentence?

(2) What is the person of the noun being replaced?
— Is the noun the person or persons speaking (first person)?
— Is the noun the person or persons spoken to (second person)?
— Is the noun the person or persons spoken about (third person)?

(3) What is the number of the noun being replaced?
— Does the noun name only one person, place, thing, or idea; that is, is the noun singular?
— Does the noun name more than one person, place, thing, or idea; that is, is the noun plural?

(4) What is the sex of the noun being replaced?
— Is the noun a woman (feminine)?
— Is the noun a man (masculine)?
— Is the noun a place, thing, or idea that has no sex (neuter)?

All of this may seem confusing, but it does not need to be. As you will see in the following pages, there are two basic groups of pronouns:

(1) a form of pronoun that names the subject or renames the subject in some way
(2) a form of pronoun that replaces a noun used in any other way

Then, there are special groups of pronouns

(1) that show ownership or relationship (possessives)
(2) that end in *self* or *selves*

We can now look at the pronouns that are in each of these groups.

(1) If the noun being replaced names the subject, or renames the subject in some way, use one of the following pronouns (called *nominative* or *subjective pronouns*):

	person speaking (first person)	*person spoken to (second person)*	*person spoken about (third person)*
singular	I	you	he, she, it
plural	we	you	they

EXAMPLES

(1) *Sara* will be at the party. (The noun is the subject.)
She will be at the party.

(2) I know that the thief is *that man.* (The noun renames the subject of the verb *is,* which is *thief;* the noun is a predicate nominative.)
I know that the thief is *he.*

(3) Those people, *Alice* and *Fred,* are never on time. (The nouns rename the subject; the nouns are appositives.)
Those people, *she* and *he,* are never on time.

(2) For all the other uses of the noun (see pages 27–28), use one of the following pronouns (called *objective pronouns*):

	person speaking (first person)	*person spoken to (second person)*	*person spoken about (third person)*
singular	me	you	him, her, it
plural	us	you	them

EXAMPLES

(1) I wouldn't go out of my way for *Ted and Susan.* (The nouns follow a connecting word, *for,* to give additional information; the nouns are the object of the preposition.)
I wouldn't go out of my way for *them.*

(2) Tom kissed *Linda* for being such a wonderful person. (The noun names the receiver of the action; the noun is a direct object.)
Tom kissed *her* for being such a wonderful person.

(3) Linda gave *Tom* a lecture for being such a romantic. (The noun names the person to whom the action is done; the noun is an indirect object.)
Linda gave *him* a lecture for being such a romantic.

(4) The boss is about to fire two people, you and *Ted.* (The noun renames the receiver of the action; the noun is an appositive attached to a direct object.)
The boss is about to fire two people, you and *him.*

(3) For nouns that show ownership or relationship (possessive nouns), use one of the following pronouns (called *possessive pronouns*):

	person speaking (first person)	*person spoken to (second person)*	*person spoken about (third person)*
singular	my	your	his, her, its
plural	our	your	their

NOTE: *Its* is spelled without an apostrophe ('). The form *it's* means only *it is* or *it has.*

If the pronoun is used alone, that is, is not attached to another word, use one of the following forms:

	person speaking (first person)	*person spoken to (second person)*	*person spoken about (third person)*
singular	mine	yours	his, hers, its
plural	ours	yours	theirs

NOTE: None of these forms is spelled with an apostrophe.

EXAMPLES

(1) Rose is worried about *Rose's* age.
Rose is worried about *her* age.

(2) It's time to quit smoking when a cigarette loses *a cigarette's* taste.
It's time to quit smoking when a cigarette loses *its* taste.

(3) *John's* hair is longer than *Joan's.*
His hair is longer than *hers.*

(4) When the action of the sentence is done by the subject to himself (or herself), use one of the following pronouns (called *reflexive pronouns*):

	person speaking (first person)	*person spoken to (second person)*	*person spoken about (third person)*
singular	myself	yourself	himself, herself, itself
plural	ourselves	yourselves	themselves

NOTE: There are no such words as *hisself* or *theirselves.*

EXAMPLES

(1) Take care of *yourself.* (Remember, the subject of a command is always *you.*)

(2) I'll do it *myself.*

(3) John talks to *himself.*

GRAMMAR AND USAGE: EXERCISE 16 (PRONOUN FORMS)

Directions: Choose the correct form from the two given and write it in the blank space on the left.

________ 1. Jack and (*me, I*) went home.

________ 2. Give it to Susan and (*they, them*).

________ 3. Because of the rain, Lance and (*him, he*) left.

________ 4. Leave the rest for the Jacksons and (*we, us*).

________ 5. The wave dragged Joan and (*she, her*) out to sea.

________ 6. Give your ticket to one of the two men at the door, John or (*he, him*).

________ 7. I know that the winner is (*her, she*).

________ 8. His car is newer than (*her's, hers*).

________ 9. The bus missed Ray and (*I, me*) by only a few inches.

________ 10. John likes to do everything (*hisself, himself*).

Answers and explanations are on page 121.

Following these basic rules will help you to solve most of the problems involved in choosing the correct pronoun. However, there are a number of special problems with which you will need to become familiar. These problems are usually in one of two areas:

(1) choosing the right kind of pronoun (subjective, objective, or possessive)
(2) choosing the right person and number of the pronoun to match the noun that is being replaced

In the following pages, the errors you are most likely to find on the GED test and in your own writing will be discussed under these two headings.

CHOOSING THE RIGHT KIND OF PRONOUN

(1) Sentences with one or more nouns and a pronoun

In a sentence that has one or more nouns and a pronoun joined together by *and* or *or,* it is sometimes difficult to decide which form of pronoun to use. A good trick for finding the right form is to leave out the noun or nouns in the sentence and to look at the sentence with the pronoun alone. This simplifies the sentence and makes choosing the right form easier.

EXAMPLES

(1) Steve and (him, he) will be in at 9:00.
He will be in at 9:00.
(pronoun used as subject)

(2) They bought some drinks for Marty and (I, me).
They bought some drinks for me.
(pronoun follows connecting word)

This same problem arises when you have two pronouns.

(3) (He, Him) and (I, me) are going to Canada.
He is going to Canada.
I am going to Canada.

(Notice that the verb had to be changed to agree with the subject.)

(2) Who or whom and whoever or whomever

The pronouns *who* and *whom* are perhaps the most difficult pronouns to use correctly. In spoken English, very few people even use the pronoun *whom*. However, on the GED test, you will be expected to know the difference between them and recognize the errors that can be made when they are used. It will help if you remember that:

who and *whoever* are used only as subjects
whom and *whomever* are used as anything except subjects.

In other words, *who* and *whoever* are used in the same way as *he* and *they; whom* and *whomever* are used in the same way as *him* and *them*. If you have trouble deciding between *who* and *whom* because the sentence sounds strange, try substituting *he* or *him* in the sentence (although you may have to reword the sentence to do this, make sure that you don't change the meaning).

(Who, Whom) is that man?
(He *is that man.*)
Who is that man?

The pronoun is the subject; therefore, use *who.*

Mr. Kelp, (who, whom) you all know, is on a fishing trip.
(Mr. Kelp, you all know him, *is on a fishing trip.)*
Mr. Kelp, *whom* you all know, is on a fishing trip.

The pronoun receives the action of the verb *know* (*you* is the subject of *know*); therefore, use *whom*. Notice that it was necessary to reword the sentence slightly to put the true subject of the verb in front of the verb; you can do this mentally if it helps you to choose the correct pronoun, although you would never write the sentence in this way.

When the sentence is as simple as the two examples above, it is fairly easy to determine which pronoun to use. All you need to do is determine whether the pronoun names the subject or renames the subject in some way. However, you will need to be careful of sentences in which an extra group of words comes between the pronoun and the verb.

(1) (Who, Whom) did you say that man is?
(2) Mr. Kelp, (who, whom) I am sure you all know, is on a fishing trip.

For sentence (1), you can mentally rearrange the question as a sentence and cross out the extra words:

~~You did say~~ that man is (who, whom).

Since the pronoun renames the subject of the verb *is, that man,* you must use the pronoun *who*.

Who did you say that man is?

For sentence (2), you can mentally cross out the extra words:

Mr. Kelp, (who, whom) ~~I am sure~~ you all know, is on a fishing trip.

The sentence is now exactly the same as it was in the earlier example, and the correct pronoun is still *whom.*

The words attached to *who* or *whom* often form a word group that may fool you. Look at the following tricky sentences:

(1) I know (who, whom) is standing by the door.
(2) I know the man (who, whom) is standing by the door.
(3) I know the man (who, whom) you met as you came in.
(4) Give this ticket to (whoever, whomever) will use it.
(5) (Who, Whom) the boss will choose for this job is a difficult question to answer.

Don't make the mistake of choosing the pronoun that seems to work for the sentence as a whole; the choice of the correct pronoun is determined by its use in the word group that begins with the pronoun.

Suppose sentence (1) had originally been written as:

I know *that man.*

If you wanted to substitute a single pronoun for the noun, you would write:

I know *him.*

The pronoun *him* is used because the pronoun receives the action of the sentence (it is the direct object).

You may be tempted to use the pronoun *whom* in the sentence, "I know (who, whom) is standing by the door." After all, the whole group of words beginning with (*who, whom*) receives the action of the verb *know*. However, the pronoun is also the subject of the verb *is standing*. Do you choose *who* because it is the subject of *is standing,* or do you choose *whom* because it is not the subject of *know?*

The rule for these sentences is:

Use the pronoun that is correct for the group of words beginning with the pronoun.

It may help to draw a box around the group of words beginning with the pronoun to keep yourself from being fooled by the sentence as a whole.

I know [(whom, whom) is standing by the door.]

Since the pronoun is the subject of the verb *is standing,* use the pronoun *who.*

I know *who* is standing by the door.

Now look at the other sentences.

I know the man [(who, whom) is standing by the door.]

The pronoun is still the subject of the verb *is standing;* the correct pronoun is *who.*

I know the man *who* is standing by the door.

I know the man [(who, whom) you met as you came in.]

You can mentally rearrange the words, putting the subject of this word group first:

you met (who, whom) as you came in

Since the pronoun names the receiver of the action of the verb *met* (that is, the pronoun is the direct object), use the pronoun *whom.*

I know the man *whom* you met as you came in.

Give this ticket to | (whoever, whomever) will use it. |

Since the pronoun is the subject of the verb *will use,* the correct pronoun is *whoever.*

Give this ticket to *whoever* will use it.

| (Who, Whom) the boss will choose for this job | is a difficult question to answer.

You can mentally rearrange the words, putting the subject of this word group first:

the boss will choose (who, whom) for this job

Since the pronoun names the receiver of the action of the verb *will choose,* use the pronoun *whom.*

Whom the boss will choose for this job is a difficult question to answer.

GRAMMAR AND USAGE: EXERCISE 17 (WHO OR WHOM)

Directions: Choose the correct form of the pronoun and write your answer in the blank at the left.

__________ 1. (Who, Whom) do you want to talk with?

__________ 2. A married man (who, whom) washes dishes is in love.

__________ 3. Tell (whoever, whomever) arrives not to wait.

__________ 4. The young child (who, whom) we saw earlier is here.

________ 5. Bill will speak to (whoever, whomever) they send.

________ 6. (Who, Whom) did he say you knew?

________ 7. The old friend (who, whom) was coming to see me telephoned me for directions.

________ 8. (Whoever, Whomever) comes will be welcome.

________ 9. He talks to (whoever, whomever) he sees.

________ 10. I know (who, whom) that is.

Answers and explanations are on pages 121–123.

(3) Pronouns that follow the verb to be

If a pronoun comes after any of the following verbs, use the subject form of the pronoun:

am	was	has been
is	were	have been
are		had been

EXAMPLES

(1) It is *I*.
(2) The former secretary was *she*.
(3) The best dressers are *they*.
(4) The tired ones were *we*.
(5) If you were *I*, what would you do?

Although these sentences may sound strange to you, remember that the underlined pronoun in each sentence renames the subject. Pronouns that rename the subject are always subject pronouns.

(4) Pronouns after the preposition between

Never use the subject pronoun after the word *between*.

WRONG: I want this secret to be just between you and I.
RIGHT: I want this secret to be just between you and *me*.
WRONG: The choice is between you and he.
RIGHT: The choice is between you and *him*.
WRONG: I can't tell the difference between Mary and she.
RIGHT: I can't tell the difference between Mary and *her*.

(5) Pronouns after than or as

Sentences that compare two people or two groups of people often look like one of the following:

(1) Tom is as funny as Bill.
(2) I know Tom better than Bill.

Parts of these sentences have been dropped to avoid repetition. If the missing parts were put back, the sentences would read:

(1) Tom is as funny as Bill is.
(2) I know Tom better than I know Bill.

Since these parts of the sentence are often dropped, you may have difficulty in choosing the correct pronoun to replace the noun. You can overcome this difficulty by mentally adding the missing part of the sentence to determine how the pronoun is used. Look at the following sentences:

(1) Tom is as funny as (he, him).
(2) I know Tom better than (he, him).
(3) Susan is older than (I, me).
(4) They are working as hard as (we, us).

By adding the missing parts of these sentences, you can choose the correct pronoun.

(1) Tom is as funny as *he* (is).
(2) I know Tom better than (I know) *him.*
(3) Susan is older than I (am).
(4) They are working as hard as *we* (are).

Notice how you would change the meaning of sentence (2) if you used *he.*

I know Tom better than *he* (does).

(6) We or us followed by a noun

When *we* or *us* is followed by another noun, mentally leave out the noun to see how the pronoun is used.

(1) Car dealers are now offering better deals to (we, us) Americans.

Car dealers are now offering better deals to *us.*

The pronoun follows a connecting word to give additional information. Since the pronoun does not name the subject or rename the subject in any way, the correct pronoun is *us*.

(2) (We, Us) children are taller than our grandparents.

We are taller than our grandparents.

The pronoun is the subject; therefore, the correct pronoun is *we*.

(7) Pronouns that end in self or selves

This special group of pronouns can be used only when the subject's "self" receives the action, as in the following sentences:

(1) I'm going to sit down and write *myself* a letter.
(2) Barbara hit *herself* in the head with her purse.

In spoken English, these pronouns are sometimes incorrectly used as the subject or the receiver of the action (direct object) of the sentence.

WRONG: Jack and myself will be there.
RIGHT: Jack and I will be there.
WRONG: How about yourself?
RIGHT: How about you?

(8) A special use of the possessive pronoun

When we studied nouns, we talked about a special kind of noun (called a gerund) that looks like a verb:

Sleeping is Paul's favorite hobby.

In this sentence, *sleeping* is used as a noun. We noted that a possessive had to be used if a noun preceded this special kind of noun:

Paul's sleeping 14 hours a day made his mother nervous.

This same rule applies to pronouns:

His sleeping 14 hours a day made his mother nervous.

Whenever a pronoun comes before a verb form that acts as a noun (a gerund), you must use the possessive pronoun:

WRONG: The musicians were annoyed by him dancing on the tables.
RIGHT: The musicians were annoyed by *his* dancing on the tables.

(9) Order of pronouns

When pronouns are connected with one or more nouns, the pronoun goes last.

WRONG: They were singing with *me and Joe.*
RIGHT: They were singing with *Joe and me.*
WRONG: *She,* Susan, and Ann went to lunch together.
RIGHT: Susan, Ann, and *she* went to lunch together.

If one of the pronouns is *I* or *me,* that pronoun goes last. This rule is a holdout from the days when people were very concerned about being polite.

WRONG: I and he took the train.
RIGHT: He and I took the train.
WRONG: The boss wanted to see me and him.
RIGHT: The boss wanted to see him and me.

GRAMMAR AND USAGE: EXERCISE 18
(CHOOSING THE RIGHT KIND OF PRONOUN)

Directions: Read each of the following sentences carefully. If the sentence is correct as written, write "correct" in the space provided. If there is an error in the sentence, write the corrected sentence in the space provided.

1. We were surprised by them arriving so late.

____

2. It was he who called you in the middle of the night.

____

3. She isn't as smart as me.

____

4. His laughing made everyone else laugh.

____

5. Now us workers pay high taxes.

____

6. The man standing between George and I is a famous songwriter.

____

7. Paul is better looking than him.

____

8. She wanted to give yourself a party on your birthday.

____

Answers and explanations are on pages 123–124.

CHOOSING THE RIGHT PERSON AND NUMBER OF THE PRONOUN

Read the following paragraph, paying special attention to the underlined words:

> When <u>a person</u> learns to ride a horse, <u>you</u> must understand the horse. <u>Their</u> fear may make <u>him</u> forget that a horse is not a machine, so <u>we</u> must be reminded to be kind to the animal underneath <u>you</u>.

The use of so many different pronouns makes this paragraph confusing. It is not clear what noun these pronouns are replacing. If all of these pronouns refer to the noun *person,* the paragraph becomes clear when it is written as follows:

> When <u>a person</u> learns to ride a horse, <u>he</u> must understand the horse. <u>His</u> fear may make <u>him</u> forget that a horse is not a machine, so <u>he</u> must be reminded to be kind to the animal underneath <u>him</u>.

All of the pronouns are singular and in the third person (the person spoken about). Since the noun these pronouns replace is both singular and the person spoken about, the pronouns are said to *agree* with the noun. Making certain that pronouns agree with the nouns they are replacing is just as important as making certain that verbs agree with their subjects.

Notice that the noun *person* does not have a specific sex; that is, the noun could apply to both men and women. Until someone invents a new pronoun that applies to both men and women (no one would like to be referred to as *it*), the rules of English grammar ask you to use the masculine pronouns *he, him,* and *his.* For all nouns that *do* have a definite sex, you must be careful to use the pronoun that *agrees* with that noun in regard to sex.

Although it is easy enough to set down the basic law of grammar that says, "A pronoun must agree with the noun it is replacing in number, person, and sex," it it not always clear how to apply this law. In the following pages, you will study the various problems you can have with noun and pronoun agreement. The errors that will be pointed out are the errors that will most likely show up on the GED test and in your own writing.

(1) When the pronoun replaces two or more nouns that are joined together by *and,* use the plural form of the pronoun.

EXAMPLES

(1) Harry and Joe are at *their* favorite bar enjoying *themselves.*
(2) Fred and his wife don't know *their* way around the city yet.

Notice that the verbs in these sentences are also plural.

(2) When the pronoun replaces two nouns joined together by *or, nor, either . . . or, neither . . . nor,* or *not only . . . but also,* the pronoun agrees with the last noun in the series.

EXAMPLES

(1) Neither Mamie nor Mimi wants *her* drink refilled.
(2) Neither Mamie nor her two sisters want *their* drinks refilled.

(Notice that the noun *drink* also had to be made plural.)

(3) Not only the players but also the coach lost *his* temper.

(3) When the pronoun replaces a collective noun (see page 62 for a list of these nouns), use a singular pronoun when the noun is

thought of as a single unit and a plural pronoun when the noun is thought of as several separate individuals or things.

EXAMPLES

(1) My favorite *team* isn't playing today; *its* union is on strike.
(2) The *crowd* showed *its* displeasure by throwing rotten eggs at the umpire.
(3) The *family* are occupied with *their* individual problems.

(4) When the pronoun replaces one of the following words, use the singular form of the pronoun:

person	someone
each	anyone
either	nobody
neither	somebody
no one	anybody
one	everybody
everyone	

EXAMPLES

(1) *Everyone* must be careful when *he* is shaving.
(2) *Someone* who lives in Hawaii should brush up on *his* swimming.
(3) A *person* interested in old records should keep *his* eyes open for sales.

Notice that the masculine pronoun is always used, even though it is impossible to know the sex of the people referred to.

(5) Use the pronoun *which* only for animals and things; use the pronouns *who* and *whom* only for people; use the pronoun *that* for either people or animals and things.

EXAMPLES

(1) The man *who* was talking was her father.
(2) The picture *that* I drew was for you.
(3) That dog, *which* is a Saint Bernard, eats twice the food that other dogs eat.

The pronoun *what* can never be used in this way.

WRONG: The woman what used to teach the class was a great teacher.

RIGHT: The woman *who* used to teach the class was a great teacher.

GRAMMAR AND USAGE: EXERCISE 19 (CHOOSING THE RIGHT PERSON AND NUMBER OF THE PRONOUN)

Directions: In each of the following sentences, two pronouns are given in parentheses. Underline the pronoun that agrees in number and person with the noun or nouns it refers to.

1. If someone doesn't pay (his, their) electricity bill, (he, they) might end up without lights.
2. The class are marking (its, their) own papers.
3. Neither Al nor his brothers want (his, their) sister to stay at the house.
4. Pat and Beverly are going to (her, their) friend's house for a party.
5. The man (which, that) used to be her husband became very rich after the divorce.

Answers and explanations are on page 124.

GRAMMAR AND USAGE: EXERCISE 20 (PRONOUN REVIEW)

Directions: If there is an error in a sentence, blacken the space under the number corresponding to it. If there is no error, blacken the space numbered (5).

1. Jim and <u>I</u> (1) met the mad scientist <u>whom</u> (2) <u>he</u> (3) had invited to have dinner with <u>himself.</u> (4) <u>No error</u> (5)

   1. 1 2 3 4 5

2. The supervisor sent <u>him</u> (1) and <u>she</u> (2) flowers because <u>he</u> (3) thought both of <u>them</u> (4) had worked very hard. <u>No error</u> (5)

   2. 1 2 3 4 5

3. If <u>you</u> (1) don't see Jeffrey, Sally, and <u>her</u> (2) sister, try to call either <u>them</u> (3) or <u>I.</u> (4) <u>No error</u> (5)

   3. 1 2 3 4 5

4. 1 2 3 4 5

4. Us New Yorkers love our city, even though it sometimes seems
1 2 3
crazy even to us. No error
4 5

5. 1 2 3 4 5

5. The judge told Harold and he that they had better change their
1 2 3
ways, or he would send them to jail. No error
4 5

6. 1 2 3 4 5

6. Jack Horner put his hand in the refrigerator, pulled out another
1
piece of cake for hisself, and he said "What a great cake this is!"
2 3 4
No error
5

7. 1 2 3 4 5

7. A person what wants to know everything might find himself in
1 2
the same situation as the man who sold his soul to the devil
3 4
for knowledge. No error
5

8. 1 2 3 4 5

8. The man whom Sarah and she met last week at the party is
1 2
sitting outside my house waving at me. No error
3 4 5

9. 1 2 3 4 5

9. Your father, her sister, and I don't care whom you choose;
1 2 3
invite whoever you want. No error
4 5

10. 1 2 3 4 5

10. The teacher that we students like least is the one who can't
1 2 3
stand us chewing gum in her classes. No error
4 5

11. 1 2 3 4 5

11. Suddenly, in the middle of our office, Pat and her, who were
1 2 3
working late, threw their typewriters on the floor. No error
4 5

12. When Mr. Thomas and his (1) wife walked into the room, they (2) felt more at home than she (3) and myself. (4) No error (5)

12. 1 2 3 4 5

13. The Smiths and us (1) have lived next to each other ever since they (2) moved their (3) whole family to our (4) neighborhood. No error (5)

13. 1 2 3 4 5

14. Our (1) house is brick, and their's (2) is one of those (3) modern houses that looks as if it's (4) made of plastic. No error (5)

14. 1 2 3 4 5

15. I (1) couldn't believe that it was them (2) who (3) took your (4) money. No error (5)

15. 1 2 3 4 5

Answers and explanations are on pages 124–125.

ADJECTIVES AND ADVERBS (WORDS THAT DESCRIBE)

Read the following paragraphs, paying special attention to the underlined words. What do these words describe?

There was a time when I could wholeheartedly agree with the kind and sensitive man who said, "I never met a man I didn't like." That was two years ago; that was before I met Ted.

Ted is one of those rare men whom you instantly dislike. Your first impression is that Ted is obviously in love with himself, that he thinks that he is the most intelligent person on this planet. His overly loud voice, his quick temper, his soldierlike walk (more a march than a normal walk), all make you fear Ted. None of these offensive qualities make you like him. If you innocently ask him what time it is, you will get a quick reply such as, "Don't you know, you stupid fool? And why are you bothering me with this ridiculous question? I have more important things on my mind!" The shock of getting an angry and hostile response to your innocent question sends you out of the room in disgust.

Why does a person behave like that? Finally, the answer comes to you. Ted does not like himself very well; he does not even consider himself as intelligent as the people with whom he works. If you don't even dare to ask him for the time, you will never discover anything about him. But, discovering why he is the way he is does not make you like him. He is still a thoroughly disagreeable person. You simply have to rewrite the old saying to read: "I have met a few men I didn't like, but I try not to meet them again."

Almost any of these sentences could be written without the underlined words. For example, the sentence in lines 7–9 could be written as:

His voice, his temper, his walk, all make you fear him.

The sentence is now made up of pronouns, nouns, and verbs. The words still form a complete sentence; that is, the words do communicate a complete thought. However, the reader has no information about *what kind* of voice, temper, and walk Ted has that would make him fear

Ted. To give this information, the writer has added words that tell *what kind:*

> *loud* voice
> *quick* temper
> *soldierlike* walk

Words that describe nouns to tell *what kind* are called **adjectives.** Adjectives can also describe nouns to tell *which one:*

> *this* planet (lines 6–7)
> *these* offensive qualities (line 9)

And, finally, adjectives can tell *how many:*

> *two* years ago (line 3)

We can now write a definition of an adjective:

An adjective is a word that describes a noun to tell what kind, which one, or how many.

When you use an adjective, you modify (that is, you give a certain meaning to) the noun. Compare these two different adjectives that were used with the same noun:

> *ridiculous* question (line 12)
> *innocent* question (line 14)

Without the adjectives, *question* would mean the same thing in both sentences. By using adjectives, you make the meaning of the noun more specific; that is, you have modified (changed) the meaning of the noun.

Nouns are not the only words that can be modified. Notice the difference between the following two sentences:

> (1) You *slowly* learn to dislike Ted.
> (2) You *instantly* learn to dislike Ted.

In these two sentences, the meaning of the verb *learn* has been modified by adding words that tell how fast you learn to dislike Ted. The words *slowly* and *instantly* are called **adverbs.** Even the meaning of these adverbs can be made more specific (that is, modified):

> (1) You *very* slowly learn to dislike Ted.
> (2) You *almost* instantly learn to dislike Ted.

In some sentences, you may want to modify an adjective:

(1) Ted has an *overly* loud voice.
(2) Ted is a *thoroughly* disagreeable person.

Notice that the same form of adverb can be used to describe either a verb or an adjective:

I *thoroughly* agree with you that Ted is a *thoroughly* disagreeable person.

Since the form of the word is the same in both cases, we can call it by the same name.

An adverb can tell *how:*

innocently ask (line 10)

It can tell *when:*

never discover (line 20)

It can tell *where:*

The car is *here.*

It can tell *to what extent:*

overly loud (line 7)
thoroughly disagreeable (lines 21–22)

We can now make up a definition of the term *adverb:*

An adverb is a word that modifies a verb, an adverb, or an adjective to tell how, when, where, or to what extent.

GRAMMAR AND USAGE: EXERCISE 21
(IDENTIFYING ADJECTIVES AND ADVERBS)

Directions: The following is a partial list of the underlined words in the paragraphs on page 92. For each word, determine whether it is an adjective or an adverb and determine what word it modifies. Write your answers in the spaces provided.

________ 1. wholeheartedly (line 1)
____

________ 2. kind (line 2)
____

________	3. rare (line 4)	________	4. first (line 5)
________		________	
________	5. overly (line 7)	________	6. offensive (line 9)
________		________	
________	7. stupid (line 11)	________	8. very (line 17)
________		________	
________	9. still (line 21)	________	10. again (line 24)
________		________	

Answers and explanations are on pages 125–126.

THE FORM OF ADJECTIVES AND ADVERBS

The difference between adjectives and adverbs is a difference in use. Adjectives describe nouns; adverbs describe verbs, adverbs, and adjectives. Look at the following two sentences:

(1) *Loud* screaming attracts attention.
(2) If you scream *loudly,* you will attract attention.

In sentence (1), *screaming* is a noun; therefore, the adjective form *loud* is used. In sentence (2), *scream* is a verb; therefore, the adverb form *loudly* is used. Notice that there is a difference between the forms of the adjective and the adverb. It is important for you to know the difference between the two, since one of the most common errors that is made with adjectives and adverbs is using one form when the usage in the sentence demands the other form.

Most adverbs are formed by adding *ly* to the end of the adjective form:

instant coffee (adjective) — *instantly* dislike (adverb)
obvious answer (adjective) — *obviously* hates (adverb)
innocent question (adjective) — *innocently* ask (adverb)

Adjectives that end in *le* are made into adverbs by changing the ending to *ly:*

simple question (adjective) — *simply* hates (adverb)
possible answer (adjective) — is *possibly* too late (adverb)

Adjectives that end in *l* are made into adverbs by adding *ly*.

actual size (adjective) — *actually* got caught (adverb)
final solution (adjective) — *finally* quit (adverb)

Adjectives that end in *ll* are made into adverbs by adding *y*.

full stomach (adjective) — *fully* expect (adverb)

Adjectives that end in *ic* are usually made into adverbs by adding *ally*.

basic education (adjective) — is *basically* true (adverb)
tragic situation (adjective) — ended *tragically* (adverb)

Some adjectives already end in *ly* and remain the same when used as an adverb.

daily newspaper (adjective) — Tom exercises *daily* (adverb)
early morning (adjective) — get up *early* (adverb)
monthly bills (adjective)—pay your bills *monthly* (adverb)

Some adjectives that do not end in *ly* remain the same when used as an adverb.

fast worker (adjective) — he works *fast* (adverb)
late night (adjective) — he worked *late* (adverb)

Other words in this group include:

hard	long
high	low
ill	straight

Some adjectives change spelling when they are made into adverbs.

true statement (adjective) — she *truly* loves him (adverb)
whole thing (adjective) — this is not *wholly* true (adverb)

Some adjectives can never be used as adverbs.

WRONG: Susan greeted me friendlily.
RIGHT: Susan greeted me in a friendly way.
WRONG: She sings lovely.
RIGHT: She has a lovely voice for singing.

Many adjectives are used as adverbs in speaking or casual writing but are not considered correct in formal English.

WRONG: She's real nice.
RIGHT: She's very nice.
WRONG: I'm feeling pretty good today.
RIGHT: I'm feeling fairly good today.
WRONG: I'm awful tired.
RIGHT: I'm awfully tired.

Make sure that you form the adverb based on the adjective form, not on the noun form:

an *accident* (noun) — an *accidental* mistake (adjective) — Fred *accidentally* cut himself (adverb)
an *incident* (noun) — *incidental* benefits (adjective) — *Incidentally,* I am free tonight (adverb)
(NOTE: although *incidentally* usually means *by the way,* it is important to remember how to form the adverb correctly)
music (noun) — *musical* chairs (adjective) — Tom is *musically* inclined (adverb)

Although the pronunciation of the adverb may sound as though you merely add *ly* to the noun form, the words *accidently, incidently,* and *musicly* are incorrect.

GRAMMAR AND USAGE: EXERCISE 22
(FORMS OF ADJECTIVES AND ADVERBS)

Directions: In each of the following sentences, four adverbs and adjectives have been underlined. If one of these adverbs or adjectives is incorrectly formed, blacken the space under the number corresponding to it. If all of the adjectives and adverbs are correctly formed, blacken the space numbered (5).

---

1. Unless you act quick (1), you obviously (2) won't find a really (3) good (4) seat in the theater. No error (5) **1.** 1 2 3 4 5

2. "The story ended happily (1)," she answered slowly (2), "with her father praising the happy (3) boyfriend enthusiasticly (4)." No error (5) **2.** 1 2 3 4 5

3. 1 2 3 4 5

3. Those (1) salesmen are usually (2) real (3) nervous. (4) No error (5)

4. 1 2 3 4 5

4. Joe, a hard (1) worker, does difficult (2) jobs cheerfully (3) and efficient. (4) No error (5)

5. 1 2 3 4 5

5. The students were almost (1) totally (2) distracted by the angry (3) loud (4) shouts. No error (5)

6. 1 2 3 4 5

6. Two old (1) men and a young (2) one walked careful (3) and slowly (4) down the street. No error (5)

7. 1 2 3 4 5

7. Lyn, who is usually (1) very well-dressed, (2) is wearing a terribly (3) ugly (4) dress today. No error (5)

8. 1 2 3 4 5

8. The older (1) carpenter hit the nail hardly (2) and squarely (3) into the younger (4) carpenter's foot. No error (5)

9. 1 2 3 4 5

9. Doris sings beautiful, (1) her songs are beautiful, (2) and she's truly (3) beautiful. (4) No error (5)

10. 1 2 3 4 5

10. This new (1) book is pretty (2) interesting but I'm too (3) tired (4) to really enjoy it. No error (5)

Answers and explanations are on page 126.

PROBLEMS WITH ADJECTIVES AND ADVERBS

In addition to knowing the difference between the adjective and adverb forms and using the correct form, there are several other kinds of problems with which you should become familiar. The errors that are pointed out in the following pages are those that are most likely to show up on the GED test and in your own writing.

(1) The Predicate Adjective

When you studied nouns, you learned about a special use of the noun called a predicate nominative. This noun renames the subject of the sentence in some new way:

Sam is an idiot.

The noun *idiot* renames the subject *Sam.* Adjectives can also be used in this way:

Sam is stupid.

The adjective *stupid* modifies the noun *Sam.* The verb merely links the subject and the adjective together; the meaning of the verb is not modified by the adjective. Watch for the following verbs that function in the same way:

is	had been
are	tastes
am	smells
was	feels
were	become (becomes, became)
has been	seem (seems)
have been	grow (grows, grew)

EXAMPLES

(1) This place smells *terrible.* (not *terribly*)
(2) This candy is awful.
(3) This candy is awfully good. (Since *awfully* modifies the adjective *good,* you *do* use the adverb form.)

(2) Well or good; badly or bad

Using a predicate adjective causes the most problems when you must decide between *well* and *good* or between *badly* and *bad.* It will help to remember which form is an adjective and which form is an adverb.

adjective	*adverb*
good	well
bad	badly

EXAMPLES

(1) My parents have been very good to me. (predicate adjective describing *parents*)
(2) The children behaved very well today. (adverb telling *how* they behaved)
(3) The apple pie smells good. (predicate adjective describing *apple pie*)
(4) Since I have a cold, I can't smell very well. (adverb telling *how* you are able to smell)
(5) When Susan wears that awful perfume, she doesn't smell very good. (predicate adjective describing *Susan*)
(6) This candy tastes bad. (predicate adjective describing *candy*)
(7) Tom is badly in need of a shave. (adverb telling *to what extent* Tom *needs* a shave)

The one exception to this rule is in sentences that describe health. To describe health, use *bad* and *well* not *badly* and *good.*

(1) I feel *bad* today.
(2) I felt *well* yesterday.

This exception is necessary since the opposite of *sick* is *well.* However, if you are describing a person's attitude, use the adjective forms *bad* and *good* not the adverb forms *badly* and *well.*

(3) She feels *bad* about what happened.
(4) He doesn't feel too *good* about it, either.

(3) The Double Negative

Be careful when you use such negative adverbs as *not, hardly,* and *scarcely,* especially when a sentence already contains a negative word such as *no, nobody, no one, nowhere,* or *neither*. Look at the following sentences; all of them contain an error in the use of a negative adverb, adjective, or pronoun.

(1) George doesn't do nothing around here.

SENTENCE REALLY MEANS: George does do something around here. (Since he does *not* do *nothing,* he must do *something.*)

SHOULD READ: George doesn't do anything around here.
George does nothing around here.

(Notice that you can choose to keep either one of the negative words, but not both.)

(2) I don't know no one here, neither.

SENTENCE REALLY MEANS: I do know someone here, as well as you don't. (Since I do *not* know *no one,* I must know *someone.* The word *neither* can only be used in a sentence such as: "You don't know anyone here, and *neither* do I." The word *neither* implies a comparison to something else that is negative.)

SHOULD READ: I don't know anyone here, either.
I know no one here, too.

(*Either* means *also* or *too.*)

(3) I haven't hardly begun to fight.

SENTENCE REALLY MEANS: I have been fighting for quite some time. (Since I have *not* only just begun—the meaning of hardly begun—I must have been fighting for some period of time.)

SHOULD READ: I haven't begun to fight.
I have hardly begun to fight.

(4) I'm not going nowhere.

SENTENCE REALLY MEANS: I am going somewhere. (Since I am *not* going *nowhere,* I must be going *somewhere.*)

SHOULD READ: I'm not going anywhere.
I'm going nowhere.

(5) I'm not going to do no work.

SENTENCE REALLY MEANS: I am going to do some work. (Since I am *not* going to do *no* work, I must be going to do *some* work.)

SHOULD READ: I'm not going to do any work.
I'm going to do no work.

By using two negative words in the same sentence, you have not written what you meant to write. Whenever you use two negatives in the same sentence, you are said to have used a *double* negative. Double negatives are always errors.

Perhaps the most difficult double negatives to remember are those involving *hardly* and *scarcely.*

(1) WRONG: I have not hardly begun to fight.
RIGHT: I have hardly begun to fight.
MEANS: I have *only just* begun to fight.

(2) WRONG: I don't hardly know you.
RIGHT: I hardly know you.
MEANS: I *just barely* know you.

(3) WRONG: I don't hardly think so.
RIGHT: I hardly think so.
MEANS: I *certainly don't* think so.

(4) WRONG: I hadn't scarcely gotten home when the phone rang.
RIGHT: I had scarcely gotten home when the phone rang.
MEANS: I had *only just* gotten home when the phone rang.

(5) WRONG: I have scarcely no money.
RIGHT: I have scarcely any money.
MEANS: I have *almost no* money.

The following table may help you to remember which pairs of words are considered double negatives, and therefore incorrect.

incorrect	*correct*
not hardly	hardly
not scarcely	scarcely
hardly no	hardly any
scarcely no	scarcely any

(4) This, that, these, those

One group of adjectives changes form depending upon the noun being modified:

this — for singular nouns that are close at hand
that — for singular nouns that are some distance away
these — for plural nouns that are close at hand
those — for plural nouns that are some distance away

EXAMPLES

(1) *This* taxi and *that* motorcycle over there were involved in an accident.
(2) *These* teenagers who are standing around me and *those* older women standing by the motorcycle saw it happen.

The most common errors that are made when using this group of adjectives are illustrated in the following sentences:

(1) WRONG: I know *this* man in Hawaii.
(Since no specific man is being pointed out, use the more general word *a*.)
RIGHT: I know *a* man in Hawaii.

(2) WRONG: *This here* problem cannot be solved.
(There is no need to use two words that point something out; use one or the other, but not both.)
RIGHT: *This* problem cannot be solved.

(3) WRONG: Look at *them* muscles.
(Never use the objective pronoun to point to something.)
RIGHT: Look at *those* muscles.

(5) A and an

The words *a* and *an* can be considered adjectives. Remember to use *an* before nouns that begin with a vowel or vowel sound (*a, e, i, o,* and *u*). For all other words, use *a*.

an apple	a book
an ugly man	a mouse

Be careful of words that begin with an unpronounced *h* or the vowels *u* or *eu* when they are pronounced like *you:*

a history book	a usual day
an hour	a European

(6) Position of Adverbs

Some adverbs can be placed in any one of several positions in a sentence without changing the meaning or making the sentence unclear:

Usually we eat dinner at seven o'clock.
We *usually* eat dinner at seven o'clock.
We eat dinner at seven o'clock, *usually*.

Sometimes, however, the position of the adverb plays an important part in the meaning of the sentence:

(1) I *only* tapped him on the shoulder.
(2) I tapped him *only* on the shoulder.

Sentence (1) could be a response to the question, "Did you punch him in the shoulder? The adverb emphasizes the fact that it was *only* a tap, not a punch. Sentence (2) could be a response to the question, "Did you tap him anywhere other than his shoulder?" The adverb emphasizes the fact that it was *only* the shoulder that was tapped, nothing else.

Sometimes, the adverb is placed too far away from the word it should emphasize.

UNCLEAR: I'll *just* give you two hours to get out of town.
IMPROVED: I'll give you *just* two hours to get out of town.

The act of *giving* is not as important as the *amount of time* given. The adverb *just* needs to be placed closer to *two hours* since that is what needs to be stressed.

UNCLEAR: He wanted you to go to the store *badly*.
IMPROVED: He *badly* wanted you to go to the store.

In the sentence labeled *unclear,* it is not clear which of the two verbs is modified by the adverb *badly*. Although the real meaning of this sentence is not difficult to understand, since it is ridiculous to think that the writer means, "He wanted you to go badly to the store," some sentences are not so clear:

UNCLEAR: Sue twisted her ankle while dancing *badly*.
IMPROVED: Sue *badly* twisted her ankle while dancing.
IMPROVED: While dancing *badly,* Sue twisted her ankle.

Notice that two very different meanings were buried in the unclear sentence even though the adverb *badly* directly followed the verb *dancing*. If the writer really means that Sue was not dancing very well, the meaning can be made clear only by placing that part of the sentence first.

GRAMMAR AND USAGE: EXERCISE 23
(ADJECTIVE AND ADVERB PROBLEMS)

Directions: In each of the following sentences, four words have been underlined. If one of these words is incorrectly used in the sentence, blacken the space under the number corresponding to it. If all of the words are used correctly, blacken the space numbered (5).

---

1. 1 2 3 4 5

1. Cowboys usually (1) prefer the open (2) spaces to them (3) tightly (4) packed cities. No error (5)

2. "I practically fainted in that steamy elevator," she said, "I really
1 2 3
feel badly with this cold." No error
4 5
2. 1 2 3 4 5

3. The friendly visitor politely asked the pretty receptionist if there
1 2 3
was an university nearby. No error
4 5
3. 1 2 3 4 5

4. The elderly woman at the candy store actually told me that this
1 2
awful fudge would taste good. No error
3 4 5
4. 1 2 3 4 5

5. He hasn't hardly been well one day out of this month because of
1 2 3
his badly injured back. No error
4 5
5. 1 2 3 4 5

6. I'll just give you five more minutes to finish this test, and then
1 2
we'll quickly find out how well you did. No error
3 4 5
6. 1 2 3 4 5

Answers and explanations are on pages 126–127.

USING ADJECTIVES AND ADVERBS FOR COMPARISON

Look at the following sentences, paying special attention to the underlined adjectives and adverbs.

(1) John is as funny as Alice.
(2) Alice is funnier than Bill.
(3) Alice is the funniest person I know.
(4) Martha is more intelligent than George.
(5) In fact, Martha is the most intelligent person I know.
(6) George is less handsome than Martha's first husband.
(7) He is not as handsome as Martha's second husband.
(8) George is the least handsome of all Martha's husbands.
(9) Ted can run as fast as I can.
(10) I can run faster than Jerry.
(11) But, Ben runs the fastest of all the people I know.
(12) Martha sang as beautifully as Jane.
(13) She sang more beautifully than her sister.

(14) She sang the most beautifully written song I have ever heard.

Almost all adjectives and adverbs can be used to compare two or more nouns or pronouns. As you can see from the sentences above, the form of the adjective or adverb changes depending upon how it is used. The following table summarizes all the ways in which these changes can be made:

To show that two nouns are equal:

as	________	*as*
John is as	funny	as Alice.
Ted can run as	fast	as I can.
Martha sang as	beautifully	as Jane.

To show that two nouns are unequal:

	____*-er*	*than*
Alice is	funnier	than Bill.
I can run	faster	than Jerry.

OR

more	________	*than*
Martha is more	intelligent	than George.
She sang more	beautifully	than her sister.

OR

less	________	*than*
George is less	handsome	than Martha's first husband.

OR

not as	________	*as*
He is not as	handsome	as Martha's second husband.

To show that three or more nouns are unequal:

the	____*-est*	
Alice is the	funniest	person I know.
But, Ben runs the	fastest	of all the people I know.

OR

the most	________	
In fact, Martha is the most	intelligent	person I know.
She sang the most	beautifully	written song I have ever heard.

OR

the least ________

George is the least handsome of all Martha's husbands.

Whenever you use an adjective or an adverb to compare nouns, you must use the form that is correct for the number of things being compared:

RIGHT: Alice is *funnier than* Bill.

WRONG: Alice and Bill are funny, but Alice is *the funniest* of the two.

RIGHT: Alice and Bill are funny, but Alice is *the funnier* of the two.

WRONG: Alice, John, and Bill are funny, but Alice is *the funnier* of the three.

RIGHT: Alice, John, and Bill are funny, but Alice is *the funniest* of the three.

You must also remember to use only one form of comparison, not two:

WRONG: Alice is *more funnier than* Bill.

RIGHT: Alice is *funnier than* Bill.

WRONG: I don't know which of these two problems is *more stupider.*

RIGHT: I don't know which of these two problems is *stupider.*

RIGHT: I don't know which of these two problems is *more stupid.*

WRONG: This is *the most stupidest* problem I have ever worked.

RIGHT: This is *the stupidest* problem I have ever worked.

RIGHT: This is *the most stupid* problem I have ever worked.

Long adjectives (three or more syllables) and all adverbs that end in *ly* can never be used with an *er* or *est* ending.

WRONG: Martha is *intelligenter than* George.

RIGHT: Martha is *more intelligent than* George.

WRONG: You'll have to work *quicklier than* you are if you expect to finish on time.

RIGHT: You'll have to work *more quickly than* you are if you expect to finish on time.

In spoken English, this last sentence might have been:

> You'll have to work *quicker than* you are if you expect to finish on time.

Notice that this sentence uses the adjective form *quicker than* rather than the adverb form *more quickly than*. The adjectives *slow* and *loud* are also frequently used in the place of the adverbs *slowly* and *loudly*—however, this usage is not considered correct in formal written English.

> SPEECH ONLY: If you work *slower*, you'll make fewer mistakes.
>
> PREFERRED FORM: If you work *more slowly*, you'll make fewer mistakes.

The only adverbs that can take the *er/est* endings are one-syllable (one vowel sound) adverbs:

> runs *fast* — runs *faster* — runs *fastest*
> plays *hard* — plays *harder* — plays *hardest*

Some adjectives and adverbs have irregular forms that are used in comparisons. The following table lists the most common irregular adjectives and adverbs.

equal	*unequal (between two)*	*unequal (among three or more)*
good	better	best
well	better	best
bad	worse	worst
badly	worse	worst
little (amount)	less	least
little (size)	smaller	smallest
many	more	most
much	more	most
far	farther	farthest
far	further	furthest

The difference between *farther* and *further* is one of use:

— use *farther* for physical distance:

> Since I moved, the school is now *farther* from my home.

— use *further* for non-physical distance:

> I have a lot *further* to go in school before I get my diploma.

The difference between *many* and *much* is also one of use:

— use *many* with nouns that can be counted:
I have *many* problems to solve.

—use *much* for uncountable nouns (see page 35):
I have *much* work to do today.

A similar problem involves the correct use of *fewer* or *less* and *fewest* or *least:*

— use *fewer* or *fewest* with nouns that can be counted:
There were *fewer* customers yesterday.
This is the *fewest* people I've ever seen at a rock concert.

— use *less* or *least* for uncountable nouns and for implied but unexpressed amounts:
On my budget, I'll have to buy *less* furniture than I would like.
Ann's doctor told her to drink *less* milk.

If the last sentence had contained some unit of measure, you would have used *fewer:*

Ann's doctor told her to drink *fewer* glasses of milk.
The milkman left *fewer* quarts of milk this week.

GRAMMAR AND USAGE: EXERCISE 24 (COMPARISONS)

Directions: In each of the following sentences, four words have been underlined. If one of these words is incorrectly used in the sentence, blacken the space under the number corresponding to it. If all of the words are used correctly, blacken the space numbered (5).

---

1. Because the movie *Teeth* is more close (1) to our house and *The Grandfather* is longer (2) and more expensive (3), we are more willing (4) to go see *Teeth.* No error (5)

1. 1 2 3 4 5

2. 1 2 3 4 5

2. Not only does Harriet interrupt people more frequently (1) and more rudely (2) than anyone else in her office (3), but she is also the loudest (4) person there. No error (5)

3. 1 2 3 4 5

3. Why don't you choose the most expensive (1) and the prettier (2) of the four dresses for yourself and give your sister the least attractive (3) and the cheapest (4) ones. No error (5)

4. 1 2 3 4 5

4. She was singing more horrible (1) and louder (2) than ever before when the rudest (3) and most cold-hearted (4) cab driver we had ever driven with told her to be quiet. No error (5)

5. 1 2 3 4 5

5. We thought we had heard the worst (1) part of the story, but the reporter continued more quickly than (2) before and told us badder (3) and more upsetting (4) facts. No error (5)

6. 1 2 3 4 5

6. He knew less (1) pretty women before he climbed further (2) toward stardom, becoming wealthier (3) and therefore more attractive (4). No error (5)

Answers and explanations are on page 127.

ANSWERS AND EXPLANATIONS—GRAMMAR AND USAGE: EXERCISES

EXERCISE 1 (SUBJECTS)

1. *Murray* is the subject of the sentence. That is the answer to the question, "*Who* is this about?"

2. *The phone company* is the subject of the sentence. The sentence is *about* the phone company, and the predicate tells what they want.

3. *You* is the subject of the sentence. The question is *about* you, and the predicate asks something about you.

4. *Freedom* is the subject of the sentence. The sentence is *about* freedom, and the predicate tells something about freedom.

5. *I* is the subject of the sentence. The sentence is *about* the writer, I, and the predicate tells what happened to the writer. *While walking through the park today* also gives information about the subject; it tells when something happened to the writer.

6. *My boss* is the subject of the sentence. The sentence is *about* that person, and the predicate tells what he did.

EXERCISE 2 (SENTENCE FRAGMENTS)

1. **(3)** *Closing the store early on holidays* is a sentence fragment. It is not possible to tell what the writer meant to say *about* closing the store early on holidays; that is, you cannot answer the question, *What about that?*

2. **(1)** It is not possible to tell what the writer meant to say *about* "the next person who comes in here to talk to me"; that is, it is not possible to answer the question, *What about that?*

3. **(3)** It is not possible to tell what happened "because John doesn't want to go to the movies"; that is, it is not possible to answer the question, *What about that?*

4. **(2)** Although this group of words may be very clear directions, there is no way to tell where these directions will take you.

5. **(5)** All of these groups of words are complete sentences.

EXERCISE 3 (IDENTIFYING NOUNS)

1. **(2)** *Picnic* is a noun; the word names a particular kind of thing and can be replaced by the word *it*.

2. **(4)** *Bus* is a noun; the word names a particular kind of thing and can be replaced by the word *it.*

3. **(4)** *Ulcer* is a noun; the word names a particular kind of thing and can be replaced by the word *one.*

4. **(3)** *Payment* is a noun; the word names a particular kind of thing and can be replaced by the word *one.*

5. **(5)** None of the underlined words are nouns; none of the words names a person, place, thing, or idea.

EXERCISE 4 (USES OF NOUNS)

1. **(2)** *Friend* renames the noun *woman,* the subject of the sentence; *friend* is a predicate nominative (use 2).

2. **(4)** *Health* follows the connecting word *with* to give additional information about the noun *person; health* is the object of the preposition *with* (use 4).

3. **(6)** *Susan* names to whom Gordon told something; *Susan* is an indirect object (use 6).

4. **(1)** *Love* is the subject of the sentence; the sentence tells something about love.

5. **(3)** *Supervisor* immediately follows and renames the noun *Henry* to give additional information about Henry; *supervisor* is an appositive (use 3).

6. **(5)** *Bill* names the receiver of the action *pay; bill* is a direct object (use 5).

EXERCISE 5 (PLURALS OF NOUNS)

1. **(2)** The plural form of *lock* is *locks,* not *lockes.* Since *lock* does not end with an *s, sh, ch, x,* or *z,* there is no need to add *es* to form the plural.

2. **(3)** The plural form of *mouse* is the irregular form *mice.*

3. **(5)** No error

4. **(4)** The plural form of *half* is *halves,* not *halfs* (see rule 9).

5. **(1)** The plural form of *hero* is *heroes,* not *heros* (see rule 8).

EXERCISE 6 (POSSESSIVE NOUNS)

1. Correct

2. The noun *sisters* is used here only as a plural noun; the relationship between *sisters* and *blond hair* is already shown by the word *have.*

The correct sentence should read, "All four sisters have blond hair."

3. Correct
4. The word *weeks* is used to express a certain quantity of *vacation;* therefore, the possessive form should be used. However, the possessive of the plural noun *weeks* is formed by adding only an apostrophe ('). The correct sentence should read, "Two weeks' vacation every year is not enough."
5. The noun *desk* is singular and indicates that there is *only one* student being talked about. The possessive form of the singular noun *student* is *student's.* The correct sentence should read, "Put this on the newest student's desk."

EXERCISE 7 (UNCOUNTABLE NOUNS)

1. This sentence is correct. The noun *alcohol* is an uncountable noun; therefore, the expression *amount of* is correct.
2. The noun *monkeys* is a countable noun; therefore, the word *much* is incorrect. The correct sentence should read, "There were many monkeys at the zoo."
3. The noun *pork* is an uncountable noun (there are many types and forms of pork, such as ham, pork chops, bacon) and can never be made plural. The correct sentence should read, "His favorite meal is rice and pork."
4. The noun *equipment* is an uncountable noun (there are many kinds of equipment) and can never be made plural. The correct sentence should read, "All the new equipment used today means new jobs for many people."
5. This sentence is correct. Although the noun *merchandise* is an uncountable noun, the noun *kinds* is countable (one kind, two kinds, etc.) and can be used with the word *many.*

EXERCISE 8 (NOUN REVIEW)

1. **(1)** The noun *deer* is not an uncountable noun; therefore, a word such as *number* should be used instead of the uncountable expression *amount.*
2. **(5)** No error
3. **(1)** There is no need to make *cities* possessive; only the plural form is required.
4. **(3)** The word *a* should never be used after the expression *kind of.*

5. **(3)** The possessive form *Jimmy's* should be used to express the relationship between that noun and the gerund *walking*.

6. **(4)** The word *cash* is an uncountable noun and does not have a plural form.

7. **(2)** The correct plural form of *mother-in-law* is formed by adding *s* to the main word, *mothers-in-law*.

8. **(2)** The plural form of *foot* should be used to show that both feet are being talked about. The possessive form should also be used to express the relationship between *feet* and *best friends*. Therefore, the correct word to use in this sentence is *feet's*.

9. **(5)** No error

10. **(2)** There is no such form as the singular of *eyeglasses;* this word only has a plural form.

EXERCISE 9 (IDENTIFYING VERBS)

1. The verbs in this sentence are: *had married; would have been. Had married* expresses an action that could have taken place at some time in the past. *Would have been* links the subject, *he,* to the description *very unhappy*.

2. The verbs in this sentence are: *became; was ringing. Became* links the subject, *Mark,* to the description *upset*. *Was ringing* expresses the action performed by the *telephone*.

3. The verbs in this sentence are: *is; creates; pollutes; wastes. Is* links the subject *traffic* to the description that follows the verb. *Creates, pollutes,* and *wastes* express the actions performed by traffic. The words *noise, environment,* and *energy* tell what these actions are performed upon.

4. The verbs in this sentence are: *can throw; is; can see. Can throw* expresses the action *Gary* performs on a *baseball*. *Is* links the word *it* (referring to *baseball*) to the word group *in the catcher's mitt*. *Can see* expresses the action performed by *you*.

5. The verbs in this sentence are: *thinks; knows; wants; has been. Thinks, knows,* and *wants* are all actions performed by *Marion,* the subject of the sentence (the word *she* refers to *Marion*). *Has been* links the word *she* (which refers to the subject) to the description *wrong*.

EXERCISE 10 (IRREGULAR VERB FORMS)

1. Hank *brought* home presents for the whole family. *Brung* is not a word and should never be used. *Brought* is the irregular past tense form of the verb *to bring*.

2. The artist *drew* a picture of the historic street. The past tense form of the verb *to draw* is the irregular form *drew*. *Drawed* is not a word and should never be used.

3. The money *lay* on the sidewalk for two hours. *Lay* is the irregular past tense form of the verb *to lie* meaning *to rest or stay in a certain position*. The other choice, *laid,* is the irregular past tense form of the verb *to lay* meaning *to put or place*. This sentence states that the money *stayed* on the sidewalk; therefore *lay* is the correct verb. NOTE: Never use the verb *laid* unless the sentence tells you *what* was laid (put).

4. They *sat* there a long time without speaking. *Sat* is the irregular past tense form of the verb *to sit*. The other choice, *set,* is the irregular past tense form of the verb *to set* meaning *to put*. Although these two verbs are often confused because they look alike, you can see that their meanings are quite different.

5. Although prices *rose,* salaries didn't. *Rose* is the irregular past tense form of the verb *to rise* meaning *to go up*. The other choice, *raised,* is the *regular* past tense form of the verb *to raise* meaning *to lift*. One way to tell the difference between these two commonly confused verbs is to remember that you should never use the word *raised* unless the sentence tells you what was raised (lifted).

6. A former student *taught* math to all the new students. *Taught* is the irregular past tense form of the verb *to teach*. The other choice, *teached,* is not a word and should never be used.

7. Alice *caught* a cold last week when she went walking in the rain without a hat or coat. *Caught* is the irregular past tense form of the verb *to catch*. The other choice, *catched,* is not a word and should never be used.

8. Bob *chose* a small black car rather than the big red one his wife wanted to buy. *Chose* is the irregular past tense form of the verb *to choose*. The other choice, *choose,* is not the past tense form of the verb. Sometimes these words are confused because they are mispronounced. Remember that *chose* rhymes with *rose;* and *choose* rhymes with *lose*.

9. The postman *laid* the mail on top of the mailbox. In this sentence the act of *putting* the mail on top of the mailbox is described; therefore, *laid,* the irregular past tense form of the verb *to lay* meaning *to put,* is the correct choice.

10. Alan *raised* his hand and *rose* to speak. The action in the first part of the sentence is Alan's *lifting* his hand; therefore, *raised,* the past tense form of the verb *to raise,* meaning *to lift* is correct. The action in the second part of the sentence is Alan's standing up; therefore, *rose,* the irregular past tense form of the verb *to rise,* meaning *to go up or get up* must be used.

EXERCISE 11 (PROBLEMS WITH VERBS)

1. **(4)** Since the rider is on a horse and *only wishes* he were in a car, the subjunctive, *were driving,* should be used.
2. **(4)** It is considered incorrect to use the word *ain't;* in this case, *am not* is the correct verb to use.
3. **(2)** The correct past form of *teach* is *taught.*
4. **(4)** The present perfect tense is formed with the past participle, not the simple past form. The correct verb is *have seen.*
5. **(3)** The verb *require* demands that the following verb be in the subjunctive. The correct verb in this sentence is *be.*
6. **(5)** No error
7. **(1)** Since the second underlined verb is in the past tense and the first verb expresses an action that was true at a time before that past time, the past perfect tense, *had been,* should be used.
8. **(5)** No error
9. **(2)** There is no need for the past participle; the simple past tense, *began,* should be used.
10. **(4)** There is no need to use the past participle; only the simple past form, *did,* should be used.
11. **(1)** The past perfect tense is formed with the past participle, not the simple past form. The correct verb in this sentence is *had rung.*
12. **(5)** No error
13. **(4)** The past participle of the verb *to lie* has been incorrectly used instead of the past participle of the verb *to lay.* The correct verb form in this sentence is *has laid.*
14. **(5)** No error
15. **(3)** The past perfect tense is formed with the past participle, not the simple past. The correct verb form is *had stolen.*

EXERCISE 12 (SUBJECT-VERB AGREEMENT)

1. A common *cure* for aches and pains *is* aspirin. The subject of this sentence is the singular noun *cure;* therefore, the singular verb *is* is correct.
2. *Mr. Johnson* together with his brother *owns* a garage. Do not be fooled by the words that only give additional information; the subject of this sentence is the singular noun *Mr. Johnson,* which requires a singular verb *owns.*

3. *One* of the secretaries *makes* coffee every morning. Don't be fooled by the words that explain the meaning of the word *one*. *One* is the singular subject of the sentence, so the singular verb *makes* is correct.

4. Not *one* of the typewriters *that were* stolen *has* been found. The subject of the first verb is *that*, which refers to the plural noun *typewriters;* therefore, the first verb must be the plural form *were*. The subject of the second verb is the singular word *one*, which makes that verb singular.

5. *Susan* as well as her sister and brother *has* decided to leave Chicago. Don't be fooled by the words that only give additional information; the subject of this sentence is the singular noun *Susan*, which requires the singular verb *has*.

6. *Sam is* one of those people *who are* always late for work. The subject of the first verb is the singular noun *Sam*, which requires a singular verb. The subject of the second verb is *who*, which refers to the plural noun *people;* therefore, the correct verb is the plural form *are*.

7. The *use* of television to educate as well as entertain and inform people *has* been very successful. Don't be fooled by the words that explain what is meant by the word *use*. *Use* is the singular subject of the sentence, and it requires a singular verb.

8. Waiting in line for unemployment checks *were* the *employees* who had been laid off. Don't be fooled by the words at the beginning of the sentence that only tell where the action of this sentence took place. The subject of this sentence is the plural noun *employees*, which requires a plural verb.

EXERCISE 13 (SUBJECT-VERB AGREEMENT)

1. There *are* about twenty *chairs* in the room. In sentences beginning with *there*, you must look for the subject after the verb, in this case, the plural noun *chairs*. Therefore, a plural verb is required.

2. *Seventy tons* of paper *is* needed to print 12,000 copies of this book. The subject of this sentence is an expression of quantity that can be thought of as a single unit; therefore, a singular verb is required.

3. Our basketball *team* always *loses* the first game of the season. The collective noun *team* is the subject of this sentence. Since the collective noun is thought of as a single unit, the singular verb is correct.

4. *Each* of these questions *is* explained at the end of the section. The subject of this sentence is the word *each*, which always takes a singular verb.

5. Every *pair* of scissors *is broken.* When *scissors* is used with the expression *pair of,* a singular verb is required.
6. *All* of the paychecks *have* arrived, but *some* of them *are* wrong. The subject of the first verb is *all,* which refers to the plural noun *paychecks;* therefore, the plural verb is correct. The subject of the second verb is *some,* which refers to the plural word *them;* therefore, the plural verb is correct.
7. *None* of these coats *look* good on me. The subject of this sentence is *none,* which refers to the plural noun *coats;* therefore, the plural verb is correct.
8. *Neither* of the movies on television tonight *is* good. The subject of this sentence is *neither,* which always requires a singular verb.

EXERCISE 14 (SUBJECT-VERB AGREEMENT)

1. *Jim and Alice don't* have the money to take a vacation. The subject of this sentence is a compound subject, *Jim and Alice.* Compound subjects joined together by *and* require plural verbs.
2. Neither Jim *nor Alice has* the money to take a vacation. The verb must agree with the part of the subject nearest to the verb when the compound subject is joined together by *neither . . . nor.* Since *Alice* is a singular noun, a singular verb must be used.
3. A bracelet *or a few records are* a good gift for her. The verb must agree with the part of the subject nearest to the verb when the compound subject is joined together by *or.* Since *records* is plural, the plural verb must be used.
4. The biggest *bargain* in the store *is* the shoes. Don't be fooled by the plural form of the predicate nominative; the subject of this sentence is the singular noun *bargain,* which requires a singular verb.
5. Not only New York *but also Chicago and Washington have* financial problems. The verb must agree with the part of the subject nearest to the verb when the compound subject is joined together with *not only . . . but also.* In this sentence that part of the subject is a compound joined together by *and,* which requires a plural verb.

EXERCISE 15 (SUBJECT-VERB AGREEMENT REVIEW)

1. Everybody here is waiting for you, but no one expects you to show up. The subject of the first verb is *everybody,* which always takes a singular verb. The subject of the second verb is *no one,* which also always takes a singular verb.
2. Four hours is too much time to take on this test; most students finish in less than an hour. The subject of the first verb is *four*

hours, an expression of an amount of time that can be thought of as a single unit; therefore, the correct form of the verb is singular. The subject of the second verb, *most students,* is plural; therefore the plural verb is used.

3. Billy Graham, together with his faithful followers, is going to offer a special service this Sunday. The subject of this sentence is *Billy Graham,* a singular subject that requires a singular verb. The additional information set off by commas has no effect on the verb.

4. Either Susan or one of her sisters is going to pick you up for the party; neither of us has the time. The subject of the first verb is *one* (in subjects joined by *either . . . or,* the verb agrees with the second part of the subject); the word group *of her sisters* only gives additional information to identify what is meant by the word *one.* Since *one* is singular, the first verb of this sentence must also be singular. The subject of the second verb in the sentence is *neither,* which always takes a singular verb.

5. Everyone who looks suspicious will be stopped by the guards, who are going to be posted at every door. The subject of the first verb is *who,* which replaces the word *everyone.* Since *everyone* always takes a singular verb, the singular verb is used in this sentence. The subject of the second part of the sentence is *who,* which refers to the plural noun *guards.* Since the meaning of the subject is plural, the plural form of the verb is used.

6. All of the audience is asleep now, although some of the people were excited when the show started. The subject of the first verb is *all,* which is connected to the collective noun *audience.* Since the meaning of *all* is singular, that is, the subject can be thought of as a single unit, the verb must also be singular. The subject of the second verb is *some,* which is connected to the plural noun *people.* Since the meaning of *some* is plural, that is, the subject is thought of as composed of a number of separate individuals, the verb must also be plural.

7. The crowd is cheering, but our group is not impressed by the convention. The subject of the first verb is *crowd,* a collective noun that requires a singular verb. The subject of the second verb is *group,* a collective noun that requires a singular verb.

8. The use of drugs in the school's buildings and on the school's grounds is forbidden. The subject of this sentence is *use;* the words that come between *use* and the verb only give information to identify what is meant by the word *use.* Since the subject of the sentence is singular, the verb must also be singular.

9. Mystery novels and collections of horror stories are Fred's idea of exciting reading. His idea of dull reading is historical novels and love stories. The subject of the first sentence is the compound *mystery novels and collections of horror stories.* A compound subject joined by *and* requires a plural verb. The subject of the second sentence is *idea,* a singular subject that requires a singular verb.

10. A thorough knowledge of mathematics is necessary if economics is your chosen field of study. The subject of the first verb is *knowledge,* a singular noun that requires a singular subject. The subject of the second verb is *economics,* a noun that has a plural form but a singular meaning. Since the meaning of the subject is singular, a singular verb must be used.

11. Neither mathematics nor physics interests him; in fact, both sciences bore him. When a compound subject is joined together with the expression *neither . . . nor,* the verb agrees with the last-named part of the subject, in this case, *physics.* Since *physics* is a noun with a plural form but a singular meaning, the singular verb must be used. The subject of the second verb is *sciences,* a plural noun with a plural meaning that requires a plural verb.

12. Behind those two-way mirrors stands a guard ready to arrest anyone who is foolish enough to try shoplifting. The subject of the first verb is *guard,* a singular noun that requires a singular verb. The words *behind those two-way mirrors* tells where the guard stands, but these words are not the subject of the sentence. The subject of the second verb is *who,* which refers to the noun *anyone.* Since *anyone* always takes a singular verb, so does *who* in this sentence.

13. One of your friends has just told me that there are beer and sandwiches in the next room. The subject of the first verb is *one,* a word that always takes a singular verb. The subject of the second verb is the compound subject *beer and sandwiches* (the subject of sentences that begin with *there is* or *there are* is always found after the verb). Compound subjects joined by *and* take plural verbs.

14. Your father and brother are waiting for you in the car, but neither of them is in a hurry. The subject of the first verb is the compound subject *your father and brother.* Compound subjects joined by *and* take plural verbs. The subject of the second verb is *neither,* a noun that always takes a singular verb.

15. George was just fired but he doesn't care because he and his wife have saved a lot of money this year. The subject of the first verb is *he,* a singular subject that requires a singular verb. The subject

of the second verb is the compound subject *he and his wife,* and compound subjects joined by *and* take plural verbs.

EXERCISE 16 (PRONOUN FORMS)

1. Jack and *I* went home. The pronoun is part of the subject of the sentence; therefore, the subjective pronoun *I* is used.
2. Give it to Susan and *them.* The pronoun follows a connecting word, *to,* to give additional information (that is, the pronoun is an object of a preposition); therefore, the objective pronoun *them* is used.
3. Because of the rain, Lance and *he* left. The pronoun is part of the subject of the sentence; therefore, the subjective pronoun *he* is used.
4. Leave the rest for the Jacksons and *us.* The pronoun follows the connecting word *for* to give additional information (that is, the pronoun is an object of the preposition); therefore, the objective pronoun *us* is used.
5. The wave dragged Joan and *her* out to sea. The pronoun receives the action of the sentence (that is, the pronoun is a direct object); therefore, the objective pronoun *her* is used.
6. Give your ticket to one of the two men at the door, John or *him.* Objective pronouns are used to give additional information after a preposition; therefore the objective pronoun *him* is used.
7. I know that the winner is *she.* Subjective pronouns are used to rename the subject in the predicate; therefore, the subjective pronoun *she* is used.
8. His car is newer than *hers.* Possessive pronouns never use apostrophes.
9. The bus missed Ray and *me* by only a few inches. When a pronoun acts as a direct object, be sure to use the objective form.
10. John likes to do everything *himself. Hisself* is not a word and should never be used.

EXERCISE 17 (WHO OR WHOM)

1. *Whom* do you want to talk with? The correct answer can be determined by rewriting the question as a sentence, putting the subject first: "You do want to talk with whom." Since the pronoun follows a connecting word to give additional information (that is, since the pronoun is an object of a preposition), the correct form is *whom.*

2. A married man *who* washes dishes is in love. The correct answer can be determined by looking only at the group of words beginning with the pronoun: "who washes dishes." Since the pronoun is the subject of the verb *washes,* the correct pronoun is *who.*

3. Tell *whoever* arrives not to wait. The correct answer can be determined by looking only at the group of words beginning with the pronoun: "whoever arrives." Since the pronoun is the subject of the verb *arrives,* the correct pronoun is *whoever.*

4. The young child *whom* we saw earlier is here. The correct answer can be determined by first looking only at the group of words beginning with the pronoun: "whom we saw earlier." Then, mentally rearrange the words in this group, putting the subject first: "we saw whom earlier." Since the pronoun is the receiver of the action of this group of words, the correct pronoun is *whom.*

5. Bill will speak to *whomever* they send. The correct answer can be determined by looking only at the group of words beginning with the pronoun: "whomever they send." Then, mentally rearrange the words in this group, putting the subject first: "they send whomever." Since the pronoun is the receiver of the action of this group of words, the correct pronoun is *whomever.*

6. *Whom* did he say you knew? The correct answer can be determined by first rearranging the question as a direct sentence: "He did say you knew whom." Then, cross out the extra words in the sentence and look only at the group of words that receives the action of the verb *say:* "you knew whom." Since the pronoun is the receiver of the action of this group of words, the correct pronoun is *whom.*

7. The old friend *who* was coming to see me telephoned for directions. The correct answer can be determined by looking only at the group of words beginning with the pronoun: "who was coming to see me." Since the pronoun is the subject of the verb *was coming,* the correct pronoun is *who.*

8. *Whoever* comes will be welcome. Perhaps the best way to determine the correct answer is to draw a box around the complete subject of the sentence as a whole:

   [Whoever comes] will be welcome.

   Since the pronoun is the subject of the verb *comes,* the correct pronoun is *whoever.*

9. He talks to *whomever* he sees. Perhaps the best way to determine the correct answer is to draw a box around the group of words beginning with the pronoun:

He talks to | whomever he sees. |

Then, mentally rearrange the words in this group, putting the subject first: "he sees whomever." Since the pronoun is the receiver of the action of this group of words, the correct pronoun is *whomever.*

10. I know *who* that is. Perhaps the best way to determine the correct answer is to draw a box around the group of words beginning with the pronoun:

I know | who that is. |

Then, mentally rearrange this group of words, putting the subject first: "that is who." Since the pronoun renames the subject of this group of words, the correct pronoun is *who.*

EXERCISE 18 (CHOOSING THE RIGHT KIND OF PRONOUN)

1. We were surprised by *their* arriving so late. In this sentence, the word *arriving* is used as a noun (the object of the preposition *by*); therefore, you must use the possessive pronoun *their* (see rule 8).

2. Correct. You can check this sentence by dividing it into parts:

   It was he   who called you in the middle of the night.

   In the first part of the sentence, the pronoun *he* renames the subject of the sentence and is, correctly, a subjective pronoun (see rule 3). In the second part of the sentence, the pronoun *who* is the subject of the verb *called* and is, correctly, a subjective pronoun (see rule 2).

3. She isn't as smart as *I.* The correct answer can be determined by mentally adding the missing part of the sentence: "She isn't as smart as I (am)." Since the pronoun is the subject of the missing verb, it should be the subjective pronoun *I* (see rule 5).

4. Correct. Since *laughing* is used as a noun in this sentence, it is correct to use the possessive pronoun *his* (see rule 8).

5. Now *we* workers pay high taxes. The correct answer can be determined by crossing out the noun and looking at the sentence only with the pronoun: "Now we pay high taxes." Since the pronoun is the subject of the verb *pay,* the subjective pronoun *we* should be used (see rule 6).

6. The man standing between George and *me* is a famous songwriter. Never use the subjective pronoun after the word *between*. The word *between* is a connecting word (a preposition), and the pronoun that follows a connecting word must be an objective pronoun (see rule 4).
7. Paul is better looking than *he*. The correct pronoun can be determined by mentally adding the missing part of the sentence: "Paul is better looking than he (is)." Since the pronoun is the subject of the missing verb, it should be the subjective pronoun *he* (rule 5).
8. She wanted to give *you* a party on your birthday. The subject of this sentence is *she*. Since the pronoun *yourself* does not refer to the subject's self, it is not correct to use this kind of pronoun (rule 7).

EXERCISE 19 (CHOOSING THE RIGHT PERSON AND NUMBER OF THE PRONOUN)

1. If *someone* doesn't pay *his* electricity bill, *he* might end up without lights. Since the pronouns are replacing the word *someone*, the singular pronoun should be used.
2. The *class* are marking *their* own papers. The pronoun replaces the collective noun *class*, which in this sentence is thought of as composed of several separate individuals performing separate and individual tasks (as indicated by the plural verb). Since the noun is plural in meaning, the plural pronoun should be used.
3. Neither Al *nor his brothers* want *their* sister to stay at home. The pronoun must agree with the last noun in a series connected by *neither . . . nor*. In this sentence, that noun is the plural noun *brothers;* therefore, the plural pronoun must be used.
4. *Pat and Beverly* are going to *their* friend's house for a party. When the pronoun replaces two nouns joined together by *and*, the plural form of the pronoun is required.
5. The man that used to be her husband became very rich after the divorce. The correct pronoun to use to replace a noun that names a person is *that; which* can only refer to animals or things.

EXERCISE 20 (PRONOUN REVIEW)

1. **(5)** No error
2. **(2)** Since this pronoun names to whom the action of the sentence is done (that is, since the pronoun is an indirect object), the objective pronoun *her* should be used.

3. **(4)** Since the pronoun names the receiver of the action of the verb *try to call,* the objective pronoun *me* should be used.
4. **(1)** Since the pronoun is the subject of the verb *love,* the subjective pronoun *we* should be used.
5. **(1)** Since the pronoun names to whom the action of the verb *told* is done, the objective pronoun *him* should be used.
6. **(2)** There is no such word as *hisself;* the correct pronoun is *himself.*
7. **(1)** The pronoun *what* can never be used to refer to a noun that comes immediately before it; the correct pronoun is either *who* or *that.*
8. **(5)** No error
9. **(4)** The correct pronoun in this sentence is *whomever.* Look only at the part of the sentence beginning with the pronoun and rearrange that part of the sentence with the subject first: "you want whomever." Since the pronoun receives the action of the verb *want,* the correct pronoun is *whomever.*
10. **(4)** Since the word *chewing* is used as a noun, the correct pronoun to use is the possessive form *our.*
11. **(2)** If a pronoun acts as the subject of a sentence, be sure to use the subjective form. In this sentence *she* would be the correct pronoun.
12. **(4)** Use a reflexive pronoun only when it refers to something the subject is doing to or for himself. In this sentence, *I* would be the correct pronoun.
13. **(1)** The subjective pronoun *we* should have been used as the subject of this sentence.
14. **(2)** Possessive pronouns are never spelled with an apostrophe. The correct spelling is *theirs.*
15. **(2)** Use the nominative pronoun *they* after any part of the verb *to be.*

EXERCISE 21 (IDENTIFYING ADJECTIVES AND ADVERBS)

1. *Wholeheartedly* is an adverb that modifies *agree* by telling *how.*
2. *Kind* is an adjective that modifies *man* by telling *what kind.*
3. *Rare* is an adjective that modifies *men* by telling *what kind.*
4. *First* is an adjective that modifies *impression* by telling *which one.*
5. *Overly* is an adverb that modifies the adjective *loud* by telling *to what extent.*

6. *Offensive* is an adjective that modifies the noun *qualities* by telling *what kind.*

7. *Stupid* is an adjective that modifies the noun *fool* by telling *what kind.*

8. *Very* is an adverb that modifies the adverb *well* (which modifies the verb *like*) by telling *to what extent.*

9. *Still* is an adverb that modifies the verb *is* by telling *when.*

10. *Again* is an adverb that modifies the verb *meet* by telling *when.*

EXERCISE 22 (FORMS OF ADJECTIVES AND ADVERBS)

1. **(1)** Since this word modifies the verb *act,* the adverb form *quickly* should be used.

2. **(4)** The adverb form of adjectives that end in *ic* are formed by adding *ally;* therefore, the correct form is *enthusiastically.*

3. **(3)** The word *real* is incorrectly used as an adverb; you should use either the adverb form *really* or the less informal adverb *very.*

4. **(4)** Since this word modifies the verb *does* by telling *how,* the adverb form *efficiently* should be used.

5. **(5)** No error

6. **(3)** The adverb *carefully* should have been used in this sentence to modify the verb *walked.*

7. **(5)** No error

8. **(2)** The adjective *hard* does not change its form when it functions as an adverb.

9. **(1)** The adjective *beautifully* should have been used in this sentence to modify the verb *sings.*

10. **(2)** The use of the word *pretty* to mean *fairly* or *rather* is unacceptable in formal writing.

EXERCISE 23 (ADJECTIVE AND ADVERB PROBLEMS)

1. **(3)** The word *them* is an objective pronoun and cannot be used as an adjective. The correct adjective in this sentence might be *those,* although you would be much better off without any adjective at all.

2. **(4)** Since this word describes a person's health, the adjective form *bad* should be used.

3. **(4)** Since the pronunciation of the word *university* begins with the sound *you,* the correct word is *a.*

4. **(5)** No error
5. **(1)** Since the verb in this sentence is already negative (*hasn't* means *has not*), the use of *hardly* creates a double negative.
6. **(1)** The adverb *just* is placed too far away from the words it should emphasize. This sentence should read: "I'll give you *just* five minutes. . . ."

EXERCISE 24 (COMPARISONS)

1. **(1)** One-syllable adverbs take an *er* ending in comparisons. The correct adverb form in this sentence is *closer.*
2. **(5)** No error
3. **(2)** Since there are four dresses being talked about, the correct adjective form is *the prettiest.*
4. **(1)** Since the comparison involves the verb *singing,* the adverb form *more horribly* should be used.
5. **(3)** The adjective *bad* is irregular; the correct form is *worse.*
6. **(1)** Since the number of women can be counted, the correct word is *fewer.*

GRAMMAR AND USAGE: REVIEW TEST

Directions: In each of the following sentences, four words have been underlined. If one of these underlined words is incorrect in any way, blacken the space under the number corresponding to it. If all of the underlined words are correct, blacken the space numbered (5).

1. 1 2 3 4 5

1. When his old Buick broked (1) down he (2) was (3) saying, "Population is greater (4) east of the Mississippi River." No error (5)

2. 1 2 3 4 5

2. Ralph, the basset hound in the red bandana, eats his (1) food enthusiastically, (2) but Pearl eats hers (3) slowly. (4) No error (5)

3. 1 2 3 4 5

3. Women's (1) position has (2) changed dramatically (3) with respect to those (4) of men. No error (5)

4. 1 2 3 4 5

4. Not only is (1) camping (2) looked down upon in the park, but it is also considered pretty (3) dangerous. (4) No error (5)

5. 1 2 3 4 5

5. Ireland and it's (1) finest (2) products, including lace or crystal, were (3) praised by (4) the trade commissioner. No error (5)

6. 1 2 3 4 5

6. While Sarah had listened (1) to her favorite record, she (2) thought (3) about the night before and laughed to herself. (4) No error (5)

7. 1 2 3 4 5

7. The purpose of these (1) memos (2) were (3) to take the attention of the press away from purely (4) political stories. No error (5)

8. The director asked her to come back the next day to audition — 8. 1 2 3 4 5
1 2
again because she had sung well in her first try-out. No error
3 4 5

9. When the sixtys gradually faded into the past, the focus of — 9. 1 2 3 4 5
1 2 3
society shifted from teenagers to politicians. No error
4 5

10. Anyone who runs more quickly than this man should send in — 10. 1 2 3 4 5
1 2 3
their name for the Olympic games. No error
4 5

11. One of the kittens were born before midnight, but it did not — 11. 1 2 3 4 5
1 2 3
live for more than four hours. No error
4 5

12. Anyone looks good in that kind of a dress. No error — 12. 1 2 3 4 5
1 2 3 4 5

13. The pilot said that neither he nor the crew want the passengers — 13. 1 2 3 4 5
1 2 3
of the plane to be afraid. No error
4 5

14. If this heat wave continues, the city will need more water and — 14. 1 2 3 4 5
1 2
oil, both of which is in short supply. No error
3 4 5

15. Joans' job is as hard as the Andersons'. No error — 15. 1 2 3 4 5
1 2 3 4 5

16. Thanks was not as important to the Lone Ranger, who never — 16. 1 2 3 4 5
1 2 3
waited to be thanked for his catching bandits. No error
4 5

17. Most people now prefer simple furniture to fancy things that — 17. 1 2 3 4 5
1 2
are more expensive and less sturdy. No error
3 4 5

18. 1 2 3 4 5

18. The little boys tooked handfuls of the cookies for themselves
1 2 3
from Mrs. Overstreet's kitchen. No error
4 5

19. 1 2 3 4 5

19. The good loser always congratulates the winner or a competitor
1
that has done better than him. No error
2 3 4 5

20. 1 2 3 4 5

20. The dog looks friendly and playfully, but be careful around him.
1 2 3 4
No error
5

21. 1 2 3 4 5

21. I think that either Mr. Smith or his children has the information
1 2 3
that you want. No error
4 5

22. 1 2 3 4 5

22. Before she went shopping, my wife asked me what kind of a
1 2 3
dinner I wanted. No error
4 5

23. 1 2 3 4 5

23. The argument that took place between she and Ethel will
1 2
probably be straightened out when they meet again tomorrow.
3 4
No error
5

24. 1 2 3 4 5

24. Neither my friends nor my family are going to be home during
1 2 3
the holidays. No error
4 5

25. 1 2 3 4 5

25. The carpenters built the companys cafeteria tables strong
1 2 3 4
enough to hold fifty pounds of food. No error
5

ANSWERS AND EXPLANATIONS—GRAMMAR AND USAGE: REVIEW TEST

1. **(1)** The past tense of *break* is *broke.*
2. **(5)** No error
3. **(4)** Since the pronoun refers to the singular noun *position,* the correct pronoun is *that.*
4. **(3)** The adjective *pretty* can not be used as an adverb; an appropriate adverb in this sentence would be *very.*
5. **(1)** *It's* means *it is* or *it has.* In this sentence, the possessive pronoun *its* should be used.
6. **(1)** There is no need to use the past perfect tense in this sentence since the two past actions occurred at the same time; the simple past tense *listened* is correct.
7. **(3)** Since the subject of this sentence is the singular noun *purpose,* the singular verb *was* should be used.
8. **(5)** No error
9. **(1)** The correct plural form of *sixty* is *sixties.*
10. **(4)** Since the pronoun replaces the word *anyone,* the singular pronoun *his* should be used.
11. **(1)** Since the subject of the verb is *one,* the singular verb *was* should be used.
12. **(4)** It is incorrect to use the word *a* with the expression *kind of.*
13. **(3)** Since the subject of this verb is joined together by *neither . . . nor,* the verb agrees with the part of the subject closest to the verb, *crew. Crew* is a collective noun that requires the singular verb *wants.*
14. **(4)** The subject of this verb is *both,* which is plural in meaning; therefore, the plural verb *are* should be used.
15. **(1)** The possessive form of a singular noun is formed by adding *'s;* therefore, the correct word in this sentence is *Joan's.*
16. **(2)** No comparison is being made in this sentence; only the adjective *important* should be used.
17. **(5)** No error
18. **(1)** The past tense of *take* is *took.*
19. **(4)** If you complete the missing part of this sentence, you will discover that the pronoun is a subject (. . . better than *he* has done).

20. **(2)** This is a predicate adjective describing the dog; *playful* is the correct word to use.

21. **(3)** In sentences using *either . . . or,* the verb should agree with the part of the subject that is closest to it. The noun *children* is plural; therefore, the verb should be *have.*

22. **(3)** The expression *kind of a* is never correct usage. The word *a* should be eliminated.

23. **(2)** Be sure to use objective pronouns after the preposition *between. Her* would be the correct pronoun to use in this sentence.

24. **(3)** In sentences using *neither . . . nor,* the verb should agree with the part of the subject that is closest to it. The collective noun *family* is singular in this sentence; therefore, the correct verb would be *is.*

25. **(3)** The possessive form *company's* should have been used in this sentence to indicate ownership.

GRAMMAR AND USAGE EVALUATION CHART

Question Type	*Review Pages*	*Question Number*	*Amount of Question Type*	*Number of Wrong Answers*
A. Noun Problems	25–38	9, 12, 15, 22, 25	5	______
B. Verb Problems	40–52	1, 6, 18	3	______
C. Subject-Verb Agreement	56–69	7, 11, 13, 14, 21, 24	6	______
D. Pronoun Problems	71–89	3, 5, 10, 19, 23	5	______
E. Adjective/Adverb Problems	92–109	4, 16, 20	3	______

PASSING SCORE: 20 right out of 25 questions

YOUR SCORE: ______ right out of 25 questions

If you have more than one question wrong in categories B or E or more than two questions wrong in any of the other categories, you should reread the explanation of that type of problem in the review pages listed in the table.

SENTENCE STRUCTURE

At the beginning of this book, we defined a complete sentence as one that has a subject and a predicate and that communicates a complete thought.

I want food.

subject *predicate*

verb *receiver of action (direct object)*

The sentence above has only one subject and one predicate and communicates only one complete thought. This kind of sentence is called a **simple sentence**—it is the simplest kind of sentence that can still be called a complete sentence.

The following paragraphs are written using only simple sentences.

> Advertising shows many things. Companies show you new products. Companies also show you their opinions. Some of these opinions concern you.
>
> Watch an evening's television commercials. You will see some opinions. The following are their opinions. First, nature obviously didn't build you very well. Your body always smells bad. Your breath always smells bad. Even your natural hair color is a mistake. Second, you are a fool. You don't eat the right things. You don't drink the right things. You don't have any energy. The third opinion is the worst. You don't have any sex appeal.
>
> You don't need to worry. These opinions shouldn't make you worry. Every company has the answer. Toothpaste companies have the answer. Deodorant companies have the answer. Buy the right products. The right products will supply your missing qualities. You can buy all these products. This might not make you perfect. This would almost certainly make you broke. You still don't have to worry. Loan companies also advertise.

Many of these simple sentences have enough in common to be made into longer, more complex sentences. Read the following revised version of these paragraphs, paying special attention to the underlined words that join the sentences together.

Through advertising, companies show you not only new products but also their opinions about you.

If you watch an evening's television commercials, you will see some of the following opinions. First, nature obviously didn't build you very well since both your body and your breath smell bad, and even your natural hair color is a mistake. Second, you are a fool because you neither eat nor drink the right things, and, as a result, you don't have any energy. Third, and worst of all, you don't have any sex appeal.

You don't need to worry about any of these opinions because every company, from toothpaste companies to deodorant companies, has the answer. If you buy the right products, they will supply your missing qualities. Buying all these products might not make you perfect, but it would almost certainly make you broke. You still don't have to worry, however, because loan companies also advertise.

The sentences have been joined together in the following ways:

(1) using a connecting word that forms a word group that acts like an adjective or an adverb:

through advertising (line 1) — modifies *show*
about you (line 2) — modifies *opinions*
of the following opinions (line 4) — modifies *some*
of all (line 9) — modifies *worse*
about any (line 10) — modifies *worry*
of these opinions (line 10) — modifies *any*
from toothpaste companies (line 11) — modifies *company*
to deodorant companies (lines 11–12) — modifies *company*

These connecting words are called **prepositions.**

(2) using a connecting word to link similar parts of two sentences:

not only new products *but also* their opinions (lines 1–2) — both *products* and *opinions* receive the action of the verb *show*
both your body *and* your breath (line 5) — both *body* and *breath* are subjects of the verb *smells*
neither eat *nor* drink (line 7) — both *eat* and *drink* are verbs with the same subject, *you.*

These connecting words are two-part **conjunctions.**

(3) using a connecting word to link two sentences that have some kind of relationship:

If you watch an evening's television commercials (line 3) — explains what you need to do to *see* (line 4)
since both your body and your breath smell bad (lines 5–6) — explains the reason behind the statement in lines 4–5
and even your natural hair color is a mistake (line 6) —adds another reason behind the statement in lines 4–5
because you neither eat nor drink the right things (line 7) — explains the reason behind the statement in lines 6–7
and, as a result, you don't have any energy (line 8) — explains the result of the actions stated in line 7
and worst of all (lines 8–9) — adds the description of the third opinion in the same sentence as the opinion itself
because every company . . . has the answer (lines 10–12) — explains why *you don't need to worry* (line 10)
If you buy the right products (line 12) — explains the condition under which the rest of the sentence will happen
but it would almost certainly make you broke (lines 14–15) — explains what would happen if you bought all the advertised products
however, because loan companies also advertise (lines 15–16) — explains why you still don't have to worry

These connecting words are called **conjunctions.**

(4) changing the verb of one sentence into a noun ending in *ing* and using the resulting sentence fragment as part of a new sentence:

Buying all these products (line 13) — this sentence fragment is then used as the subject of the verb *might*

By using these four methods of combining sentences, the writer has avoided unnecessary repetition and has made logical connections.

REPEATED SUBJECT AND VERB

Companies show you new products. Companies also show you their opinions.

Companies show you not only new products but also their opinions.

LOGICAL CONNECTIONS

Buy the right products. The right products will supply your missing qualities.

If you buy the right products, they will supply your missing qualities.

Whenever two or more simple sentences share some common bond (if, for example, they have the same subject or if they have a cause-and-effect relationship), you should consider combining them. In the following pages, we will examine seven basic methods of combining sentences. Study each method carefully, paying special attention to the common errors that are pointed out. The errors that are pointed out in this section are those that are most likely to show up on the GED test.

Method 1. Use a prepositional phrase.

Prepositions are connecting words that are used to form a word group, called a **prepositional phrase,** that acts like an adjective or adverb.

The man *on the motorcycle* is my father. (The prepositional phrase is used to describe or modify the noun *man.*)

I would like to look *at your book.* (The prepositional phrase is used to tell *where* the writer wants to look; in other words, it functions as an adverb modifying the verb *would like to look.*)

You can also use a prepositional phrase to express time:

in six hours
by tomorrow
at seven o'clock

to show location:

on the motorcycle
in the car
into the house

or to show ownership or relationship (like a possessive):

property *of* mine
property *of* the church
owner *of* the store

Many pairs of sentences can be combined by making one of the sentences a prepositional phrase:

(1) Joe succeeded. He got the job.
Joe succeeded *in* getting the job.
(2) They were happy. They liked the house.
They were happy *with* the house.

The position of the prepositional phrase is very important. Look at the following two sentences in which the position of the prepositional phrase creates an error in meaning:

WRONG: On top of the building, we saw a very strange statue.
WRONG: Watch for your cousin's arrival with the binoculars.

In the first sentence, the position of the phrase leads your reader to believe that the subject, *we,* is on top of the building. In the second sentence, the position of the phrase *with the binoculars* indicates that the phrase modifies the word *arrival;* in other words, the meaning of this sentence is that the cousin is bringing a pair of binoculars. These two sentences should be written as:

RIGHT: We saw a very strange statue on top of the building.
RIGHT: With these binoculars, watch for your cousin's arrival.

Always place the prepositional phrase next to the word it modifies.

The most common error that is made when using prepositional phrases is the use of the wrong preposition. Study the following misused prepositions; you will be expected to recognize these errors on the GED test.

(1) *different from* NOT *different than*

WRONG: New Yorkers are different than Chicagoans.
RIGHT: New Yorkers are different from Chicagoans.

The strict law of grammar demands that you never use *different than.*

(2) *was (were) in* or *was (were) at* NOT *was (were) to*

WRONG: Jerry and Tim were to New Orleans for Mardi Gras.
RIGHT: Jerry and Tim were in New Orleans for Mardi Gras.
WRONG: Ray was to my house for dinner last night.
RIGHT: Ray was at my house for dinner last night.

(3) *like* can be used only to mean *resembles* or *is similar to*

RIGHT: Susan looks like her mother.
WRONG: Very few people think like you do.
RIGHT: Very few people think as you do.

(4) use *between* for phrases involving two nouns; use *among* for phrases involving three or more nouns

WRONG: This secret is just among the two of us.
RIGHT: This secret is just between the two of us.
WRONG: When my father dies, his money will be divided equally between his four sons.
RIGHT: When my father dies, his money will be divided equally among his four sons.

(5) *borrow from* NOT *borrow off*

WRONG: Can I borrow a pencil off you?
RIGHT: Can I borrow a pencil from you?

(6) *around* does not mean *approximately* or *about*

WRONG: There were around twenty people at last night's meeting.
RIGHT: There were about twenty people at last night's meeting.

(7) *off* NOT *off of*

WRONG: He jumped off of the train at the last minute.
RIGHT: He jumped off the train at the last minute.

(8) never use *should of, would of,* or *could of;* use *should have, would have,* or *could have*

WRONG: I would of been here hours ago if I could of been.
RIGHT: I would have been here hours ago if I could have been.

In addition to remembering the correct preposition to use, you will also be expected to know that the rules of English grammar demand that you never end a sentence with a preposition. Although ending a sentence with a preposition seems to be acceptable in speech and informal writing, this practice is considered an error in formal writing and on the GED test.

WRONG: She is the person he is in love with.
RIGHT: She is the person with whom he is in love.
WRONG: Whom am I speaking to?
RIGHT: To whom am I speaking?

SENTENCE STRUCTURE: EXERCISE 1 (PREPOSITIONAL PHRASES)

Directions: If there is an error in the following sentences, rewrite the sentence correctly in the space provided. If there is no error in a sentence, write "correct" in the space provided.

1. Is that the person whom he had a fight with?

____

2. Jane's feelings about this problem are different than mine.

____

3. I was to a rock concert last night.

____

4. I am not like you; I can't do things like that.

____

5. We'll have to divide the pizza between the four of us.

____

6. I'll be home around seven o'clock.

____

7. Get off of the phone and let someone else use it.

____

8. If you don't have enough money, you can always borrow off me.

____

Answers and explanations are on page 168.

Method 2: Form a compound.

If two or more sentences are the same except for the subjects, you can often combine the subjects:

> John is out to lunch. Jane is out to lunch.
> John *and* Jane are out to lunch.

When a sentence has two subjects, it is said to have a **compound subject.** Notice that the verb has been made plural to agree with the compound subject.

If two or more sentences have the same subject but different predicates, you can often combine the predicates:

> John ran out to the store. John got the beer for the party.
> John ran out to the store *and* got the beer for the party.

When a sentence has two predicates, it is said to have a **compound predicate.**

If two or more sentences are the same except for the verbs, you can often combine the verbs:

> I searched for the missing book. I found the missing book.
> I searched for *and* found the missing book.

When a sentence has two or more verbs, it is said to have a **compound verb.**

If two or more sentences are the same except for one part of the sentences, you can often combine the different parts:

> I would like a piece of cake. I would also like a piece of pie
> I would like *not only* a piece of cake *but also* a piece of pie.
> Jack is giving me a hard time. Jack is giving you a hard time, too.
> Jack is giving you *and* me a hard time.

In the first pair of sentences, there is a **compound direct object;** in the second pair, there is a **compound indirect object.**

When the ideas of two or more sentences are related in some way, you can often combine the sentences:

> Sam is going to the party. I am not.
> Sam is going to the party, *but* I am not.
>
> I have a lot of work to do. I am staying late.
> I have a lot of work to do, *so* I am staying late.

When two or more complete sentences are joined together, the resulting sentence is called a **compound sentence.**

The words that are used to form compounds are called conjunctions. Conjunctions may be only one word:

and	or
but	nor
yet	so
as	

or more than one word:

not only . . . but also	neither . . . nor
both . . . and	either . . . or
rather . . . than	

Whenever you use one of these last pairs of words as conjunctions, make sure that you use both parts of the pair and only the words that belong to the same pair. In other words: use *nor* only with *neither;* use *or* only with *either;* and make sure that you use *but also,* not *also* alone, with *not only.*

> WRONG: *Neither* she *or* I know what is going on.
> RIGHT: *Neither* she *nor* I know what is going on.
> WRONG: I *not only* need to pass this test, I *also* want to.
> RIGHT: I *not only* need to pass this test, *but* I *also* want to.

Not every pair of sentences can be combined as a compound. The sentences must be related in some way. Look at the following compound sentence:

> The President is in London today, and it is raining in Ohio.

Although the sentence is grammatically correct, the idea in the first part of the sentence has nothing to do with the idea in the second part.

Before you make any pair of sentences into a single compound sentence, make sure that the resulting sentence will make sense. Remember that the purpose of a sentence is to communicate a complete thought; you must make certain that your reader can understand your thought. If the sample sentence had been used in the following context, however, the sentence would make sense:

> The President was fond of saying that it would be a rainy day in Ohio before you would see him in London. Well, the President is in London today, and it *is* raining in Ohio.

Another problem in forming compounds is choosing the conjunction that helps you express your thought. Look at the following pair of compound sentences in which the conjunction plays an important part in the meaning:

> WRONG: Don't come in here, *and* you'll ruin the surprise.
> RIGHT: Don't come in here, *or* you'll ruin the surprise.

The first sentence could be correct only in the following context:

> When we called out into the living room for Tom to come into the kitchen, he said that he didn't want to come. So I said, "All right, don't come in here, *and* you'll ruin the surprise."

Placing the conjunction at the wrong spot in the sentence may also get in the way of your meaning. Look at the following pair of sentences and the ways in which they have been combined:

> The hail stopped. The rain also stopped.
> WRONG: The hail *not only* stopped *but also* the rain.
> RIGHT: *Not only* the hail *but also* the rain stopped.

In the version of the sentence labeled *wrong,* the first part of the conjunction is attached to the verb, and the second part of the conjunction is attached to a subject. In the version of the sentence labeled *right,* the two parts of the conjunction are attached to the two subjects. Conjunctions can only be used to join two similar parts of a sentence. Don't be fooled by the expression *rather . . . than:*

> RIGHT: I would *rather* see a bad movie *than* read a bad book.
> RIGHT: I would *rather* see Ben *than* Jane.

In the first sentence, the two parts of the conjunction are connected to verbs. It may seem as though the two parts of the conjunction in the second sentence are connected to two different kinds of words, the first to a verb and the second to a noun. However, this is not the case. The second sentence can also be written as:

> I would *rather* see Ben *than* see Jane.

Because the repetition of the verb is not necessary to make the meaning of the sentence clear, the second verb can be left out. However, you will need to remember that the second verb is understood and that this use of the conjunction *rather . . . than* is grammatically correct.

When you use a conjunction to connect three or more similar parts of a sentence, do not use a conjunction for each part:

> WRONG: Martha felt confused *and* frightened *and* nervous.
> RIGHT: Martha felt confused, frightened, *and* nervous.

Notice the way this sentence has been punctuated. You must place a comma between each part if you have three or more parts. Notice, too, that there is no comma before the first item in the series and that the final comma comes before the conjunction.

In some sentences, several pairs of words that are treated as units are connected in a series. Look at the following example of this kind of sentence, noting how the sentence is punctuated:

> Among the most famous lovers in history are Romeo and Juliet, Anthony and Cleopatra, and Richard Burton and Elizabeth Taylor.

There is no punctuation between the individual names in each pair (Romeo and Juliet), but there is a comma between each complete pair.

If there are only two similar parts of a sentence joined by a conjunction do not use a comma:

> Martha felt confused by what had happened and frightened that it might happen again.

This sentence has a compound predicate; no punctuation should be used. However, you must use some mark of punctuation if the conjunction joins two complete thoughts, that is, if you have a compound sentence.

WRONG: First the man told us to leave the building then I heard the explosion.
WRONG: First the man told us to leave the building and then I heard the explosion.
RIGHT: First the man told us to leave the building, and then I heard the explosion.

You must use both a conjunction and a comma to join two complete thoughts. However, you may use a semicolon to replace both the comma and the conjunction:

RIGHT: First the man told us to leave the building; then I heard the explosion.

Some compound sentences require a stronger connecting word that will make the relationship between the two parts of the sentence clear:

I am very tired this evening; however, I will still go to Frank's party.
I am very tired this evening; therefore, I will not go to Frank's party.

The words *however* and *therefore* connect the two complete thoughts of these sentences (that is, they act as conjunctions) as well as describe the relationship between the thoughts (that is, they act as adverbs). Notice that the use of these words requires stronger punctuation than the use of the simple conjunctions. Compare the following sentences, noting the difference in punctuation:

(1) I am very tired this evening, but I will still go to Frank's party.
(2) I am very tired this evening. However, I will still go to Frank's party.
(3) I am very tired this evening; however, I will still go to Frank's party.
(4) I will go to Frank's party this evening; however, I am very tired.

In sentence (1), the use of a simple conjunction requires only a comma. In sentence (2), the compound sentence has been divided into two separate sentences. Notice that a comma is placed after the word *however* since it is an extra word that cannot be tied to any one part of the sentence; *however* modifies the sentence as a whole. When the two sentences are joined together as a compound, as in sentence (3), a strong mark of punctuation is needed to replace the period. You must always use a semicolon between the two parts of a compound sentence of this type. Notice how the use of *however* has been changed in sentence (4). *However* modifies *I am tired* and is separated from that part of the sentence by a comma; a semicolon is used to separate the two complete thoughts that make up the compound sentence.

You may use any one of the following words or groups of words to join the two parts of a compound sentence:

however	besides
therefore	in fact
moreover	for example
nevertheless	on the other hand
consequently	as a result
then	

Whenever you use a word or group of words from this list, be sure to use a semicolon to separate the two complete thoughts of the sentence and a comma to separate the connecting word from the part of the sentence it modifies.

> My boss was very friendly today; in fact, he has been friendly all week.

Joining two or more sentences together by forming a compound sentence is perhaps the easiest way to join sentences. Because it is so easy, you may be tempted to run the following related thoughts together:

> I am happy today, *and* Ann is sad, *but* something tells me that I'll end up being in her mood, *as* she is a very strong person, *and* she usually wins, *but* I'll try to avoid her *so* I can stay in a good mood.

This kind of a sentence is called a **run-on sentence** because it runs on and on and on. Allowing a sentence to run for this long is always considered an error. You should break up the sentence into several sentences to avoid tiring and confusing your reader.

> Although I am happy today, Ann is sad. Since Ann is a very strong person who usually wins, I could end up being in her mood. However, I'll try to avoid her so that I can stay in a good mood.

Notice that, by breaking up the run-on sentence, you have actually used fewer words and have made it easier for your reader to follow your thoughts.

SENTENCE STRUCTURE: EXERCISE 2 (FORMING COMPOUND SENTENCES)

Directions: Make one sentence out of each pair of sentences given below by choosing one of the two connecting words given under each pair of sentences. Write your answer in the space provided.

1. (a) Salesmen usually use a hard-sell approach.
   (b) Most people are suspicious about buying something new.

   or
   so

   ____

   ____

2. (a) You need proteins for good health.
   (b) You need vitamins for good health.

   not only . . . but also
   either . . . or

   ____

   ____

3. (a) They traded in their old television set for a big color set.
   (b) They wanted to enjoy football games at home.

   and
   so

   ____

   ____

4. (a) Bill moaned about his problems.
   (b) Bill groaned about his problems.

   however
   and

   ____

   ____

5. (a) The food is good in that store.

(b) It is better in this one.

but
so

____

____

6. (a) I don't want to work.
(b) I will work.

and
however

____

____

7. (a) You might win $2,000 in the lottery.
(b) You might lose the price of the ticket.

or
so

____

____

8. (a) Bob barbecues the chicken.
(b) Marilyn eats it.

either . . . or
and

____

____

Answers and explanations are on pages 168–169.

SENTENCE STRUCTURE: EXERCISE 3
(PROBLEMS WITH CONJUNCTIONS AND PREPOSITIONS)

Directions: In each of the following sentences, four words have been underlined. If one of these words is incorrectly used, blacken the space under the number corresponding to it. If all of the words are correctly used, blacken the space numbered (5).

1. 1 2 3 4 5

1. Both (1) Susan, Ted, and (2) Henry would rather (3) see Jeff than (4) Jack. No error (5)

2. 1 2 3 4 5

2. Your child wanted neither (1) chicken nor (2) hamburger for lunch. He said he was angry, and (3) felt sick, and (4) wanted to go home. No error (5)

3. 1 2 3 4 5

3. January, but (1) not February, looks like (2) a difficult month to schedule neither (3) parties or (4) celebrations. No error (5)

4. 1 2 3 4 5

4. The perfect man was described as brave but (1) careful, strong but (2) tender, and (3) aggressive but (4) tolerant. No error (5)

5. 1 2 3 4 5

5. Before (1) he left, he both (2) lifted the table and (3) the chair to prove how (4) strong he was. No error (5)

6. 1 2 3 4 5

6. Black, white, and (1) red were chosen by (2) the director for (3) the costumes. He doesn't approve to (4) wild, flashy colors. No error (5)

7. 1 2 3 4 5

7. A good actor not only (1) changes the history of (2) theater or (3) film, but also (4) excites the audience. No error (5)

8. 1 2 3 4 5

8. "To what can this sudden change of (1) heart and (2) strong feelings be attributed to?" (3) asked the surprised clerk of (4) his old employer. No error (5)

9. 1 2 3 4 5

9. People are willing to (1) pay a large sum of money to (2) be steamed and (3) exercised on (4) health clubs. No error (5)

10. Neither rain or the gloom of night is supposed to keep postmen from performing their duties. No error
(1: Neither; 2: or; 3: to; 4: from; 5: No error)

10. 1 2 3 4 5

Answers and explanations are on pages 169–170.

Method 3: Use a connecting word to turn one of the sentences into a sentence fragment that gives the reason for, shows a contrast to, expresses a time relationship with, or expresses the conditions for the rest of the sentence.

Look at the following pair of sentences and the ways in which they have been combined:

> Sam is always late for work. He doesn't have an alarm clock.
>
> Sam doesn't have an alarm clock, *so* he is always late for work.
>
> Sam is always late for work *because* he doesn't have an alarm clock.

The sentences can be combined as a compound sentence joined by the conjunction *so.* The sentences can also be combined by using the connecting word *because.* Notice that, when you use this last method, you have formed a sentence fragment:

> because he doesn't have an alarm clock

Although you still have a subject and a verb, the addition of the word *because* demands that you give more information to communicate a complete thought. The fragment alone does not communicate a complete thought; the reader does not know *what happens* because Sam doesn't have an alarm clock.

Any of the following words can be used to connect two sentences by this method:

connecting word	*use*
because	to show the reason for something
since	to show the reason for something
so that	to show the reason for something
in order that	to show the reason for something
whereas	to show contrast
although	to show contrast
though	to show contrast
even though	to show contrast

connecting word	*use*
as though	to show contrast
as if	to show contrast
in spite of the fact that	to show contrast
despite the fact that	to show contrast
before	to express a time relationship
after	to express a time relationship
while	to express a time relationship
when	to express a time relationship
as soon as	to express a time relationship
as long as	to express a time relationship
until	to express a time relationship
if	to express the conditions under which something may happen
unless	to express the conditions under which something may happen

The sentence fragment that you form by using one of these connecting words may be placed either before or after the rest of the sentence:

The President speaks well. His speeches are not broadcast nationwide.
Although the President speaks well, his speeches are not broadcast nationwide.
The President's speeches are not broadcast nationwide *although* he speaks well.

Notice that a comma is required when the fragment begins the sentence, but there is no comma when the fragment ends the sentence.

When the President speaks well, his rivals worry.
His rivals worry *when* the President speaks well.

SENTENCE STRUCTURE: EXERCISE 4 (METHOD 3 COMBINATIONS)

Directions: Make one sentence out of each pair of sentences given below by choosing one of the connecting words given under each pair of sentences. Use sentence (a) as the first sentence. Write your answer in the space provided.

1. (a) You give me a dollar.
   (b) The Brooklyn Bridge will be yours.

   although
   if
   whereas

2. (a) The blues singer didn't smoke.
   (b) He accepted the cigarette.

   as soon as
   because
   even though

3. (a) The boss speaks.
   (b) The secretary takes notes.

   while
   despite the fact that
   unless

4. (a) Water dripped through the ceiling.
   (b) Pat called the landlord.

   after
   if
   despite the fact that

5. (a) She quit her job.
   (b) The boss was unreasonable.

   because
   whereas
   unless

Answers and explanations are on page 170.

Method 4: In sentences with the same subject, you can use the predicate of one sentence to modify the complete second sentence.

Using the methods of sentence combination that you have studied so far, you can combine the following pair of sentences in a number of ways.

The dancer nodded her head.
She turned toward the audience.

METHOD 2 COMBINATION: The dancer nodded her head, and she turned toward the audience.
METHOD 3 COMBINATION: After the dancer nodded her head, she turned toward the audience.
METHOD 3 COMBINATION: The dancer nodded her head as she turned toward the audience.

Notice that, in all of these combined sentences, the subject is repeated (*she* refers to *the dancer*). Although each of these sentences is grammatically correct, there is a way to avoid repeating the subject. Look at the following two ways in which these sentences have been combined:

Nodding her head, the dancer turned toward the audience.
Turning toward the audience, the dancer nodded her head.

The verb in one of the two sentences has been changed into a special form that ends in *ing; nodded* became *nodding,* and *turned* became *turning*. The resulting sentence fragment was then attached to the remaining sentence, and a comma was inserted between the two parts of the sentence as a whole. (In traditional grammar books this kind of sentence fragment is called a *participial phrase*).

Whenever you use this method of combining sentences, keep the form of the most important sentence exactly the way it is, and change the form of the less important sentence. Study the following pairs of sentences. How could these sentences be combined without repeating any words?

(1) The actor was wearing an old pair of jeans.
He looked like a student.
(2) Jack stretched out on the couch.
Jack realized how tired he was.
(3) Farmer Dell saw the fox.
The fox was running off with a chicken.

These sentences could be combined in the following ways:

(1) *Wearing* an old pair of jeans, the actor looked like a student.
(2) *Stretching* out on the couch, Jack realized how tired he was.
(3) Farmer Dell saw the fox *running* off with a chicken.

In each of these combined sentences, a fragment of one sentence has been placed next to the noun it describes in the second sentence. Since the fragments describe the subject in sentences (1) and (2), the fragment comes first. Since the fragment in sentence (3) describes the noun *fox,* the fragment must be placed at the end of the sentence.

WRONG: Running off with a chicken, Farmer Dell saw the fox.

This version of the sentence is wrong because it says, in effect, that *Farmer Dell* was running off with a chicken when he saw the fox.

This same method can be used for sentences that contain descriptions. Look at the following pairs of sentences and the ways in which they have been combined.

The dog was *happy to see his owner.*
The dog leaped into the car.
Happy to see his owner, the dog leaped into the car.

The manager was *upset over the team's mistakes.*
The manager screamed at the players.
Upset over the team's mistakes, the manager screamed at the players.

In these two sentences, the predicate of one of the simple sentences is a description of the subject. When the simple sentences were combined, only the description was used as a fragment to begin the sentence. The general rule to follow is:

FOR ACTIONS THAT OCCUR AT THE SAME TIME — change the verb of the less important sentence to a verb ending *ing* and leave the rest of the predicate exactly as it is
FOR DESCRIPTIONS — drop the verb and leave the predicate exactly as it is

The most common errors that are made in combining sentences using Method 4 involve misplacing the sentence fragment or incorrectly using a sentence fragment. Look at the following sentence. Can you tell why it is wrong?

> WRONG: Walking into the cemetery, the tombstones looked frightening.

This sentence actually says that the tombstones were walking into the cemetery. This error can be avoided by looking for the subjects of the original simple sentences:

> *We* walked into the cemetery.
> *The tombstones* looked frightening.

Since the subjects are not the same, you cannot combine them by using Method 4. You could combine these two sentences by using Method 3:

> As we walked into the cemetery, the tombstones looked frightening.

However, the implied meaning of this combined sentence is that the tombstones did not look frightening at any other time. You could change the second sentence to have the same subject as the first and then combine them by using Method 4:

> *We* walked into the cemetery.
> *We* were frightened by the tombstones.
> Walking into the cemetery, we were frightened by the tombstones.

A similar confusion occurs when a group of words describing something or someone has wandered too far from the person or thing it is supposed to describe. For example:

> Sam hunted alligators wearing tennis shoes.

Who was wearing tennis shoes, Sam or the alligators? In this sentence, the fragment *wearing tennis shoes* should be close to Sam since it is describing him, not the alligators. The description is placed correctly in the following two sentences:

> Wearing tennis shoes, Sam hunted alligators.
> Sam, wearing tennis shoes, hunted alligators.

SENTENCE STRUCTURE: EXERCISE 5 (METHOD 4 COMBINATIONS)

Directions: Make one sentence out of each pair of sentences given below by Method 4. Write your answer in the space provided.

1. Sam watched an old movie on television.
   Sam fell asleep.

   ____

   ____

2. We were sad to see the evening end.
   We tearfully said goodbye.

   ____

   ____

3. We sat in the balcony.
   We had a great view of everyone on stage.

   ____

   ____

4. I read the newspaper.
   I noticed an interesting story about Mexico.

   ____

   ____

5. Frank was angry about losing so much money.
   He swore that he would never gamble again.

   ____

   ____

Answers and explanations are on page 170.

Method 5: When one sentence gives some kind of additional information about a word in another sentence or another sentence as a whole, you can often insert that sentence in the middle of the combined sentence.

Look at the following pairs of sentences and notice how they have been combined.

(1) The type of music called the blues was first sung in Mississippi.
Blues was the forerunner of jazz.

The type of music called the blues, the forerunner of jazz, was first sung in Mississippi.

(2) The Declaration of Independence was signed on July 4.
This was the document that announced the American Revolution.

The Declaration of Independence, the document that announced the American Revolution, was signed on July 4.

(3) Bald men are strong.
This is what I have been told.

Bald men, I have been told, are strong.

(4) This strike will be settled in a week.
This is what the workers argue.

This strike, the workers argue, will be settled in a week.

Notice that these additional information groups must be set off by commas.

Method 6: In some sentences, a group with a possessive pronoun, the possessed noun, and either the ing form or the past participle of a verb can replace a sentence and be linked to the other by a comma.

Look at the following pairs of sentences and notice how they have been combined:

(1) The old man limped away.
His cane was dragging behind him.

The old man limped away, *his cane dragging behind him.*

(2) His job had been completed.
He went into the kitchen for a sandwich.

His job completed, he went into the kitchen for a sandwich.

Method 7: Change the verb or predicate adjective of one sentence into a noun and use it as the subject of the second sentence.

By adding a suffix (see page 257), nouns can sometimes be formed from other types of words and used to combine sentences. Look at the following pairs of sentences and notice how they have been combined.

(1) Jeff arrived.
This made us leave.

Jeff's arrival made us leave.

(2) Susan was late.
This resulted in her losing her job.

Susan's lateness resulted in her losing her job.

Notice that the subject of the first sentence in each pair became possessive in the combined sentence.

SENTENCE STRUCTURE: EXERCISE 6 (MORE SENTENCE COMBINATIONS)

Directions: Combine each of the following pairs of sentences by using the method indicated. Write your answer in the space provided.

1. The girls were beginning to suspect the driver.
The girls decided to watch him carefully.
(Use Method 4)

____

____

2. The President approved.
He admired the plan.
(Use Method 1)

____

____

3. The astronaut was badly shaken.
The astronaut was taken to headquarters.
(Use Method 3)

____

____

4. The runner dashed over the finish line.
His body was covered with perspiration.
(Use Method 6)

____

____

5. Ted is lazy.
Ted is also careless.
(Use Method 2)

____

____

6. John asked for the evidence.
John was the man accused of the crime.
(Use Method 5)

____

____

7. The couple doesn't have a penny.
They enjoy living in the city.
(Use Method 3)

____

____

8. The children had bad table manners.
This made their mother angry.
(Use Method 7)

____

____

9. Sam was nervous about the job interview.
Sam forgot to buckle his belt.
(Use Method 4)

____

____

10. A rich man used to own that house.
That is what I have been told.
(Use Method 5)

____

____

Answers and explanations are on pages 170–171.

INTERNAL CONSISTENCY

When a person behaves in exactly the same way every time a certain situation comes up, his behavior is said to be consistent, that is, always the same. If a person behaves in a different way every time the same situation comes up, his behavior is said to be inconsistent, that is, never the same. Sentences, like people, can also be described as either consistent or inconsistent; that is, the structure and the various kinds of words that make up a sentence can be either the same throughout or different throughout. Unlike people, sentences must always be consistent. Look at the following sentences and notice the kinds of inconsistencies that are pointed out:

INCONSISTENT:	Sam's favorite hobbies are *bowling, swimming,* and *to chase* women.
CONSISTENT:	Sam's favorite hobbies are *bowling, swimming,* and *chasing* women.
INCONSISTENT:	Ernie *breaks* down the door and *charged* into the room.
CONSISTENT:	Ernie *broke* down the door and *charged* into the room.
INCONSISTENT:	Once a *person* learns to ride a bicycle, *you* never forget how.
CONSISTENT:	Once a *person* learns to ride a bicycle, *he* never forgets how.

The first sentence is labeled *inconsistent* because the words in the series at the end of the sentence are not all the *same kind of word.* This error, called lack of parallel structure (to be discussed in this section), can be cleared up by changing the form of the last item in the series. The second inconsistent sentence has two different verb tenses. Even though both actions occurred in the past, the writer has mistakenly used the present tense for the first verb. This error, called improper sequence of tenses (to be discussed in this section), can be cleared up by using the same tense (the past tense) for both verbs. You should recognize the error in the third inconsistent sentence. The writer has shifted from the third person singular (*person*) to the second person singular (*you*) in the same sentence. This is an error in noun-pronoun agreement. (If you do not remember the rules of noun-pronoun agreement, turn back to page 86 for review.)

Parallel Structure

One of the most common errors in sentence structure, and one that you will be expected to recognize on the GED test, is the error of not using a parallel structure. The word *parallel,* when used to describe sentence structure, means that similar parts of a sentence have the same form.

Look at the following application for a computer dating service, paying special attention to the answers to the three questions.

Application for True Love

NAME: Eddie Ego
AGE: 29

Answer the following questions honestly so that the computer can match you with your ideal mate.

1. What three things do you look for in a woman?

   a good personality
   if she is pretty
   laughs at my jokes

2. Name your strong points.

   I am very handsome
   successful in business
   good jokes

3. What do you want from life?

   lots of money
   my name should be famous
   being a movie star

Eddie's answers are not parallel; that is, he has not used the same form for each item in his lists of three answers. His answers could be made parallel in any one of the following ways:

using three complete predicates:

has a good personality
has a pretty face and figure
has a good sense of humor

using three adjectives:

handsome
successful
funny

using three nouns:

wealth
fame
stardom

The rule of using parallel structure also applies to any compound part of a sentence:

NOT PARALLEL:	*Asking* for advice and *if you follow* it are two different things.
PARALLEL:	*Asking* for advice and *following* it are two different things.
NOT PARALLEL:	Susan is not only *intelligent* but also *has a good sense of humor.*
PARALLEL:	Susan is not only *intelligent* but also *funny.*
NOT PARALLEL:	Fred is a man *with* seven children and *who* works two jobs to support them.
PARALLEL:	Fred is a man *who* has seven children and *who* works two jobs to support them.
PARALLEL:	*Fred is* a man with seven children, and *he must work* two jobs to support them. (Notice that a compound sentence, a sentence with a subject and verb in each part, is considered parallel.)

SENTENCE STRUCTURE: EXERCISE 7 (PARALLEL STRUCTURE)

Directions: Correct the lack of parallel structure in each of the following sentences by rewriting the underlined parts of the sentence.

---

1. She is my best friend because she is a good listener, has a strong sense of responsibility, and is interesting.

   She is my best friend because she is a good listener, ____________

   ____________________, and ____________________.

2. I used to love to swim, playing ball, and when we would go fishing when I was a child.

   I used to love to swim, ______________, and ______________ when I was a child.

3. What they need, wanting, and things they have are three different things.

   What they need, ____________________, and ____________________ are three different things.

4. Harry will never leave Susan because she is beautiful, her sense of humor, and has money.

   Harry will never leave Susan because she is beautiful, ____________

   ____________, and ____________________________.

5. This diet stops you from eating ice cream, you can't drink beer, and not to sleep more than seven hours a day.

   This diet stops you from eating ice cream, ______________________,

   and ___________________.

Answers and explanations are on page 171.

Sequence of Tenses

Before you read this section, turn back to page 46 and review the basic tenses of verbs.

When you write a simple sentence, you must choose the tense of the verb that places the sentence in the proper time period. However, when you combine sentences, the verb in one part of the sentence will have an effect on the verb in the other part of the sentence. Study the following seven sentences, paying special attention to the verb tenses:

(1) I *smoke* too much when I *work*.
(Both verbs are in the present tense since this is a statement that is always true.)

(2) I *smoked* too much when I *worked* yesterday.
(Both verbs are in the past tense since both actions occurred in the past.)

(3) I *think* I *smoked* too much yesterday.
(The first verb is in the present tense since it describes what the writer thinks *now;* the second verb is in the past tense since it describes an action that occurred in the past.)

(4) I *had smoked* two whole packs of cigarettes before I *realized* it.

(The first verb is in the past perfect tense since it describes the earlier of the two past actions; the second verb is in the past tense since it describes the more recent of the two past actions.)

(5) I *will quit* smoking when I *am* ready.
(The first verb is in the future tense since it describes an action that has not yet taken place; the second verb is in the present tense since it describes a state that must be present before the other action takes place.)

(6) I *would quit* smoking if I *were* ready.
(The verbs in this sentence will be discussed below.)

(7) If I *had smoked* one more cigarette, my lungs *would have* collapsed.
(The verbs in this sentence will be described below.)

From your review of the discussion of the basic tenses of verbs, you should know when it is correct to use the past perfect tense (as well as when to use the present perfect and future perfect tenses). There is one special verb tense that is mainly used in sentences that use the conjunction *if* to express the conditions under which something may take place. The verbs *would quit* and *would have collapsed* in sentences (6) and (7) are in this special tense called the conditional. The following table will show you when to use this special tense:

tense of verb following if	*tense of other verb*
subjunctive (*were*)	would/should
past perfect (*had smoked*)	would have/should have

EXAMPLES

(1) If I *were* the President, I *would know* what to do.

(2) If I *had been* there, I *would have known* what to do.
(Notice that the past participle of the verb *to know* is used.)

(3) If you *walk* to work every day, you *will develop* strong legs.
(Notice that the verb in the *if* part of the sentence is in the present tense; therefore, the second verb is in the future tense, not the conditional.)

(4) If you *had walked* to work every day, you *would have developed* strong legs.

When a verb consists of a group of words, all of the words except the last one are called helping or auxiliary verbs (EXAMPLES: *would have* known; *might have* helped). These helping verbs can often cause problems if you do not recognize which ones are used for the past tense. The following table should help you solve this problem:

not in the past	*in the past*
am/is	was
are	were
have/has	had
can	could
may	might
must	had to
will	would
shall	should

Knowing that *would* is the past form of *will* makes it possible to adjust the tenses correctly in the following sentences:

> I *think* you *will feel* better after you *take* your medicine.
> I *thought* you *would feel* better after you *took* your medicine.

SENTENCE STRUCTURE: EXERCISE 8 (SEQUENCE OF TENSES)

Directions: In each of the following sentences, four verbs have been underlined. If one of these verbs is in the wrong tense, blacken the space under the number corresponding to it. If all of the verbs are correct, blacken the space numbered (5).

---

1. 1 2 3 4 5

1. Mama always said (1) there will (2) be days like this when I could (3) hardly remember where I came (4) from. No error (5)

2. 1 2 3 4 5

2. Before the guard turned (1) around, the visiting teenager had pushed (2) the kitten into the monkey's cage. Afterwards, she was (3) sorry to do (4) it. No error (5)

3. 1 2 3 4 5

3. The flag is (1) more than a piece of red, white, and blue cloth. It represents (2) and united (3) many people who come (4) to patriotic ceremonies. No error (5)

4. The four bored children $\underset{1}{\underline{\text{decided}}}$ $\underset{2}{\underline{\text{to ask}}}$ the pilot if they $\underset{3}{\underline{\text{may}}}$ fly the plane when he $\underset{4}{\underline{\text{got}}}$ tired. $\underset{5}{\underline{\text{No error}}}$ **4.** 1 2 3 4 5

5. $\underset{1}{\underline{\text{To have lived}}}$, many people $\underset{2}{\underline{\text{say}}}$, it $\underset{3}{\underline{\text{is}}}$ necessary $\underset{4}{\underline{\text{to have loved.}}}$ $\underset{5}{\underline{\text{No error}}}$ **5.** 1 2 3 4 5

Answers and explanations are on page 171.

UNCLEAR WRITING

Frequently, when you combine sentences, you will find it necessary to use a pronoun in one part of the sentence. If you are not careful, your meaning may not be clear. Examine the following sentences and notice how the same sentence can mean two very different things.

UNCLEAR: Joe took us to the party, *which* we thought was very nice.
CLEAR: We thought Joe's taking us to the party was very nice.
CLEAR: We thought the party to which Joe took us was very nice.

UNCLEAR: The cowboy fired at the Indian, and then *he* fell to the ground.
CLEAR: The cowboy fired at the Indian and then fell to the ground.
CLEAR: The cowboy fired at the Indian, who then fell to the ground.

In the sentences labeled *unclear,* the pronouns *which* and *he* could refer to two different words in the first part of the sentence. Only by rewriting the sentences can you make the reference clear. However, you may find that it is impossible to use pronouns that will have clear references:

UNCLEAR: Sam asked Fred if *he* thought *he* had done a good job.
CLEAR: Sam asked Fred if Fred thought Sam had done a good job.
CLEAR: "Do you think I have done a good job?" Sam asked Fred.
*CLEAR: Sam asked Fred if Fred thought Fred had done a good job.

CLEAR: "Do you think you have done a good job?" Sam asked Fred.

Although it may seem awkward to repeat the nouns, especially in the sentence marked with an asterisk (*), it may be the only way to make your meaning clear. Perhaps the best way to avoid repeating the nouns is to rewrite the sentence as a direct quote.

Constantly connecting sentences with *and* or *so* will not make the relationship between the parts of a sentence clear. Effective sentence combinations using such conjunctions as *because, although, when, after,* or *before* and such pronouns as *who, which,* and *that* will make your sentences clearer. Compare the following pair of sentences:

WEAK: This weekend is a holiday, and we are going to visit friends in Chicago. And they will come back to Kansas with us.

IMPROVED: Because this weekend is a holiday, we are going to Chicago to visit friends who will be coming back to Kansas with us.

SENTENCE STRUCTURE: EXERCISE 9 (UNCLEAR WRITING)

Directions: In each of the following sentences, four groups of words have been underlined. If one of these groups of words is unclear or misplaced, blacken the space under the number corresponding to it. If the sentence is clear as written, blacken the space numbered (5).

1. 1 2 3 4 5

1. If the lamp (1) should happen to fall (2) on the glass table, (3) see that it is fixed. (4) No error (5)

2. 1 2 3 4 5

2. They say (1) that women are healthier (2) than men (3) and also live longer. (4) No error (5)

3. 1 2 3 4 5

3. He gave her (1) a birthday present, (2) so she married him, (3) which made her happy. (4) No error (5)

4. Sarah told (1) her boss (2) that she was tired (3) and wanted to go home. (4) No error (5)

4. 1 2 3 4 5

5. Frank said (1) that he was going to wear a red velvet suit (2) to the Christmas party, (3) which he knew was strange. (4) No error (5)

5. 1 2 3 4 5

Answers and explanations are on page 171.

ANSWERS AND EXPLANATIONS— SENTENCE STRUCTURE: EXERCISES

EXERCISE 1 (PREPOSITIONAL PHRASES)

1. Is that the person *with* whom he had a fight? A sentence must never end with a preposition.
2. Jane's feelings about this problem are *different from* mine. It is never correct to use the expression *different than.*
3. I was at a rock concert last night (*or* I went to a rock concert last night). It is never correct to use the expression *was to.*
4. This sentence is correct. In both cases, the word *like* means *similar to.*
5. We'll have to divide the pizza *among* the four of us. *Between* is used only for two people or things; *among* is used for groups of three or more.
6. I'll be home *about* seven o'clock. *Around* does not mean *approximately.*
7. Get *off* the phone and let someone else use it. It is never correct to use the double preposition *off of.*
8. If you don't have enough money, you can always borrow *from* me. It is never correct to use the expression *borrow off.*

EXERCISE 2 (FORMING COMPOUND SENTENCES)

1. Most people are suspicious about buying something new, *so* salesmen usually use a hard-sell approach. (You might combine these two sentences as: Salesmen usually use a hard sell approach, *so* most people are suspicious about buying something new.) The order in which you combine these sentences will depend upon how you view the situation, that is, which sentence is the cause and which sentence is the effect. However, the relationship between the two sentences is cause and effect; therefore, the best conjunction is *so.*
2. You need *not only* proteins *but also* vitamins for good health. Since these two sentences are exactly alike except for the receivers of the action of the verb *need* (the direct objects), you can combine these two different parts of the sentence and leave the rest of the sentence alone. You need both vitamins and proteins, not one or the other; therefore, the correct conjunction is *not only . . . but also.*
3. They wanted to enjoy football games at home, *so* they traded in their old television set for a big color set. Since the desire to watch

football games at home was the reason for the trade, sentence (b) comes first. The conjunction *so* shows the relationship of reason to event much more clearly than the weak conjunction *and.*

4. Bill moaned *and* groaned about his problems. Since the two sentences are exactly alike except for the verbs, and since the two verbs mean very much the same thing, the sentences can be combined with the conjunction *and* between the two verbs.

5. The food is good in that store, *but* it is better in this one. Sentence (b) expresses a contrast to sentence (a), a relationship that can be shown by combining the two sentences with the conjunction *but.*

6. I don't want to work; *however,* I will work. Sentence (b) expresses the opposite thought to the one expressed in sentence (a), a relationship that can best be shown by joining the two sentences with the word *however.*

7. You might win $2,000 in the lottery, *or* you might lose the price of the ticket. The two sentences express two different things that may happen if a person purchases a lottery ticket, a relationship that can be shown by combining the two complete sentences with the conjunction *or.*

8. Bob barbecues the chicken, *and* Marilyn eats it. The two sentences express two different but related actions, a relationship that can be shown by joining the two complete sentences with the conjunction *and.*

EXERCISE 3 (PROBLEMS WITH CONJUNCTIONS AND PREPOSITIONS)

1. **(1)** The conjunction *both* can be used only with two persons or things.
2. **(3)** Since there are three related groups of words joined together, only the last conjunction should be used.
3. **(3)** There is no negative meaning in this part of the sentence; therefore, the correct conjunction is *either.*
4. **(5)** No error
5. **(2)** Since *the table* and *the chair* receive the action of the same verb, *lifted,* these are the two words that should be joined by conjunctions. In this sentence, the word *both* should come after the verb.
6. **(4)** The correct preposition to use with the verb *approve* is *of.*
7. **(5)** No error

8. **(3)** It is incorrect to end a sentence with a preposition. (Remember that the end of the quote signals the end of the sentence that was spoken.)
9. **(4)** The correct preposition is *in*.
10. **(2)** The negative form *nor* should be used with *neither*.

EXERCISE 4 (METHOD 3 COMBINATIONS)

1. *If* you give me a dollar, the Brooklyn Bridge will be yours. *If* expresses the condition under which the Brooklyn Bridge will become yours.
2. *Even though* the blues singer didn't smoke, he accepted the cigarette. *Even though* expresses the contrast between the two sentences.
3. The boss speaks *while* the secretary takes notes. *While* expresses the time relationship between the two sentences.
4. *After* water dripped through the ceiling, Pat called the landlord. *After* expresses the time relationship between the two sentences.
5. She quit her job *because* the boss was unreasonable. *Because* shows the reason for the action expressed in sentence (a).

EXERCISE 5 (METHOD 4 COMBINATIONS)

1. Watching an old movie on television, Sam fell asleep. OR: Sam fell asleep watching an old movie on television.
2. Sad to see the evening end, we tearfully said goodbye.
3. Sitting in the balcony, we had a great view of everyone on stage.
4. Reading the newspaper, I noticed an interesting story about Mexico.
5. Angry about losing so much money, Frank swore that he would never gamble again.

EXERCISE 6 (MORE SENTENCE COMBINATIONS)

1. Beginning to suspect the driver, the girls decided to watch him carefully.
2. The President approved of the plan.
3. Since the astronaut was badly shaken, he was taken to headquarters.
4. The runner dashed over the finish line, his body covered with perspiration.
5. Ted is not only lazy but also careless. OR: Ted is both lazy and careless.
6. John, the man accused of the crime, asked for the evidence.

7. Even though the couple doesn't have a penny, they enjoy living in the city.
8. The children's bad table manners made their mother angry.
9. Nervous about the job interview, Sam forgot to buckle his belt.
10. A rich man, I have been told, used to own that house.

EXERCISE 7 (PARALLEL STRUCTURE)

1. She is my best friend because she is a good listener, a responsible person, and an interesting person.
2. I used to love to swim, to play ball, and to go fishing when I was a child.
3. What they need, want, and have are three different things. (You might also want to repeat the whole word group for emphasis: What they need, what they want, and what they have are three different things.)
4. Harry will never leave Susan because she is beautiful, funny, and rich.
5. This diet stops you from eating ice cream, drinking beer, and sleeping more than seven hours a day.

EXERCISE 8 (SEQUENCE OF TENSES)

1. **(2)** Because the main verb is past, the past form *would* is needed.
2. **(4)** The action happened before the time of the verb, so the past infinitive *to have done* is the correct form.
3. **(3)** There is no reason for switching from the present to the past tense. *Unites* is the correct form.
4. **(3)** The main verb *decided* is past, so the helper *may* should be *might*.
5. **(5)** No error

EXERCISE 9 (UNCLEAR WRITING)

1. **(4)** The pronoun *it* could refer to either the lamp or the table.
2. **(4)** This group should precede group (3).
3. **(4)** It is not clear which event made her happy, the birthday present or the marriage.
4. **(5)** No error
5. **(4)** It is not clear which would be strange, Frank's wearing a red velvet suit or the Christmas party.

SENTENCE STRUCTURE: REVIEW TEST

Directions: One of the sentences in each of the following groups may have an error in sentence structure. If you identify an error in one of the sentences, blacken the space under the number corresponding to it. If all of the sentences in the group are correct as written, blacken the space numbered (5).

1. 1 2 3 4 5

1. (1) Whirling Dervish is a nickname given to a Turkish religious group whose sacred ritual consists of spinning around, repeating the name "Allah."
   (2) All over three regions of Turkey and beyond, sixty years after the leader died.
   (3) Scientists say that the spinning has the same effect as drinking liquor or taking certain drugs.
   (4) Many children whirl around to have fun, not for any religious reason.
   (5) No error

2. 1 2 3 4 5

2. (1) Avocados grow well in southern California, as well as citrus fruit.
   (2) When planting avocados became a money-making business, many people moved to California.
   (3) They wanted to make a fortune quickly, and they also wanted protection from taxation, which agriculture provides.
   (4) Thousands of acres of avocados are being planted in spite of the fact that few people in America like the taste of this strange fruit.
   (5) No error

3. 1 2 3 4 5

3. (1) More women than ever are professional competitors in sports; there seems to have been a change in the attitude toward women athletes.
   (2) The most famous woman tennis player in America, a leader in women's liberation, has brought about certain changes by speaking out over the years.
   (3) Now the sex of the players is not considered as important as before, and men and women, women and women, and men and men play to equally large crowds.
   (4) As more women become successful in professional sports, golf has been played in Scotland for centuries.
   (5) No error

4. 1 2 3 4 5

4. (1) The art of knotting to make designs or useful objects, called macrame, is an ancient one.
   (2) The most popular macrame products now are plant hangers

and wall decorations, bought by enthusiastic people, made of rope.
(3) Macrame was invented on long voyages by sailors who made knots to pass the long, quiet hours.
(4) Macrame is easy and fun to learn.
(5) No error

5. (1) Many photographs in *Life* magazine won awards, some of which were taken in Vietnam.
(2) A dramatic picture of a mother carrying a wounded baby stands out in my mind.
(3) Photographs certainly do bring an event to life and make a person feel as if he is witnessing it first hand.
(4) Why do men repeat mistakes that they see recorded in black and white and living color?
(5) No error

5. 1 2 3 4 5

6. (1) Davy Crockett was an adventurer.
(2) One legend says, that he killed a bear at the age of three.
(3) According to another well-known story, he patched the crack in the Liberty Bell.
(4) He died in the battle against Mexico, which took place at the Alamo.
(5) No error

6. 1 2 3 4 5

7. (1) Traveling in a jungle can be a strange experience for someone not used to the environment.
(2) Huge insects appearing on monstrous plants make an outsider jump with fright.
(3) It is said that jungle Indian tribes still practice the ancient rituals that an American cannot begin to understand.
(4) But, if the spirit is strong and you have a healthy body, a jungle adventure can be fascinating.
(5) No error

7. 1 2 3 4 5

8. (1) Although most people do not take it seriously, snoring can be a serious problem.
(2) Take, for example, the case of the fireman who was shaken awake because of his heavy snoring and shot the man that had awakened him.
(3) What is the main cause of snoring?
(4) Respiratory diseases, according to my doctor.
(5) No error

8. 1 2 3 4 5

9. 1 2 3 4 5

9. (1) Around the neighborhood, J. J. Bentley is treated like a king.
(2) This is only proper. If you think of what Bentley has meant to the neighborhood in recent years.
(3) Bentley is now 72 and president of three social clubs; he has come a long way, indeed, since the early days on lower Broadway.
(4) These days, he enjoys his existence as one of the community leaders.
(5) No error

10. 1 2 3 4 5

10. (1) Familiar phrases and gestures are part of every society, and they help people get used to their surroundings.
(2) Phrases such as "The more the merrier" and gestures such as hand-shaking make people more comfortable with each other.
(3) It is possible that people who lived long ago repeated words and copied gestures to establish a social order.
(4) While some young people rebel against their parents' way of life, most follow patterns they are familiar with.
(5) No error

11. 1 2 3 4 5

11. (1) Elevators are truly amazing creatures.
(2) They operate with no respect for man, who is dependent on them.
(3) While some slam eager doors in an attempt to capture a human victim, others move slowly up or down to various floor levels.
(4) Elevators have a wide range of personalities but they are almost always people-haters.
(5) No error

12. 1 2 3 4 5

12. (1) Living on islands off the coast of Panama, the Cuna Indians are known for their beautiful cloth designs.
(2) Cuna society is unusual, women have all the power and wealth in the family.
(3) A gold ring that each woman wears tells the world how rich her family is.
(4) Palm trees and a large number of children also are an indication of great wealth.
(5) No error

13. 1 2 3 4 5

13. (1) Near the Texas border are several good Mexican restaurants.
(2) Most serve beans, rice, chili, tamales, and tequila.
(3) Tequila is taken from the cactus a plant that lives in the desert.

(4) A strong liquor, tequila is drunk with lime and salt by many Americans who want to get the real Mexican flavor.
(5) No error

14. (1) President Lincoln was seeing a play entitled "Our American Cousin" when he was shot at Ford's Theatre in April, 1865. **14.** 1 2 3 4 5
(2) Since the Civil War had recently ended with Lee's surrender at Appomattox, Lincoln had begun feeling optimistic about the atmosphere in Washington.
(3) In fact, right before they arrived at the theatre, he told his wife Mary Todd Lincoln, to take back a statement she had made.
(4) She had mentioned that she felt the presence of enemies all around her and that she was frightened.
(5) No error

15. (1) Malaria, a disease carried by a certain type of mosquito, still exists in many parts of the world. **15.** 1 2 3 4 5
(2) It is difficult to control because mosquitos reproduce very quickly under certain conditions.
(3) If a person catches malaria, he should see a doctor immediately for proper medication.
(4) Chills, fever, and nausea are the symptoms; the long range effects are the inability to donate blood, and it may recur.
(5) No error

16. (1) Fantasy allows us to escape from the pressures of everyday life. **16.** 1 2 3 4 5
(2) Nowadays, more people than ever are going to movies and reading books about imaginary people and events.
(3) Mysteries and adventure stories have become popular with adults as well as children.
(4) Realistic, true-to-life stories, seem to be less popular.
(5) No error

17. (1) Advertising is one of the main ways that our culture is created and spread. **17.** 1 2 3 4 5
(2) All over the country, advertisers are telling Americans how they should look and smell, what to eat, and places that are nice to go.
(3) Advertising is supposed to serve our needs by informing us about needed goods and services, but, actually, it often creates false needs or makes unimportant ones seem important.
(4) When things are bought for the status they bring the owner, a false need has been met.
(5) No error

18. 1 2 3 4 5

18. (1) How different the United States would be today if the French, not the British, had won the French and Indian War!
(2) We would probably be saying "bonjour" instead of "good morning," and "merci" instead of "thank you."
(3) French food would be eaten everyday, and not not just by rich people.
(4) Because New Orleans was the capital of the French territory in this country, Napoleon's code of law would probably be the law of the land.
(5) No error

Answers and explanations are on pages 177–178.

ANSWERS AND EXPLANATIONS— SENTENCE STRUCTURE: REVIEW TEST

1. **(2)** This is a sentence fragment. The group of words that come before the comma tell where something happened, and the group of words that come after the comma tell when something happened. But there is no way to tell what happened.

2. **(1)** This sentence should be written as: "Avocados, as well as citrus fruit, grow well in southern California." By placing the words *as well as citrus fruit* at the end of the sentence, you have placed it too far away from the word it is meant to modify and have created an unlikely meaning: "Avocados grow well in southern California, and they grow well in citrus fruit, too."

3. **(4)** There is no logical connection between the two parts of this sentence.

4. **(2)** The description *made of rope* should be next to what it describes (*plant hangers and wall decorations*), not next to *people.*

5. **(1)** The description *some of which were taken in Vietnam* does not describe *awards.* It should be placed next to the word *photographs.*

6. **(2)** No comma should be used to separate the subject from the complete predicate.

7. **(4)** This sentence contains a non-parallel structure. The sentence should read: "But, if the spirit is strong and *the body is healthy,* a jungle adventure can be fascinating."

8. **(4)** This is a sentence fragment.

9. **(2)** These two sentences should be made into one sentence. As they are written, the second sentence is a sentence fragment.

10. **(5)** No error

11. **(4)** This is a compound sentence and should be joined with a comma before the conjunction *but.*

12. **(2)** A comma is not strong enough to join the two parts of a compound sentence. You must either use a semicolon in place of the comma or add a conjunction of some kind.

13. **(3)** Since the words *a plant that lives in the desert* add extra information about the noun *cactus,* they should be separated from the rest of the sentence by a comma.

14. **(3)** Since the name Mary Todd Lincoln is used to rename the noun *wife,* it should be set off by commas.

15. **(4)** The words *it may recur* are not parallel to *the inability to donate blood.* To make this group parallel, you would have to write, "the possibility of a recurrence."

16. **(4)** Never divide the subject and the predicate of a complete sentence with a comma.

17. **(2)** This sentence lacks parallel structure. It should read: "All over the country, advertisers are telling Americans how they should look and smell, what they should eat, and where they should go."

18. **(4)** No logical connection between the two parts of this sentence has been established.

SENTENCE STRUCTURE EVALUATION CHART

Question Type	*Review Pages*	*Question Number*	*Amount of Question Type*	*Number of Wrong Answers*
A. Sentence Fragments	19–23; 149–150	1, 8, 9	3	____
B. Misplaced Description	152–154; 165–166	2, 4, 5	3	____
C. Logical Connections	141–142	3, 18	2	____
D. Punctuation in Compounds	143–145	6, 11, 12, 16	4	____
E. Parallel Structure	159–161	7, 15, 17	3	____
F. Punctuation with Additional Information	156	13, 14	2	____

PASSING SCORE: 14 right out of 18 questions

YOUR SCORE: ____ right out of 18 questions

If you have more than one question wrong in any category, you should reread the explanation of that type of problem in the review pages listed in the table.

PUNCTUATION

Punctuation is to writing what gestures, facial expressions, tone of voice, and stress are to speaking. Every mark of punctuation carries some meaning, either by adding emphasis or by keeping thoughts separate on paper. Punctuation gives hints about how to read written English. A comma indicates a pause; a question mark represents a rise in the voice at the end of a sentence; and an exclamation point adds special emphasis to the sentence.

Look at the underlined punctuation in the following passage to discover the uses of the various punctuation marks.

When Sgt. Marsh opened the bathroom door at 4:32 P.M., he was struck by a number of unusual details: an uncapped tube of toothpaste, a woman's shoe in the bathtub, and a bloodstain on the faucet. He was sure of one thing: something unusual had happened in old Mrs. Johnson's apartment in the last forty-eight hours. He heard a sudden noise. The door—the one to the hall—was opening! Who could it be? The old lady had been missing since Feb. 16; moreover, Mrs. Johnson, who was practically a hermit, didn't have any relatives or friends who visited her. While running to the closet to hide, Sgt. Marsh tripped over Mrs. Johnson's Bible, which was opened to Deut. 1:3.

A loud voice rang out: "Who's there?" Sgt. Marsh didn't answer. He heard a man whisper to a barely visible figure that it must have been a mouse. As the detective tried to hear the whispered conversation, he felt with horror two powerful hands close around his neck. Oh no! Someone had gone into the closet before him!

Here are the major uses of specific punctuation marks.

The Period

1. To end a statement

    He heard a sudden noise. (line 6)

2. At the end of abbreviations

    Feb. 16 (February) (line 8)
    Deut. (Deuteronomy) (line 11)
    Sgt. (Sergeant) (line 1)

3. As a decimal point

    1.1 (one and one-tenth)

4. To separate dollars from cents

    $23.58

5. Three periods show that part of a sentence or passage has been left out.

    They answered . . . that they had.

The Exclamation Point !

1. To indicate strong emotion

    Oh no! (line 16)
    Someone had gone into the closet before him! (lines 16–17)

The Question Mark ?

1. To end a question

    Who could it be? (line 7)
    "Who's there?" (line 12)

    NOTE: Do not use a question mark at the end of a statement that only states the question but does not ask it.

    I asked you if you thought it was a good idea.
    I asked, "Do you think it is a good idea?"

    NOTE: Do not use a comma after a question mark that falls in the middle of a sentence.

    Sam asked, "Is anyone here?" and then left the room.

PUNCTUATION: EXERCISE 1
(THE PERIOD, EXCLAMATION POINT, AND QUESTION MARK)

Directions: In each of the following sentences, insert the necessary periods, exclamation points, and question marks in the blank spaces.

---

1. The man ran out of the building yelling, "There's a fire on the fifth floor__"
2. I asked you if you wanted to go to the movies__
3. I think that Gen__ Jones runs a very tight ship.

4. Do you believe everything you read__
5. "I give up__" she screamed__

Answers and explanations are on page 189.

The Comma ,

1. To divide more than two items

   an uncapped tube of toothpaste, a woman's shoe in the bathtub, and a bloodstain on the faucet (lines 2–4)
   I hate to eat, drink, and run.
   I hate to eat and run. (No comma between only two items)

2. Before a conjunction (*and, but, yet, as, or, nor, so*) to connect two closely related complete thoughts (a compound sentence)

   Osgood is the smartest foreman in the plant, but Henry works the hardest.
   I don't want to go to work, yet I feel that I must.
   I am very tired, and I want to go home.
   I am very tired and want to go home. (This is not a compound sentence; it is a sentence with a compound predicate, which does not require a comma.)

3. After a sentence fragment that begins a sentence, but only when the rest of the sentence could stand by itself

   While running to the closet to hide, Sgt. Marsh tripped . . . (lines 9–10)
   As the detective tried to hear the whispered conversation, he felt . . . (lines 14–15)
   Happy to be home at last, I collapsed in the nearest chair.
   Walking home late at night, we were frightened.
   But:
   Walking home late at night is frightening. (This is not an introductory sentence fragment; *walking home late at night* is the complete subject of the sentence and should not be separated from the predicate.)

4. Before a sentence fragment that falls at the end of a sentence, but only when that fragment could be omitted without altering the meaning of the sentence

   I hate to get up in the morning, especially on Monday.
   I'll finish this project in three days, not two.

BUT: I didn't invite Ted to the party because he is so rude. (The underlined fragment cannot be omitted without altering the writer's complete thought. See pages 149–150 for a discussion of this kind of sentence.)

5. Around groups of words that interrupt the sentence to give additional information that is not essential to the meaning of the sentence

    She spoke to her father, a jazz pianist, yesterday.
    He walked into the room which, he happened to notice, was painted black.
    I want you to know, Bert, that I think you're wonderful. (The name of the person being spoken to is set off by commas.)
    BUT: The man who is standing in the corner is my father. (The underlined group of words gives more than additional information; it makes the subject of the sentence more specific.)
    Martha, who is never on time for work, showed up early today. (The underlined group of words interrupts the complete thought of the sentence to give additional information.)

6. To break down large numbers into readable units

    23,800 (twenty-three thousand eight hundred)

7. To separate the day from the year

    Nov. 12, 1948

8. To separate city or town from state or country

    Pamplona, Spain
    St. Louis, Missouri

9. To set off a speaker from his exact words

    "Not much," she said.

10. To set off the name of a person being addressed

    Martha, come here.
    I told you so, Sam.

Because a comma shows where you would pause if you were reading aloud, a good test for comma versus no comma is to read to yourself. If you stop for a second when you are reading, a comma is probably needed. Remember—punctuation reflects common sense!

The Semicolon ;

1. To combine two closely related complete thoughts that are joined by such words as *however, therefore, moreover* (see page 144 for a discussion of this kind of sentence)

   The old lady had been missing since Feb. 16; moreover, Mrs. Johnson . . . (lines 7–9)

   We had hoped to be on time; however, the heavy traffic slowed us up.

2. To combine two closely related complete thoughts that are not joined together by a conjunction

   The party was a great success; there were seventy people who showed up.

   I never tell a lie; I only tell half-truths.

3. To separate items in a list when commas would be confusing

   Four people were in the bar: Mary, a doctor; Susan, a factory worker; Leslie, a social worker; and Joan, a housewife.

PUNCTUATION: EXERCISE 2 (THE COMMA AND SEMICOLON)

Directions: Rewrite each of the following sentences, inserting commas and semicolons where they are needed. If a sentence is correct without additional punctuation, write "correct" in the space provided.

---

1. I decided to buy a stereo a television set and a new car with the money I won in the lottery.

   ____

   ____

2. I am very nervous today I don't know the reason for it.

   ____

   ____

3. We wanted to finish up our work before 7:00 therefore we worked through lunch.

   ____

   ____

4. Three people showed up for the job: a woman from Albany New York a man with a 1000-page résumé and a senior citizen who said that he was born December 25 1888.

____

____

5. While marching in a parade the President stepped on his shoelace and fell.

____

____

Answers and explanations are on pages 189–190.

The Colon :

1. After the greeting in a formal letter

   Dear Sir:

2. To separate hours from minutes in clock time

   4:32

3. Between two complete thoughts when the second serves to explain the first

   He was sure of one thing: something unusual had happened. . . (lines 4–5)

4. Before a direct quotation (usually used only when two or more quoted sentences follow)

   A loud voice rang out: "Who's there?" (line 12)

5. Before a list of items

   Many pieces of music were played: a symphony, a concerto, and two sonatas.

6. To separate chapter and verse in Bible notations

   Deut. 1:3

The Apostrophe

1. To show ownership

a. By a singular person or thing: add *'s*

woman's
Mrs. Johnson's
Ross's

b. Plural person or thing ending in *s*: add the apostrophe alone

babies'
Johnsons'

c. Plural person or thing not ending in *s*: add *'s*

men's
children's

Some words show possession without an apostrophe.

his
hers
theirs
its (*it's* means *it is* or *it has*)
ours
yours
whose

2. To show that a letter has been left out in a combination of two words

didn't = did not
who's = who is

3. In plurals of numbers, specific words, letters, and symbols

Mind your p's and q's.
He used a lot of if's.
There are four i's in Mississippi.

The Hyphen -

1 To join the two parts of numbers or fractions

forty-eight
one-fifth

2. In a two-part description of words

emerald-green feathers
rose-colored glasses

3. After certain prefixes

anti-American
self-appointed leader

The Dash —

1. For shift in thought or break in idea

   The door—the one to the hall—was opening!

Parentheses ( )

1. Explanations or information not considered central to the idea expressed

   Steaming mad, John coughed loudly. (He always coughed when he was angry.)

   The bacteria in question (see Illustration III) can have one of three shapes.

PUNCTUATION: EXERCISE 3
(THE COLON, APOSTROPHE, HYPHEN, DASH, AND PARENTHESES)

Directions: Rewrite each of the following sentences, inserting colons, apostrophes, hyphens, dashes, and parentheses where they are needed. If a sentence is correct without additional punctuation, write "correct" in the space provided.

---

1. At exactly 537 he was always very precise about time the well dressed man walked in front of a bus.

   ____

   ____

2. Mike didnt like to drive up Forty eighth Street the street with all the red lights because the traffic was too heavy.

   ____

   ____

3. The restaurant owners family always had dinner with the waiters John, Jack, Jim, and Jerry.

   ____

   ____

4. None of the childrens classes finished before 600 mine always finished late too, so dinner was always late.

   ____

   ____

5. Its ridiculous to make statements such as the following one "Things always get worse before they get better."

Answers and explanations are on page 190.

Quotation Marks " "

1. Around a person's exact words

   "Who's there?" he asked.
   He said, "I will gladly do it."
   Who said, "I will gladly do it"?

   NOTE: Periods and commas at the end of a quotation *always* go *inside* the quotation marks. Question marks and exclamation points go inside the quotation marks when the quotation is a question or an exclamation; when the sentence as a whole is a question or an exclamation, but the quotation is not, the question mark or exclamation point goes outside the quotation marks. Semicolons and colons always go outside the quotation marks.

2. Around titles of shorter written pieces—essays, articles, chapters, poems, and songs

   Who wrote "Body and Soul"?
   Lucy Morton wrote "How to Catch a Wiggle-eyed Wallabuck" in the latest issue of *Field and River.*

PUNCTUATION: EXERCISE 4 (QUOTATION MARKS)

Directions: Rewrite each of the following sentences adding quotation marks where they are needed. If no quotation marks are necessary, write "correct" in the space provided.

1. This car is dangerous, warned the mechanic.

2. The fireman yelled, Jump!

3. Who wrote the song Bad Luck?

____

____

4. I read an interesting article entitled Survival in the 70's.

____

____

5. Won't you try to come home tonight? she asked sadly.

____

____

Answers and explanations are on pages 190–191.

ANSWERS AND EXPLANATIONS—PUNCTUATION: EXERCISES

EXERCISE 1 (THE PERIOD, EXCLAMATION POINT, AND QUESTION MARK)

1. The man ran out of the building yelling, "There's a fire on the fifth floor!" An exclamation point is used in this sentence to express a strong emotion—fear.
2. I asked if you wanted to go to the movies. A period is used to punctuate this sentence. Don't be confused by the fact that this sentence describes someone asking a question. The sentence itself is not a question; it is a statement.
3. I think that Gen. Jones runs a very tight ship. Two periods are necessary in this sentence: the first one to indicate an abbreviation; the second one to indicate the end of a statement.
4. Do you believe everything you read? This sentence is clearly a question and should end with a question mark.
5. "I give up!" she screamed. Use an exclamation point for emphasis after the quoted statement. Use a period to end the complete sentence.

EXERCISE 2 (THE COMMA AND SEMICOLON)

1. I decided to buy a stereo, a television set, and a new car with the money I won in the lottery. A comma is used to separate items in a series.
2. I am very nervous today; I don't know the reason for it. A semicolon is used to separate two complete thoughts that can stand independently and are closely linked in meaning.
3. We wanted to finish up our work before 7:00; therefore, we worked through lunch. Two punctuation marks are necessary in this sentence: the semicolon to separate two independent but closely linked thoughts and the comma after the conjunction *therefore* to connect closely related thoughts.
4. Three people showed up for the job: a woman from Albany, New York; a man with a 1,000-page résumé; and a senior citizen who said that he was born December 25, 1888. You needed to add five additional punctuation marks to this sentence: a comma to separate the name of a city from its state *Albany, New York;* two semicolons to separate items in a list where commas would be confusing; a comma in the number *1,000* to make it more readable; and a comma to separate the day from the year.

5. While marching in a parade, the President stepped on his shoelace and fell. A comma is used to separate a sentence fragment that begins a sentence when the rest of the sentence could stand by itself.

EXERCISE 3 (THE COLON, APOSTROPHE, PARENTHESES, DASH, AND HYPHEN)

1. At exactly 5:37 (he was always very precise about time) the well-dressed man walked in front of a bus. Three punctuation marks are needed in this sentence: a colon to separate hours from minutes in expressions of clock time; parentheses to indicate extra information that is not central to the meaning of the sentence; and a hyphen for two-part descriptions of words.
2. Mike didn't like to drive up Forty-eighth Street—the street with all the red lights—because the traffic was too heavy. Four punctuation marks are needed in this sentence: an apostrophe for the short form of *did not* (*didn't*); a hyphen between the two parts of the street number; and two dashes to indicate a break in idea.
3. The restaurant owner's family always had dinner with the waiters: John, Jack, Jim, and Jerry. Two additional punctuation marks are needed in this sentence: an apostrophe to indicate the possessive noun *owner's* and a colon to introduce a list of names.
4. None of the children's classes finished before 6:00 (mine always finished late too), so dinner was always late. The apostrophe is needed to show that the noun *children* is possessive in this sentence. The colon is needed in expressions of clock time. The parentheses are used to set off information that is not central to the meaning of the sentence.
5. It's ridiculous to make statements such as the following one: "Things always get worse before they get better." In this sentence, you should have added the apostrophe to *it's* so that it means *it is* and not the possessive form of the pronoun *it* (*its*). You should have also added a colon to precede a direct quotation.

EXERCISE 4 (QUOTATION MARKS)

1. "This car is dangerous," warned the mechanic. You should have added quotation marks around the mechanic's words, including the comma. Remember, commas always go inside quotation marks.
2. The fireman yelled, "Jump!" Quotation marks should go around the fireman's words. However, the exclamation point must be inside the quotation marks since the whole sentence is not meant to get special emphasis, only the fireman's word.

3. Who wrote the song "Bad Luck"? Quotation marks go around the titles of songs. However, the question mark should go outside the quotation marks since the whole sentence is a question.
4. I read an interesting article entitled "Survival in the 70's." Quotation marks are used around titles of articles. Be sure that you always put periods *inside* quotation marks.
5. "Won't you try to come home tonight?" she asked sadly. Quotation marks should go around the words of the speaker. The question mark should go inside the quotation marks because *her* sentence is a question, not the entire sentence.

PUNCTUATION: REVIEW TEST

Directions: In each of the following sentences, four marks of punctuation have been underlined. If one of these marks of punctuation is incorrect, blacken the space under the number corresponding to it. If all of the punctuation is correct, blacken the space numbered (5).

1. 1 2 3 4 5

1. The doctor said,(1) "The plague's(2) been killing people throughout the ages;(3) it's(4) effect has been felt by many civilizations." No error(5)

2. 1 2 3 4 5

2. The desk (her room included several pieces of furniture)(1) had three nice features:(2) it was large,(3) beautiful,(4) and clean. No error(5)

3. 1 2 3 4 5

3. The blue-(1)eyed farmer screamed,(2) "(3)What do you want from me.(4)" No error(5)

4. 1 2 3 4 5

4. Rev.(1) Jones delivered a hot sermon last Sunday (2) and then he drove to Detroit,(3) Michigan.(4) No error(5)

5. 1 2 3 4 5

5. When food prices go up,(1) the American housewife looks for money-saving measures:(2) forming food co-ops,(3) cooking with less expensive ingredients,(4) and boycotting high-priced items. No error(5)

6. 1 2 3 4 5

6. What a relief!(1) The dam,(2) on the swollen river (3) held and protected the Smiths'(4) house. No error(5)

7. Capt. Bark realized the purpose of the invasion at 4-15 A.M.: Jupiter's army was trying to take over Earth! No error
1 2 3 4 5

7. 1 2 3 4 5

8. Steven's father smelled smoke—he realized with horror that The Daily Planet distribution plant was on fire. No error
1 2 3 4 5

8. 1 2 3 4 5

9. The manager said that "he didn't want to hear any but's. No error
1 2 3 4 5

9. 1 2 3 4 5

10. Can you imagine that. Fifty-six bottles of beer, twelve pounds of potato salad, and thirty chocolate cakes were eaten at the party. No error
1 2 3 4 5

10. 1 2 3 4 5

11. At 8:35 P.M. the comet is expected to be over Duluth; Minnesota, and it will move on to Canada from there. No error
1 2 3 4 5

11. 1 2 3 4 5

12. Gypsies never live in one place for more than three weeks; traveling, and adapting are a way of life for them. No error
1 2 3 4 5

12. 1 2 3 4 5

13. The domestic skills such as cooking and sewing, have become very important for men to learn; these skills are no longer considered women's work. No error
1 2 3 4 5

13. 1 2 3 4 5

14. 1 2 3 4 5 — 14. There are many basketball players in big cities'[1] like New York_[2] because basketball is one of the few sports_[3] that can be played on a small asphalt court.[4] No error[5]

15. 1 2 3 4 5 — 15. It is strange_[1] that ancient arts of self-[2]defense,[3] such as judo and karate,[4] are popular today. No error[5]

16. 1 2 3 4 5 — 16. Kevin_[1] will you please look for some screws,[2] a hammer,[3] and a few nails?[4] No error[5]

17. 1 2 3 4 5 — 17. There are some good schools near here:[1] Benson High School, Bawlin High School,[2] and Potter's[3] School for Girls?[4] No error[5]

18. 1 2 3 4 5 — 18. The police had a few suspects:[1] Jeffrey,[2] an enemy of the victim,[3] Howard, the victim's secretary;[4] and Lewis, his nephew. No error[5]

19. 1 2 3 4 5 — 19. Its[1] easy to forget that,[2] at one time,[3] water was an important source of energy_[4] and a means of transportation. No error[5]

20. 1 2 3 4 5 — 20. It's[1] terrific![2] Everyone passed the Civil Service Examination for secretaries'[3].[4] No error[5]

Answers and explanations are on pages 195–196.

ANSWERS AND EXPLANATIONS— PUNCTUATION: REVIEW TEST

1. **(4)** *It's* is a contraction for *it is* or *it has;* there is no apostrophe in the possessive pronoun.

2. **(5)** No error

3. **(4)** The quotation is a question and, therefore, should end with a question mark.

4. **(2)** A comma must be used with a conjunction, in this case *and,* to connect two complete thoughts.

5. **(5)** No error

6. **(2)** The word group *on the swollen river* gives more than additional information; it identifies exactly which dam is being talked about.

7. **(1)** A colon is used to separate minutes from hours in figures that express time.

8. **(2)** A dash is used to show a shift in thought or a break in idea; it is too weak to join two complete sentences.

9. **(1)** Quotation marks are used only when the exact words a person said or wrote are given.

10. **(1)** Since the first sentence is a question, it should end with a question mark.

11. **(2)** A comma is used to separate a city and a state.

12. **(4)** Two items connected by *and,* in this case a compound subject, are not separated by a comma.

13. **(1)** The words *such as cooking and sewing* add extra information—they only give two examples—and should be set off by commas.

14. **(1)** The noun *cities* is plural; it is not a possessive. Therefore, no apostrophe is needed.

15. **(5)** No error

16. **(1)** In direct address, a name is separated from the rest of the sentence by a comma.

17. **(4)** This is a statement, not a question, and should end with a period.

18. **(3)** A semicolon is needed to separate each complete item in the series since each individual item is divided into two parts with a comma.

19. **(1)** *Its* is the possessive pronoun; *it's* means *it is.* Since the meaning of the word in this sentence is *it is,* the apostrophe must be inserted.

20. **(3)** The possessive is not needed here; the simple plural form *secretaries* is correct.

PUNCTUATION EVALUATION CHART

Question Type	*Review Pages*	*Question Number*	*Amount of Question Type*	*Number of Wrong Answers*
A. Apostrophe	184–185	1, 14, 19, 20	4	_______
B. Quotation Marks	187	3, 9	2	_______
C. Comma	181–182	4, 6, 11, 12, 13, 16	6	_______
D. Colon	184	7	1	_______
E. Dash	186	8	1	_______
F. Question Mark	180	10	1	_______
G. Period	179–180	17	1	_______
H. Semicolon	183	18	1	_______

PASSING SCORE: __16__ right out of 20 questions

YOUR SCORE: ______ right out of 20 questions

If you have more than two questions wrong in category C or any questions wrong in any of the other categories, you should reread the explanation of that type of problem in the review pages listed in the table.

CAPITALIZATION

Although there are some individual capitalization rules that you must memorize, most capitalization questions can be answered by remembering one basic principle:

General names are not capitalized, but specific ones are.

Read through the following paragraphs to test this principle. Also, see if you can arrive at other capitalization rules for yourself by paying attention to the underlined letters.

New York, New York, is, at best, an unusual place. This island city is not only the largest in the state but also the largest in the country. Because it is a complicated system of concrete and steel structures, New York is often called a jungle. And, because of the high crime rate, many people laughingly say that the Amazon Jungle is much safer than the asphalt one. Certainly the rivers in the green jungles are cleaner than the Hudson, Harlem, and East Rivers that surround New York on three sides.

In spite of what New York's critics say, some people remain devoted to it. A middle-aged doctor who lives and works on Manhattan's East Side swears he would not live anywhere else. Dr. Robert Morton really enjoys city living. He can walk to the hospital where he works, Mt. Sinai, and stop by a museum on his way home. The Metropolitan and the Guggenheim Museums are both within walking distance. For dinner, he and his wife, Congresswoman Lucy Morton, sometimes go out to a restaurant where they can get good food from another country. They really enjoy Spanish food and Italian specialties, as well as the home-cooking of the American South. In their spare time, the Mortons go to the movies. And they both love sports. Lucy Morton just finished writing an article for the magazine *Field and River* entitled "How to Catch a Wiggle-eyed Wallabuck." Neither Robert nor Lucy can imagine living anyplace else!

The following pairs of general and specific names have been taken from the passage above to show you how this rule works for many types of names.

General Names	*Specific Names*
city (line 2)	New York (line 1)
state (line 2)	New York (line 1)
jungle (line 4)	the Amazon Jungle (line 6)
rivers (line 7)	Hudson, Harlem, and East Rivers (line 8)
doctor (line 11)	Dr. Robert Morton (line 13)
hospital (line 14)	Mt. Sinai (line 14)
magazine (line 22)	*Field and River* (line 22)

CAPITALIZATION RULES

1. The first word of a sentence is capitalized.

   In spite of what New York's critics say, some people remain devoted to it.

   Neither Robert nor Lucy can imagine living anyplace else.

2. Geographic names and words derived from them are capitalized.

   New York
   the Amazon Jungle
   the East River
   the United States of America
   Spanish food

3. Names of streets and parts of a town, as well as regions of a country, are capitalized.

   Manhattan
   the East Side
   the South
   the Far East
   Forty-second Street (When the name of a street is a hyphenated number, only the first number is capitalized.)

   When *north, south, east,* and *west* are used as part of a name, they are capitalized. Otherwise, when used as directions, they are not.

   Chicago's South Side
   They drove west.

4. Special titles used as part of a name are capitalized.

   Dr. Morton
   Congresswoman Morton
   Mr. Smith

5. In the title of something written—a magazine, an article, a book, a composition, a poem, a movie, a play, or a song—the first and last words are always capitalized, as well as all important words between. Short words such as *the, a, an, and, for, of, at, in* are only capitalized when they occur at the beginning or the end of a title.

   Field and River
   "How to Catch a Wiggle-eyed Wallabuck" (Only the first word of a hyphenated word is capitalized.)
   The New York Times

6. Names of important buildings are capitalized.

   Mt. Sinai Hospital
   the White House

7. Names of companies are capitalized, as well as the names of specific products.

   the Ambex Corporation
   Xerox

CAPITALIZATION: EXERCISE 1

Directions: Check each of the following sentences for capitalization errors. If there is a mistake, blacken the space under the number corresponding to it. If there is no error, blacken the space numbered (5).

1. The writer of the song "Stranded(1) in the jungle(2)" understood the elements of popular American(3) music(4). No error(5)

   1. 1 2 3 4 5

2. People in the Northeast(1) enjoy Southern(2) fried chicken as much as people living in the deep(3) South(4). No error(5)

   2. 1 2 3 4 5

3. On Fifty-Seventh(1) Street(2) in Toledo, Wyoming(3), you can still occasionally see a cowboy(4) on a horse. No error(5)

   3. 1 2 3 4 5

4. 1 2 3 4 5

4. I read that Dr. (1) Johnson, the famous old doctor (2), finally published an article in the Magazine (3) *Newsweek* (4). No error (5)

5. 1 2 3 4 5

5. The spices used in west (1) African and Indian food were spread to the Caribbean (2) by sea captains (3) in the 19th century (4). No error (5)

Answers and explanations are on page 204.

The following passage is a conversation between two women. Look at the underlined letters and try to formulate more rules of capitalization.

Mrs. Pirani ran into her neighbor, Mrs. Montag, at the laundromat.

"Were you at the P.T.A. meeting last night?" asked Mrs. Pirani.

"No, I wasn't," Mrs. Montag replied. "Was it at the elementary school or one of the high schools?"

"It was at East High School. You won't believe what happened! An escaped baboon got into the building somehow," reported Mrs. Montag excitedly, "and was leaping around for about forty minutes. One lady from the Board of Education fainted, and Mr. Manzell, the principal, hid under the speaker's table the whole time."

"How strange! Was the baboon from the zoo?"

"No. From the circus visiting town—Jingley Brothers."

"Did someone finally catch it?"

"The young man who teaches American History 101, along with a Russian-speaking friend, cornered it in the coatroom."

"I'm really sorry I missed that."

"Yes. It's too bad. It was without a doubt the best meeting I've ever been to."

Notice that the general-specific principle of capitalization applies here, too.

General Names	*Specific Names*
high school	East High School
circus	Jingley Brothers

MORE CAPITALIZATION RULES

8. Specific organizations' names are capitalized.

    the P.T.A.
    the Board of Education

9. Names of specific courses are capitalized.

    American History 101
    Plane Geometry II

10. Names of languages, races, and religions are capitalized.

    Russian-speaking
    Jewish tradition

11. Any word used as part of a special name is capitalized.

    Aunt Jane
    Cousin Mildred

12. In a direct quotation, the first word is capitalized.

    "Were you at the meeting?"
    "No, I wasn't there."

    The second part of a divided quotation begins with a capital letter only when a new sentence is begun.

    "No, I wasn't," Mrs. Montag replied. "Was it at the elementary school?"
    "A baboon got into the building somehow," reported Mrs. Montag excitedly, "and was leaping around."

13. Any words referring directly to God begin with a capital letter.

    Trust Him.
    In the words of Jesus Christ.
    There is no God but God, and Mohammed is His prophet.

14. General words used in the place of specific names are capitalized.

    Yes, Father.
    Please, Mama.
    What is it , Doctor?

    EXCEPTIONS: dear, honey, darling, young man, friend, madam, sir, waiter

15. Abbreviated titles after a name are capitalized.

    Stan Smart, Sr. (Senior)
    David Aaron, Ph.D. (Doctor of Philosophy)

Look at the underlined words in this letter for more capitalization rules.

November 18, 1976

Mr. M. Manzell
Principal
East High School
Charlestown, Tennessee

Dear Sir:

We at Jingley Brothers sincerely regret the inconvenience caused you by our baboon Wanda last Tuesday.

Have a pleasant Thanksgiving.

Sincerely yours,

Jim Jingley
Executive Director

MORE CAPITALIZATION RULES

16. In a letter, each word of the opening greeting is capitalized except *and*.

    Dear Sir:
    Dear Mom and Dad,

    The first word of the closing is capitalized.

    Sincerely yours,
    Love you always,

17. Names of the months and days of the week are capitalized.

    November
    Tuesday

    BUT: tomorrow, today, this month

18. Names of holidays and special days, weeks, months, or years are capitalized.

Memorial Day
National Letter Writing Week
African-American History Month
National Year of the Disabled

but not the seasons of the year: fall, winter, spring, summer

19. *I* is always capitalized.

So do I.

CAPITALIZATION: EXERCISE 2

Directions: Check each of the following sentences for capitalization errors. If there is a mistake, blacken the space under the number corresponding to it. If there is no error, blacken the space numbered (5).

1. "Why, (1) Jim, (2) why," She (3) asked, "must (4) we fight every night?" No error (5) — 1. 1 2 3 4 5

2. Dear (1) Sir: (2) enclosed (3) you will find a copy of President (4) Smith's policy statement. No error (5) — 2. 1 2 3 4 5

3. The note read: "We (1) cannot be married because Mama (2) cannot accept the difference in our religious (3) backgrounds. Goodbye, Dear." (4) No error (5) — 3. 1 2 3 4 5

4. Do community (1) Colleges (2) offer courses (3) in English? (4) No error (5) — 4. 1 2 3 4 5

5. 1 2 3 4 5

5. Dear Ann Banter:

How in the name of god (1) can you get a divorce and continue to write this column advising people how to save their marriages?

Yours (2) truly, (3)

Disillusioned (4) No error (5)

Answers and explanations are on page 204.

ANSWERS AND EXPLANATIONS—CAPITALIZATION: EXERCISES

CAPITALIZATION: EXERCISE 1

1. **(2)** Because it is an important word in a song title, *jungle* should begin with a capital letter.
2. **(3)** Since *deep* is part of the name of a region, it should be capitalized.
3. **(1)** In a hyphenated number of a street name, only the first number is capitalized.
4. **(3)** Because the word *magazine* is being used here in a general sense, it should not be capitalized.
5. **(1)** *West Africa* is a geographic name, so *west* should begin with a capital letter.

CAPITALIZATION: EXERCISE 2

1. **(3)** *She* does not begin a sentence or refer to a specific person, so it should not be capitalized.
2. **(3)** The body of a letter should begin with a capital letter.
3. **(4)** Most words used in place of a specific name are capitalized, but *dear* is an exception.
4. **(2)** No specific school is named; therefore, *community colleges* is correct.
5. **(1)** *God* and direct references to Him are always capitalized.

CAPITALIZATION: REVIEW TEST

Directions: If there is a capitalization error in a sentence, blacken the space under the number corresponding to that of the mistake. If there is no error, blacken the space numbered (5).

1. “The doctor just called, Professor Kane,” said the nurse, “And said not to worry.” No error
   (1 = doctor, 2 = Professor, 3 = nurse, 4 = And, 5 = No error) — **1.** 1 2 3 4 5

2. The geography book tells us that the Mississippi and Amazon Rivers are the longest on their Continents. No error
   (1 = geography, 2 = the, 3 = Rivers, 4 = Continents, 5 = No error) — **2.** 1 2 3 4 5

3. Westbeth school’s principal kept seven students after class for calling him “Hotshot Harold.” No error
   (1 = school’s, 2 = principal, 3 = Hotshot, 4 = Harold, 5 = No error) — **3.** 1 2 3 4 5

4. “On Christmas Day,” remembered Mr. Peters, “the Cathedral bells rang in honor of the birth of Jesus.” No error
   (1 = Day, 2 = the, 3 = Cathedral, 4 = Jesus, 5 = No error) — **4.** 1 2 3 4 5

5. Folk customs of Russia are very similar to those of slavic countries. No error
   (1 = customs, 2 = Russia, 3 = slavic, 4 = countries, 5 = No error) — **5.** 1 2 3 4 5

6. Dear sir: Your cousin Martha and I will arrive next Wednesday. No error
   (1 = sir, 2 = cousin, 3 = I, 4 = Wednesday, 5 = No error) — **6.** 1 2 3 4 5

7. In New York City, Fifth avenue runs from Washington Square Park to Harlem. No error
   (1 = City, 2 = avenue, 3 = Park, 4 = Harlem, 5 = No error) — **7.** 1 2 3 4 5

8. Have you read the article “Elements Of Snobbery” by Samuel Snit, Ph.D? No error
   (1 = article, 2 = Of, 3 = Ph, 4 = D, 5 = No error) — **8.** 1 2 3 4 5

9. 1 2 3 4 5

9. In Tokyo, capital of Japan, there are eleven daily newspapers,
(1: In; 2: capital; 3: newspapers,)
none of which is as interesting as *the Daily Gossip*. No error
(4: the Daily Gossip; 5: No error)

10. 1 2 3 4 5

10. A famous American once said: "Go west, young man." No error
(1: Go; 2: west; 3: young; 4: man; 5: No error)

11. 1 2 3 4 5

11. The two women asked If there was a train to Detroit on Easter
(1: If; 2: train; 3: Detroit; 4: Easter)
morning. No error
(5: No error)

12. 1 2 3 4 5

12. The reporter quoted the famous dancer's comment as: "we of
(1: dancer's; 2: we)
the Community Ballet are happy to be in your city." No error
(3: Ballet; 4: city; 5: No error)

13. 1 2 3 4 5

13. The magazine, *Design of cities*, printed an interesting article on
(1: magazine; 2: Design; 3: cities)
housing in downtown Philadelphia. No error
(4: downtown; 5: No error)

14. 1 2 3 4 5

14. In the 30's, during the depression, a number of American people
(1: In; 2: depression; 3: American; 4: people)
almost starved to death. No error
(5: No error)

15. 1 2 3 4 5

15. A small group is going to California to play with a rock band
(1: California; 2: rock; 3: band)
this Summer. No error
(4: Summer; 5: No error)

Answers and explanations are on page 207·

ANSWERS AND EXPLANATIONS—CAPITALIZATION: REVIEW TEST

1. **(4)** In a divided quotation, the first letter of the second part is not capitalized if it does not start a new sentence.
2. **(4)** No specific continent is mentioned. Since this is a general term, it should not be capitalized.
3. **(1)** Any word that is used as part of a specific name or title is capitalized.
4. **(3)** *Cathedral* is a general term, not part of a specific name, in this sentence and should not be capitalized.
5. **(3)** Races, religions, and words derived from them are capitalized.
6. **(1)** Each important word in the opening greeting in a letter begins with a capital letter.
7. **(2)** *Avenue* should be capitalized since it is part of the specific name.
8. **(2)** In titles of publications, small, unimportant words are not capitalized unless they appear first or last.
9. **(4)** The first word of a publication's title is always capitalized.
10. **(5)** No error
11. **(1)** The first word of a quotation begins with a capital letter only if the speaker's exact words are used.
12. **(2)** The first word in a direct quotation is capitalized.
13. **(3)** Each important word in a title should be capitalized.
14. **(2)** Names of specific periods in history should be capitalized.
15. **(4)** The names of the four seasons are not capitalized.

CAPITALIZATION EVALUATION CHART

Question Type	*Review Pages*	*Question Number*	*Amount of Question Type*	*Number of Wrong Answers*
A. Capitalization Rules 1–7	198–199	2, 7, 8, 9, 13	5	______
B. Capitalization Rules 8–15	200–202	1, 3, 4, 5, 11, 12, 14	7	______
C. Capitalization Rules 16–19	202–203	6, 15	2	______

PASSING SCORE: 12 out of 15 questions YOUR SCORE: _____ out of 15 questions

If you have more than two questions wrong in either category A or B or either question wrong in category C, you should reread the explanation of that type of problem in the review pages.

STYLE AND DICTION

Generally speaking, style is simply a way of doing or saying something. The way a person wears his hair, or the way he dances and dresses, is called his style. We usually think of having style as having special characteristics that make something or someone different from other members of his group. For example, the style of modern music is very different from the style of music written 100 years ago.

A change has also taken place in the style of written English. Clear, direct language is now considered better than the complicated, wordy sentences that used to be considered good English style. A more informal approach to writing is now accepted. Which of each of the following pairs of sentences do you think demonstrates a more modern style?

1. Angela, the termination of your studies is a source of grave disappointment to your parents.
2. Angela, your mother and I are upset about your dropping out of school.

Your answer: ________

1. I would like to inquire as to whether or not you are desirous of an after-dinner drink.
2. Would you like an after-dinner drink?

Your answer: ________

The directness and greater informality of the second sentence in each pair is clearly more in keeping with the principles of modern English style.

MAKE YOUR STYLE FIT YOUR PURPOSE

Because modern English is generally simpler and more informal than the language used to be, there is more than one acceptable way to say the same thing. Style is not a question of right or wrong. It depends on the purpose of your writing and how you want to express yourself. There are as many writing styles as there are people who write. The best style is the style that helps communicate *your* meaning and that gives exactly the impression you want to create.

Before deciding on a particular writing style, be sure to consider such factors as your purpose in writing, your subject, and the people for whom you are writing. Compare the following two versions of a sentence in a letter from a lawyer to a judge. Which one has the style that best fits the situation?

1. I've gotta get to that crook before that little jerk of a D.A. does.
2. I intend to cross-examine the witness before the district attorney questions him.

Your answer: ________

The first version is too informal for a legal situation, which calls for an extremely formal tone. Slang and casual expressions such as *jerk* and *gotta* are unprofessional and should not be used in formal writing. The second sentence is therefore better.

A writer expresses an attitude about his subject when he writes, and this attitude is shown in the words he uses. For example, when writing about the death of a great leader for a news magazine, a writer would most likely deal with the subject matter in a straightforward way and use rather formal words. The same writer writing in the same magazine about a baby gorilla's birthday party would probably use a very casual, possibly humorous style. Whatever the style of a piece of writing is, it should be consistent throughout, because a shift is usually confusing to the reader.

STYLE AND DICTION: EXERCISE 1 (CHOOSING A STYLE)

Directions: If there is a word that does not fit the general style of the sentence, blacken the space under the number corresponding to it. If the style is consistent, blacken the space numbered (5).

1. We were so sorry (1) to hear about the infirmity (2) of your cute (3) puppy (4). **1.** 1 2 3 4 5

   No change (5)

2. Regarding the transfer (1) of the aforementioned (2) car (3), a registered letter should be popped (4) into the mail at the earliest possible date. **2.** 1 2 3 4 5

   No change (5)

3. 1 2 3 4 5

3. To make(1) a milkshake, first(2) put milk, eggs, sugar, and ice into a shaker. Agitate(3) and then pour(4) into a glass. No change(5)

4. 1 2 3 4 5

4. Her grandfather was a mischievous(1) old dude(2) who would tell(3) joke after joke to his laughing(4) children. No change(5)

5. 1 2 3 4 5

5. His school friend(1) conversed(2) with him about ways(3) to make(4) money. No change(5)

Answers and explanations are on page 228.

CHOOSE YOUR WORDS CAREFULLY

The best style involves choosing the best words to do a job, that is, the words that express the meaning most exactly. By selecting the best words, it is easy to avoid using unnecessary ones.

Words that give you a clear picture or sensation communicate most effectively. For example, the words *march, stagger, limp,* and *strut* all mean *walk,* but each creates a different picture. Look at the following pairs of sentences:

GOOD: The man *walking slowly and sloppily* down the street was drunk.
BETTER: The man *shuffling* down the street was drunk.

GOOD: The child *not eating much of* her dinner is my daughter.
BETTER: The child *picking at* her dinner is my daughter.

The great number of words that describe slight variations in meaning make it possible for a writer to express himself exactly. Be aware that some common words, such as *great, fine, interesting, good,* and *bad,* are either too general or too often used to communicate meaningfully.

When writers overuse nouns, adjectives, and adverbs, a sentence becomes weak. The verb represents the heart of a sentence and should therefore be carefully chosen. In the interest of strengthening a sentence, the weaker verbs *be, seem, feel,* and *become* should be used only when necessary. Others, such as *go, have,* and *get,* lack forcefulness because of overuse and generality. In most sentences, the most direct verb has the greatest impact on the reader. Compare the following pairs of sentences:

WEAK:	His wife's friends *are a threat to him.*
IMPROVED:	His wife's friends *threaten him.*
WEAK:	Let's *go and have a good time in honor of* your promotion.
IMPROVED:	Let's *celebrate* your promotion.

STYLE AND DICTION: EXERCISE 2 (CHOOSE YOUR WORDS CAREFULLY)

Directions: Choose the word that could best replace the underlined words in the sentence and blacken the space under the number corresponding to it.

1. Because of the heavy rain, our clothes were <u>extremely wet</u>. **1.** 1 2 3 4 5

   (1) heavy (2) drenched (3) tired (4) ruined (5) stale

2. The woman <u>spoke irrationally and excitedly</u>. **2.** 1 2 3 4 5

   (1) cursed (2) shouted (3) raved (4) murmured
   (5) lectured

3. His horse <u>walked unsteadily and clumsily</u>. **3.** 1 2 3 4 5

   (1) pranced (2) fell (3) dragged (4) shook
   (5) wobbled

4. The army has a well-stocked <u>storehouse for arms and military equipment</u>. **4.** 1 2 3 4 5

   (1) arsenal (2) weapon (3) camp (4) missile
   (5) warehouse

5. The speech was <u>boring because it was the same throughout</u>. **5.** 1 2 3 4 5

   (1) tedious (2) terrible (3) ineffective (4) monotonous
   (5) long

Answers and explanations are on page 228.

Words That Are Commonly Confused

J. J. Silver has just been voted the most well-spoken member of his club. Since J. J. is unable to be at the club meeting tonight, he has asked his friend D. J. Tonguetwist to accept the award for him. During D. J.'s speech, many of the club members in the audience start to laugh.

The underlined words in this copy of the speech will help you understand why they laughed.

> I know I don't talk too good, but I'll try and express how happy I am to except this reward on behalf of my friend. I don't have anything pacific to say, and don't know how to say nothing with a morale. As I was laying down last night, I thought about the amount of people who would be setting here tonight, and I got very nervous. Just among you and me, J. J. seems pretty lucky to attain this trophy without giving a speech. All kidding besides, gentlemen, this is a great honor.

D. J. has made a number of very common errors that result from two or more words' sounding alike or having a similar use. He has confused many words with others, and, as a result, he uses them incorrectly. Some of these errors you will recognize because they are grammatical ones that you have studied in other chapters. Others come from the similarities in the sound of certain words. Here is a list of D. J.'s errors paired with the words he should have used.

D. J.'s words	*correct words*
good	well
try and	try to
except	accept
reward	award
pacific	specific
nothing	anything
morale	moral
laying	lying
amount	number
setting	sitting
among	between
attain	obtain
besides	aside

Following is a list of pairs of words that, because of similarities in sound, structure, or meaning, are often confused with each other. Study them carefully because many of them often appear on the GED test.

accept: receive willingly
except: excluding; but

The operator asked if he would *accept* the charges.
Everyone *except* Ben is happy with the results.

advice: recommendation
advise: say something to help someone

She is not looking for *advice.*
Please *advise* me in this matter.

affect: have an influence on
effect: result (as a noun); cause (as a verb)

Did the movie *affect* you?
The *effect* of heavy smoking on your health is still being studied.
He hoped to *effect* some changes in his department.

aggravate: make a bad situation worse
irritate: annoy; create a bad situation

The noise of the traffic will *aggravate* a headache.
Her loud voice didn't *irritate* him.

all ready: prepared
already: previously; by now

The children are *all ready* to go.
Annette has *already* read that book.

all right: an expression meaning that everything is correct; okay
alright: an incorrect spelling of the first term; remember that "alright" is never *all right*

I'm feeling *all right* today.
The answers were *all right.*

all together: at the same time
altogether: completely

Sing now, *all together.*
She was *altogether* exhausted.

around: near; in a circular path
about: approximately

He walked *around* the house.
We will arrive *about* three hours late.

attain: reach [a goal]
obtain: get [something]

Education can help a person *attain* many of his goals.
To *obtain* a pass, you have to speak to the guard.

because: a transition word signaling a result or an effect
being that: an incorrect term that should *never* be used to replace *because*

RIGHT: Humphrey must be right *because* he is more intelligent.
WRONG: Humphrey must be right *being that* he is more intelligent.

beside: to one side of
besides: in addition; moreover

The challenger stood *beside* his opponent.
It costs too much. *Besides,* I don't like it.

breath: air taken into the lungs (used only as a noun)
breathe: take air into the lungs; inhale and exhale (used only as a verb)

Take a deep *breath.*
Breathe slowly and deeply.

bring: carry to
take: carry away

Please *bring* that note here.
Take me to your leader.

can: physically capable of doing something
may: having permission to do something

The boss says that you *may* leave early today if you *can* finish your work before you go.

capitol: the building in which a state legislature meets; Capitol refers to the building in Washington in which Congress meets.
capital: the city in which the heads of a state or federal government are located

They're tearing down the old-fashioned state *capitol* and building a modern one.
Springfield is the *capital* of Illinois.

choose: pick (present and future tenses)
chose: picked (past tense)

People who enjoy Italian food usually *choose* this dish.
The President *chose* his running mate yesterday.

clothes: collective noun meaning things that people wear
cloths: pieces of material

Some people can afford to buy new *clothes* every week.
She had to use several *cloths* to polish the furniture.

continual: happening again and again
continuous: without stopping

His *continual* interruptions upset the speaker.
The showings of the movie are *continuous.*

costume: decorative clothes for special occasions; clothes worn by an actor for a film or play
custom: habit or tradition

Lenny's Halloween *costume* was frightening.
Eating turkey on Thanksgiving is an American *custom.*

council: a group of people who meet for legislative purposes
counsel: advice (noun); advise (verb)

The employee relations *council* will be made up of three members of management and three union members.
The doctor *counseled* me to get more rest.

discover: find out that something is true or exists
invent: create for the first time

When will she *discover* his true identity?
Maybe cavemen didn't dream that anyone could *invent* something like the wheel.

disinterested: impartial; without prejudice
uninterested: not interested

A judge must be *disinterested* to try a case fairly.
Marge is so self-centered that she is completely *uninterested* in other people.

each other: between two
one another: among three or more

Kim and Jill call *each other* often.
The members of the team were told to cooperate with *one another.*

everywhere: in all places
everywheres: this is not a word and should not be used

RIGHT: After the flood, there was water *everywhere.*
WRONG: After the flood, there was water *everywheres.*

farther: at a greater physical distance
further: at a greater non-physical distance

He throws the ball *farther* than Sam.
Nothing could be *further* from the truth.

flout: not pay attention to laws or customs
flaunt: show off something

City drivers sometimes *flout* parking laws.
If you've got it, *flaunt* it.

imply: hint or suggest
infer: draw a conclusion

The newspaper article *implied* that the mayor was dishonest.
Based on her statement, we *inferred* that she was unhappy.

itch: (verb) produce an uncomfortable sensation that causes the desire to scratch; (noun) the sensation itself
scratch: (verb) run something along a surface, such as skin; (noun) a slight flesh wound

These bug bites *itch*.
Why don't you *scratch* them?

it's: short form of *it is* or *it has*
its: possessive pronoun

It's too late to go swimming.
The dog chased *its* tail.

lay: put or place something somewhere
lie: rest or recline

I will *lay* my packages on the hall table.
I'm so tired that I've got to *lie* down.

NOTE: The past and past participles of these verbs are irregular.

present	*past*	*past participle*
lay	laid	laid
lie	lay	lain

I don't know where I *laid* my glasses.
I *have laid* a copy of the test on each student's desk.
I just couldn't *lay* down and go to sleep last night.
I *had* just *lain* down when the phone rang.

Notice that the verb *lay* is used when the subject performs an action *on* something else; the verb *lie* is used when the subject is performing the action.

like: used as a preposition meaning *resembles* or *is similar to*
as: used as a conjunction to join two sentences together

I am not *like* you; I can't do things *like* that.
Susan looks *like* her mother.
As I was saying, no one understands me.
I will redo my work *as* it should have been done in the first place.

lose: misplace or get rid of
loose: not tight

Many people are trying to *lose* weight.
Loose clothing is the most comfortable in summer.

moral: right or ethical (as an adjective); principle (as a noun)
morale: mental state

He was a man of high *moral* standards.
The candidate's *morale* sank after his defeat.

pacific: peaceful; calm
specific: definite

The meeting seemed *pacific;* no one even raised his voice.
She has nothing *specific* in mind.

personal: private; relating to someone exclusively
personnel: the employees of an organization

My feelings about the war are too *personal* to discuss.
All office *personnel* must have identification cards.

principal: the head of a school (noun); main or most important (adjective)
principle: a basic truth; a rule of conduct

The *principal* reason for reading this book is to pass the GED.
In order to pass the GED, you must learn the *principles* of sentence structure.

quite: rather; very
quiet: not loud

Betty was *quite* pretty as a young girl.
Libraries are *quiet* places

raise: lift
rise: get up; go up

In a well-run meeting, people *raise* their hands to get permission to speak.

Raise the window shades and let a little light in this room.
Prices continue to *rise* every week.
I believe in the old saying, "Early to bed, early to *rise,* makes a man healthy, wealthy, and wise."

regardless: in spite of
irregardless: this is not a word in the English language and is never considered acceptable

RIGHT: *Regardless* of what happens, I'll still be your friend.
WRONG: *Irregardless* of what happens, I'll still be your friend.

reward: something given in exchange for something that was done
award: something given to honor someone

Hal is offering a large *reward* for his lost dog.
The "Best Film" *award* is given every year.

set: put or place something somewhere
sit: take a sitting position

I have to *set* these heavy packages down for a moment.
I have to *sit* down for a moment.

NOTE: The past and past participles of these verbs are irregular.

present	*past*	*past participle*
set	set	set
sit	sat	sat

Notice that the verb *set* is used when the subject performs an action on something else; the verb *sit* is used when the subject is performing the action.

their: possessive pronoun
they're: short form of *they are*
there: someplace at a distance, not here

Their speech was not clear.
They're obviously tired.
Sit down over *there*.

then: afterwards
than: a word used before the second part of a comparison

We stayed for two hours, *then* we went home.
She is fatter *than* she was before.

to: preposition indicating direction
two: the number that follows one
too: also; overly

Come *to* the party.
Two people can't be there.
They are *too* busy.
I am busy, *too*.

try to: attempt something
try and: do not use this form for *try to;* the conjunction can be used only if there is a compound verb

I will *try to* make it work by nine o'clock.
I know he tried, but he failed. I have *tried and* failed many times myself.

whether: if
weather: the conditions outside, such as temperature and humidity

They don't know *whether* we have left.
The *weather* seems to be clearing up.

who's: a short form for *who is*
whose: the possessive form of the pronoun *who*

Who's the man at the door?
Whose coat is lying on the chair?

DICTION AND STYLE: EXERCISE 3 (WORDS COMMONLY CONFUSED)

Directions: If there is an error in a sentence, blacken the number under the space corresponding to it. If there is no error, blacken the space numbered (5).

---

1 Except (1) for when the last award (2) was presented, there (3) was no effect (4) on the audience. No error (5)

1. 1 2 3 4 5

2\. A number (1) of interesting points were raised (2) by the group of people we chose (3) to decide on the customs (4) for the masquerade. No error (5)

2. 1 2 3 4 5

3. 1 2 3 4 5

3. Regardless (1) of what she says, being that (2) she has flouted (3) the law, she must try to (4) cooperate. No error (5)

4. 1 2 3 4 5

4. Sometimes when the children want to itch (1) their (2) chickenpox, the two (3) of them complain to each other (4). No error (5)

5. 1 2 3 4 5

5. Beside (1) the beautiful house there (2) stood two (3) people who were starting to aggravate (4) each other. No error (5)

6. 1 2 3 4 5

6. If you had gotten the same bad advice, (1) you would have (2) flaunted (3) your jewels, too. (4) No error (5)

7. 1 2 3 4 5

7. They said that it was alright (1) to park their (2) car about (3) three blocks farther (4) from the house. No error (5)

8. 1 2 3 4 5

8. Bring (1) me to any quiet (2) place you choose, (3) and then (4) let's talk about it. No error (5)

9. 1 2 3 4 5

9. Its (1) altogether (2) too (3) expensive to buy new clothes (4) this year. No error (5)

10. 1 2 3 4 5

10. It's (1) to (2) late to (3) do anything about those two (4) checks that bounced. No error (5)

Answers and explanations are on pages 228–229.

DON'T REPEAT YOURSELF

One principle that seems to apply to every aspect of modern and effective English style is that redundancy, or unnecessary repetition of words or ideas, should be avoided. Be aware of the commonly made repetition mistakes such as, "In my opinion, I think this is good." Since the two underlined groups mean exactly the same thing, only one is necessary.

Errors of repetition are often made with adjectives and adverbs, as illustrated in the following sentences:

REPETITIOUS: The Mexican man who is from Mexico opened a restaurant.
CORRECTED: The man from Mexico opened a restaurant.

REPETITIOUS: The fresh, wholesome, healthy, all-American type is often seen on magazine covers.
CORRECTED: The all-American type is often seen on magazine covers.

The repetition in these sentences comes from the use of an extra adjective or adjectives that add no new information to the sentence.

Another example of redundancy is the word group *equally as good.* Since *equally* and *as* have the same meaning, only one of them is necessary to show that two things are the same.

WRONG: This movie is *equally as good as* television.
RIGHT: This movie is *as good as* television.

The word group *reason is (or was) because* is an example of the same error.

WRONG: Why did she leave? The *reason was because* she had an appointment.
RIGHT: Why did she leave? The *reason was that* she had an appointment.

OR

She left *because* she had an appointment.

Watch out for the double negative. Only one word with a negative meaning is needed in a sentence. Two negatives actually make a statement positive. Certain words like *hardly, barely, scarcely, no one, nothing, none,* and *never* are negative *without* the addition of *no* or *not.* Don't add *no* or *not* to these words.

WRONG: I *don't* know how to say *nothing.*
RIGHT: I don't know how to say *anything.*

OR

I know how to say *nothing.*

WRONG: She *can't scarcely* stand up.
RIGHT: She can *scarcely* stand up.

WRONG: He is*n't hardly* taller than you.
RIGHT: He is *hardly* taller than you.

STYLE AND DICTION: EXERCISE 4
(AVOIDING UNNECESSARY REPETITION)

Directions: If there is an error in a sentence, write the correction on the lines provided. If there is no error, write "correct."

1. They had heard nothing about that.

____

____

2. The actress can't scarcely remember her own name, much less her lines.

____

____

3. Please never tell no one this secret.

____

____

4. He was equally as famous as his neighbor.

____

____

5. His father said the reason he was not there was because he was at a party.

____

____

Answers and explanations are on page 229.

BE CAREFUL WHEN YOU USE FIGURES OF SPEECH

The patterns formed by clouds can resemble sheep, boats, people, or any number of things. A train's whistle can sound like the sad cry of a woman or the screech of an angry bird. Whenever such a comparison is made, a *figure of speech* is being used. For example, in a description of a fire, a newspaperman might write about the flames *licking* the building. Because the movement of the flames resembles that of a tongue, fire is compared to a living creature that is able to lick, something that a fire doesn't really do. *Licking flames* is a figure of speech.

Figures of speech are stylistic devices that are used in everyday speech as well as in writing. A figure of speech can create a vivid picture and save words because, if the comparison is well chosen, further description is unnecessary.

The most commonly used figures of speech are the **simile,** which is a direct comparison using the words *like* or *as,* and the **metaphor,** which is an implied, indirect comparison in which two things are presented as being the same thing.

SIMILE: Bob's legs were *like rubber.*

The crowd became as angry *as a swarm of hornets.*

METAPHOR: *The pink balloon* between Jan's shoulders opened to speak. (The comparison is between a pink balloon and a face.)

John can be a *mule* when he is asked to do something he doesn't like. (John's stubbornness is being compared to that of a mule, though, of course, John does not really turn into a mule.)

Another useful figure of speech is **personification,** in which nonhuman things, such as animals, events, and general ideas, are discussed as though they had human characteristics and abilities. Here are some examples of personification:

The bull *danced into the ring and bowed politely to the crowd.*
A gentle wind *combed the trees.*

Whenever figures of speech are used, the following problems must be avoided.

1. Avoid common, overused comparisons, or clichés. Tired figures of speech have no real impact because the reader is so familiar with these expressions that he doesn't stop to think about them. The purpose of a figure of speech is to allow a writer to make fresh

comparisons, not to use old formulas. Here are some examples of overused and tired figures of speech.

> She is *as dead as a doornail.*
> That movie is *a lemon.*
> Harry is no *spring chicken.*

2. Avoid using too many figures of speech in any one piece of writing. If you use too many, they become ineffective.

3. Avoid mixed comparisons. If you make a comparison, continue it for as long as the thing being compared is discussed. For example, if a train is compared to a snake, it would be correct to describe it slithering and weaving its way down the track. However, to describe the train as galloping over the hills would be mixing one comparison with another; the train has been compared to a snake but has been described using an action performed by a horse.

STYLE AND DICTION: EXERCISE 5 (FIGURES OF SPEECH)

Directions: In each of the following sentences, one part of the sentence has been underlined. If the underlined part of the sentence is a figure of speech, blacken the space under the number of the answer choice that tells what kind of figure of speech it is. If the underlined words are not a figure of speech, blacken the space under choice (4).

1. 1 2 3 4

1\. It was a blisteringly hot, smotheringly muggy day.

(1) simile
(2) metaphor
(3) personification
(4) not a figure of speech

2. 1 2 3 4

2\. The tire screeched like a wounded cat.

(1) simile
(2) metaphor
(3) personification
(4) not a figure of speech

3. 1 2 3 4

3\. The sun smiled upon the world today.

(1) simile
(2) metaphor
(3) personification
(4) not a figure of speech

4. When Walt gets on the basketball court, he is a tiger. **4.** 1 2 3 4

(1) simile
(2) metaphor
(3) personification
(4) not a figure of speech

5. The bread is as soggy as pudding. **5.** 1 2 3 4

(1) simile
(2) metaphor
(3) personification
(4) not a figure of speech

Answers and explanations are on page 229.

VARY YOUR SENTENCE PATTERNS

Variety also contributes to good English style. Reading sentences that are of the same length and structure becomes monotonous, so all writers ought to explore the different writing styles that are available to them. Interesting sentence patterns can spice up any type of written material. The following six sentence patterns will add style to your writing.

1. Variety in sentence beginnings gets the reader's interest and can emphasize important information. A plain sentence can be made more interesting by placing unexpected types of groups first.

   Preposition and noun groups can begin a sentence.

   In the last minute, ten points were scored.

   What is normally a mid-sentence group can be shifted to the beginning of the sentence.

   A natural leader, Sam inspired the crowd.

   Other types of sentence fragments are often placed at the beginning of a sentence.

   Having read the book, she wanted to see the movie.

2. Parallel structure in a sentence can create emphasis or can underline a comparison or contrast. Compare the effectiveness of the two versions of this sentence.

   We loved tenderly; our hate was violent.
   PARALLEL: We loved tenderly; *we hated violently.*

3. A sentence can be constructed to highlight a certain piece of information by beginning the sentence with *it is* or *it was.* The position immediately after the *be* verb is the focus of attention, so the key element of the sentence should be placed in it. Notice how the structure of each highlighted sentence draws attention to a different part of the original sentence.

	Mrs. Wilton solved the murder case.
HIGHLIGHTED:	It was *Mrs. Wilton* who solved the murder case.
HIGHLIGHTED:	It was *the murder case* that Mrs. Wilton solved.

4. To create suspense and hold the reader's interest, the key part of a sentence can be delayed by placing less important matter first. Compare the effect of these two sentences.

	A man knows when his life is about to change drastically.
SUSPENSEFUL:	When his life is about to change drastically, *a man knows.*

5. To economize on words and produce a special effect, a sentence dealing with a cause-effect relationship can be reduced to a pattern of *"the + comparison, the + comparison"* in which the second half is a result of the first. Notice the greater economy and effectiveness of the second sentence in this pair.

	As a person learns more, he begins to question more.
THE + COMPARISON:	*The more* a person learns, *the more* he questions.

6. Certain phrases can make a sentence hold a great deal of informa tion. Notice how the use of the *one of whom* phrase allows two sentences to be combined without affecting the meaning at all.

	He met several people at the party last week. One of the people he met was a diplomat.
COMBINED:	He met several people at the party last week, one of whom was a diplomat.

STYLE AND DICTION: EXERCISE 6 (VARY YOUR SENTENCE PATTERNS)

Directions: Rewrite the sentences using the pattern indicated.

1. He left the movies after the first five minutes. (pattern 1)

____

____

2. The daughter killed him in the kitchen. (Emphasize *in the kitchen* by using pattern 3)

____

____

3. As you get richer, you spend more money. (pattern 5)

____

____

4. She took two books to work. One book was a mystery. (pattern 6)

____

____

5. His heart was beating quickly; it felt as though his brain were exploding. (pattern 2)

____

____

6. He never speaks on the topics of religion or politics. (pattern 4)

____

____

Answers and explanations are on page 229.

ANSWERS AND EXPLANATIONS— STYLE AND DICTION: EXERCISES

EXERCISE 1 (CHOOSING A STYLE)

1. **(2)** *Infirmity* is a much more formal word than the others in the sentence.
2. **(4)** The short, casual word *popped* does not fit this extremely formal, legal-sounding sentence.
3. **(3)** *Agitate* is too formal for the situation.
4. **(2)** *Dude* is the only slang word in the sentence. Slang is considered appropriate only in casual conversation or in friendly letters.
5. **(2)** *Conversed* is more formal than the other words in this sentence.

EXERCISE 2 (CHOOSE YOUR WORDS CAREFULLY)

1. **(2)** *drenched* is a vivid way of saying extremely wet.
2. **(3)** *raved,* in one strong word, means spoke irrationally and excitedly.
3. **(5)** *wobbled* can easily replace walked unsteadily and clumsily.
4. **(1)** *arsenal* expresses precisely the phrase storehouse for arms and military equipment.
5. **(4)** *monotonous* is a clear way to say boring because it was the same throughout.

EXERCISE 3 (WORDS COMMONLY CONFUSED)

1. **(5)** No error
2. **(4)** *Customs,* meaning *habits,* has been confused with *costumes,* meaning *clothes worn for special occasions.*
3. **(2)** *Being that* is an incorrect substitution for *because* or *since.*
4. **(1)** *Itch* has been confused with *scratch. To itch* refers to the physical sensation that produces the desire to scratch; *to scratch* refers to the action that is performed to relieve an itch.
5. **(4)** *Aggravate* means *make a bad situation worse. Irritate,* meaning *annoy,* is the correct word to use in this sentence.
6. **(5)** No error
7. **(1)** *Alright* is an incorrect spelling of the expression *all right.*
8. **(1)** *Bring* means *carry to* the speaker or writer. *Take,* meaning *carry away* from the place the speaker or writer is now, is the correct word in this sentence.

9. **(1)** *Its* is the possessive form of the pronoun *it*. The correct word in this sentence is *it's*, the short form of *it is*.

10. **(2)** The word *too*, meaning *overly*, should be used in this sentence.

EXERCISE 4 (AVOIDING UNNECESSARY REPETITION)

1. Correct
2. The actress *can scarcely* remember her own name, much less her lines.
   OR
   The actress *can't* remember her own name, much less her lines.
3. Please *never* tell *anyone* this secret.
   OR
   Please tell *no one* this secret.
4. He was *as famous as* his neighbor.
5. His father said that *the reason* he was not there *was that* he was at a party.
   OR
   His father said that he was not there *because* he was at a party.

EXERCISE 5 (FIGURES OF SPEECH)

1. **(4)** This is not a figure of speech; the words are simply adverbs and adjectives used to describe the day.
2. **(1)** This is a simile, a direct comparison using the word *like*.
3. **(3)** This is an example of personification since the sun can't really smile.
4. **(2)** This is an example of a metaphor; although Walt is not really a tiger, the implied comparison is that Walt is as ferocious and aggressive as a tiger.
5. **(1)** This is an example of a simile, a direct comparison using the word *as*.

EXERCISE 6 (VARY YOUR SENTENCE PATTERNS)

1. After the first five minutes, he left the movies.
2. It was in the kitchen that the daughter killed him.
3. The richer you get, the more money you spend.
4. She took two books to work, one of which was a mystery.
5. His heart was beating quickly; his brain was exploding.
6. On the topics of religion or politics, he never speaks.

STYLE AND DICTION: REVIEW TEST

Directions: If the style or word choice of the underlined part of a sentence is improved in one of the answers, blacken the space under the number corresponding to that answer. If the style or word choice cannot be improved, blacken the space numbered (5). This test will also require you to draw on information you have learned in the Sentence Structure section of this book.

1. 1 2 3 4 5

1. The city planted three trees. One tree was an oak.
   (1) , and one was an oak.
   (2) . One tree planted was an oak.
   (3) , one of which was an oak.
   (4) . One, it seems, was an oak.
   (5) No change

2. 1 2 3 4 5

2. Their friend has some memory of that party.
   (1) is a man who has some memory of
   (2) remembers
   (3) does not remember
   (4) thinks about
   (5) No change

3. 1 2 3 4 5

3. A knowing smile crossed the waitress's face. A knowing smile showed her understanding of the situation.
   (1) Crossing the waitress's face, a knowing smile
   (2) Because it crossed the waitress's face, a knowing smile
   (3) The knowing smile that crossed the waitress's face
   (4) As a knowing smile crossed the waitress's face, the smile
   (5) No change

4. 1 2 3 4 5

4. Larry judged the movie to be enjoyable.
   (1) was pleased with the movie.
   (2) enjoyed the movie.
   (3) found the movie enjoyable.
   (4) thought the movie was the best he had ever seen.
   (5) No change

5. 1 2 3 4 5

5. When she got the news she slumped in her chair.
   (1) sank down with limp muscles
   (2) fell
   (3) bounced
   (4) was no longer alert
   (5) No change

6. As was his custom on Sunday, the minister invited several church members to chew the fat with him. **6.** 1 2 3 4 5

(1) talk
(2) be so kind as to converse
(3) rap
(4) verbalize abstractions
(5) No change

7. That old man looks at the girls sideways as though he is thinking evil thoughts. **7.** 1 2 3 4 5

(1) glances at the girls.
(2) stares at the girls.
(3) glimpses at the girls.
(4) leers at the girls.
(5) No change

8. Her husband is nice, charming, and good company. **8.** 1 2 3 4 5

(1) nice.
(2) good.
(3) charming.
(4) quite a fine person.
(5) No change.

9. The child was fascinated by the parade. **9.** 1 2 3 4 5

(1) The child was pleased with the parade.
(2) The child did not enjoy the parade.
(3) The child felt fascinated by the parade.
(4) The parade fascinated the child.
(5) No change

10. She was sure that the statue winks at her. **10.** 1 2 3 4 5

(1) had closed an eye quickly
(2) winked
(3) will wink
(4) blinks
(5) No change

ANSWERS AND EXPLANATIONS— STYLE AND DICTION: REVIEW TEST

1. **(3)** By adding the expression *one of which,* the two sentences can neatly be made into one.
2. **(2)** One "exact" word is generally preferable to a group of words that means the same thing.
3. **(3)** Since the subject of the two sentences is the same, the two sentences should be combined to avoid the repetition of the subject. Choice (1) would eliminate the repetition, but the use of *crossing the waitress's face* as the first words of the sentence creates an awkward use of personification—that is, a smile does not really walk across someone's face. By beginning the sentence as in choice (3), the writer avoids both the repeated subject and the awkward use of personification.
4. **(2)** This phrase saves words and expresses the idea more directly.
5. **(5)** No change
6. **(1)** *Talk* is more in keeping with the style of the sentence.
7. **(4)** *Leers* expresses the same idea much more clearly and more concisely (with fewer words).
8. **(3)** One well-chosen word should be used instead of three that mean roughly the same thing. Of those given, *charming* is the clearest.
9. **(5)** No change
10. **(2)** To be consistent with the first verb in the sentence, *was,* the second verb should also be in the past tense (*winked*).

STYLE AND DICTION EVALUATION CHART

Question Type	*Review Pages*	*Question Number*	*Amount of Question Type*	*Number of Wrong Answers*
A. Vary Your Sentence Patterns	225–226	1, 3, 4	3	______
B. Choose Your Words Carefully	210–211	2, 7	2	______
C. Make Your Style Fit Your Purpose	208–209	6	1	______
D. Don't Repeat Yourself	221–222	8	1	______
E. Use of Verb Tenses	48–49; 162	10	1	______

PASSING SCORE: 8 out of 10 questions YOUR SCORE: ______ out of 10 questions

If you have any question wrong in any category, you should reread the explanation of that type of problem in the review pages.

LOGIC AND ORGANIZATION

THE PARAGRAPH

A paragraph is a group of sentences, or sometimes only one sentence, the first line of which is indented, or begun farther to the right on the page than the others. The purpose of writing in paragraphs is to make the thought structure of a piece of writing clear by dividing it into separate thoughts. By indenting, the writer gives the reader a visual clue that a new thought is going to be discussed. Each paragraph contains one topic of a larger subject or one part of a topic. Most paragraphs consist of a *statement of the central idea,* or **topic sentence,** and support or proof of that statement in the form of specific details, facts, examples, incidents, or reasons. Thus a paragraph is a blend of specific and general statements.

The Topic Sentence

The following paragraph has no topic sentence. What is the effect? Does it communicate the idea as effectively as possible?

> If the apartment or house is messy, you can tell the inhabitant is disorganized or lazy. If a great deal of care in decoration is obvious, you can be sure a person with a strong need to express himself lives there. An apartment that is neat and orderly has the mark of a well-organized person.

The three sentences offer support for an idea that is not expressed in the paragraph. A topic sentence would make the writer's purpose clear. A good topic sentence might be: "You can tell a great deal about a person by the apartment in which he lives." This sentence could be placed either at the beginning or at the end of the paragraph.

LOGIC AND ORGANIZATION: EXERCISE 1 (THE TOPIC SENTENCE)

Directions: If one sentence is a good topic sentence for the group, blacken the space under the number corresponding to it. If none is a good topic sentence, blacken the space numbered (5).

1. 1 2 3 4 5

1. (1) Babies practice making sounds they will need for speech.
(2) Moving around in a crib gives a baby the skill he needs to crawl.
(3) The statement "Babies just lie around all day long" is nonsense.
(4) Touching everything in his immediate environment trains a baby to know textures and temperature through his fingertips.
(5) None is the topic sentence.

2. 1 2 3 4 5

2. (1) Indians used every part of the buffalo for a specific purpose.
(2) All the uses of an object might not be immediately obvious.
(3) George Washington Carver found hundreds of uses for the peanut.
(4) An old egg carton can be used to start small house plants.
(5) None is the topic sentence.

3. 1 2 3 4 5

3. (1) The example of the bus comes to mind immediately.
(2) People who usually behave in a civilized way change into antisocial monsters.
(3) Normally sweet old ladies jab people with umbrellas when they are trying to reach seats.
(4) As many as twenty people can be competing for the one empty seat on a bus.
(5) None is the topic sentence.

4. 1 2 3 4 5

4. (1) Farmers live close to the forces of nature.
(2) The sun and the moon together are his clock.
(3) At the mercy of the weather, a farmer hopes for rain and sunshine at critical times.
(4) The animals and plants that surround the farmer illustrate the various stages of the life cycle.
(5) None is the topic sentence.

5. 1 2 3 4 5

5. (1) Why does a photographer choose to cover the front lines of a war?
(2) Why do stunt men choose to make their livings acting out catastrophes?
(3) Why are many people attracted to death and destruction?
(4) Why do tourists seek out the sites of terrible tragedies?
(5) None is the topic sentence.

Answers and explanations are on page 246.

METHODS OF PARAGRAPH DEVELOPMENT

Once a writer has defined his purpose in a topic sentence, a number of techniques of paragraph development are available to him. The purpose of all of the methods is to allow the writer to put flesh on the bones of the topic sentence and build a full supporting structure for the main idea.

Method 1: Comparison and Contrast

To compare is to point out similarities between two or more items. To contrast is to point out differences. The method of development that involves comparison and contrast works well in many situations because two things or people are never completely identical, but never completely different, either.

Examine the following example of comparison and contrast:

> The two accountants at Janus Baby Shoe Company were equally good at their jobs, but very different in personality. Both Johnson and Edwards were hard workers, but, while Johnson did a good part of his work at home, Edwards stayed in the office from 8 A.M. to 9 P.M. Johnson preferred to communicate with other employees by letter, in contrast to Edwards's preference for face-to-face communication. Johnson, cautious since birth, could never understand Edwards's freewheeling attitude and eagerness for change.
>
> Fortunately, the two men had no occasion to work together since their responsibilities were different. They would never have agreed on anything.

The similarities as well as the differences between the two men were discussed point by point. Notice that, instead of dealing with the men separately, their personality traits were presented together, creating a more easily readable paragraph. If one man were discussed first, the reader might lose the train of thought. This combination of similar and different elements is the best approach to comparison and contrast.

Method 2: Classification

If someone were asked to write on the subject of transportation, how would he do it? To write a meaningful piece on transportation, an extremely broad topic, he would have to approach it carefully. The method of development called "classification," or logical division, would probably be the best approach. In classification, a subject is broken down into parts within a framework that includes the most important elements of the topic. Choosing the framework is the first step. A writer must be prepared to reject a framework if it does not include the factors he wants to express and to look for another that does. Here are some examples of possible frameworks for the topic "Transportation":

(1) classification according to which type of energy is used (oil, steam, water, human energy, or wind)
(2) classification according to the people who use the means of transportation
(3) classification according to speed
(4) classification according to economy
(5) classification according to popularity
(6) classification according to historical era

The best framework would allow a writer not only to include the most important means of transportation but also to make distinctions among them. If all people use all means of transportation, framework (2) would not be helpful in classifying the various means of transportation. If, however, this framework makes it possible to discuss the topic of transportation by breaking the subject into parts, it might be a good approach.

The following example of classification uses framework (2).

> Even in the jet age, every means of transportation is being used in some part of the world. Rich people everywhere travel by private jet and chauffeured limousine, but poor people still use the most ancient and simple means—foot. In many underdeveloped countries and in rural areas of some developed countries, those who are a little better off travel by means of animals. In the cities of developed countries, most people use the public systems of transportation, buses and trains. In the suburbs, however, people who can afford them depend on automobiles to get around.
>
> One means of transportation that seems to have dropped in popularity is travel by boat. Formerly used by great numbers of people from the very rich to the very poor, travel by boat is becoming limited to people with plenty of money and time on their hands.

Notice that, by organizing these paragraphs according to the people who use the various means of transportation, the important means of transportation and some of the distinctions among them were brought out.

Method 3: Sequence of Events

A sequence of events or steps is a useful framework whenever different stages are involved. Tracing the history of something, telling a story, explaining a process, and giving directions should include the order of events, from the first to the last.

The following paragraph is developed by showing the sequence of events.

> My friend Shelby has developed an art of eating pizza. He first sees to it that there is an acceptable amount of tomato sauce and cheese on the piece he is considering eating. After sprinkling the chosen piece with a large number of hot pepper flakes, he makes sure that his glass of soda is within easy reach. He then curls the pizza triangle and scoops it into his mouth, where almost half of it neatly disappears. He immediately returns the remaining half to his plate with his left hand while his right hand grabs his soda. After a few slurps and pleased noises, the process is repeated until the pizza is gone.

Notice that the underlined words determine the way in which one step logically proceeds from the previous one.

Method 4: Location

Sometimes it is important for a writer to help his readers picture a scene. In order to write an accurate description, he must choose a logical order of presenting details. In a physical description, the actual location of things can provide the best means of presentation. To help the readers see through his eyes, a writer must choose a starting point, usually the most prominent or striking feature, and move consistently in some direction around the scene presenting the features of the scene in relation to one another.

Examine the following description of a room.

> The first impression I got was that of a dark room with two windows punched out at the far end. Around the windows I could see the outlines of hanging plants with leaves hanging almost to the floor. When my eyes adjusted to the dim light, I noticed that the room was filled with an amazing number of strange, beautiful things. Between the windows were three colorful pictures. On the floor in front stood two tribal statues from Africa. The bottom half of the brick wall to the left was covered by bookshelves containing a large number of books. Above the bookshelves, old fishing nets had been hung from

> the wall. As I stood in the doorway, I noticed to my immediate left a grandfather clock with a strange face of a moon painted on it. On the wall opposite the brick one, there were many photographs of odd-looking people, in front of which lay a shabby mattress.

In this paragraph, each detail grows out of the preceding one. The word picture develops from the most prominent point, the windows, around the room moving from right to left. Other possible methods of organization are from left to right, top to bottom, bottom to top, front to back, depending on what is being described.

Method 5: Cause and Effect

Using the method of development known as "cause and effect" means explaining why something is true or why something happened. A cause is what produces a result or effect. The connection between an effect and its cause must be clear.

Failure to establish a connection between a cause and an effect is a common error in everyday life as well as in paragraph development. For example, John knew that his friend, Fred, had been arguing with his wife all week. When John ran into Fred at the movies on Friday, he noticed that Fred looked extremely depressed. Assuming that the cause for Fred's depression had been the argument, John didn't bother to ask Fred what was wrong. Actually, Fred was depressed because he had lost his job, not because of his arguments with his wife. John could have been a better friend if he had established the connection between the effect and its cause.

The following paragraph is an example of organization by cause and effect.

> According to leading psychologists, environment is the main influence on personality, and the home environment, the family, has a far greater effect than the total environment of society as a whole. Because a young child does not know enough about the world to formulate his own opinions, he must use those of his parents or the people closest to him until he is able to understand life for himself. Even if he rejects them later in life, the personalities and character traits of the people who brought him up leave their mark on him.

This paragraph uses the authority of psychologists to show a cause and effect relationship between the home environment of a child and his personality. As usually happens in a cause-effect relationship, there is more than one cause for an effect and more than one effect of each cause. This paragraph deals with only one aspect of a very complicated series of causes and effects.

LOGIC AND ORGANIZATION: EXERCISE 2
(METHODS OF PARAGRAPH DEVELOPMENT)

Directions: For each topic given, decide which method of paragraph development would be most effective and blacken the space under the number corresponding to it. If no method listed would be appropriate, blacken the space numbered (5).

1. "Why Grass Is Green" **1.** 1 2 3 4 5
   (1) Comparison and Contrast
   (2) Classification
   (3) Sequence of Events
   (4) Cause and Effect
   (5) None is appropriate

2. "Two American Presidents" **2.** 1 2 3 4 5
   (1) Comparison and Contrast
   (2) Classification
   (3) Location
   (4) Cause and Effect
   (5) None is appropriate

3. "Animals" **3.** 1 2 3 4 5
   (1) Comparison and Contrast
   (2) Classification
   (3) Sequence of Events
   (4) Location
   (5) None is appropriate

4. "How to Ride a Motorcycle" **4.** 1 2 3 4 5
   (1) Classification
   (2) Sequence of Events
   (3) Location
   (4) Cause and Effect
   (5) None is appropriate

5. "My Grandmother's Kitchen" **5.** 1 2 3 4 5
   (1) Comparison and Contrast
   (2) Classification
   (3) Sequence of Events
   (4) Cause and Effect
   (5) None is appropriate

Answers and explanations are on page 246.

PROBLEMS WITH PARAGRAPH CONSTRUCTION

Irrelevancy—Sentences That Don't Fit into the Paragraph

To be effective a paragraph must be unified. This means that all of the sentences in a paragraph must be working toward a common purpose, the communication and discussion of one thought. All parts of a paragraph, whether they are incidents, facts, examples, or reasons, must refer to the main idea of the paragraph. Check the following paragraph to see whether any irrelevant sentences are included.

> [1]The Browns had a wonderful party last night. [2]Many people stopped by, and everybody seemed to have a good time. [3]Wine, fried chicken, and potato salad were served. [4]Almost everybody danced, and several new friendships were started. [5]The party is a social institution that exists in one form or another in all cultures.

All of the sentences except sentence 5 work to support the general statement that the Browns had a good party. The last sentence is not related to this idea. It is irrelevant to the main idea and interferes with the unity of the paragraph

LOGIC AND ORGANIZATION: EXERCISE 3 (IRRELEVANCY)

Directions: If one sentence in a paragraph is not related to the central idea stated or suggested by the others, blacken the space under the number corresponding to it. If all sentences refer back to one main idea, blacken the space numbered (5).

---

1. 1 2 3 4 5

1. [1]Zoos should be abolished. [2]Scientists benefit from the existence of zoos. [3]Animals are treated miserably, and many cannot reproduce in captivity regardless of the conditions. [4]From a practical point of view, it should also be considered that few people enjoy seeing animals in cages. [5]None of the sentences is irrelevant.

2. 1 2 3 4 5

2. [1]Street life is growing in America. [2]In big cities there are more outdoor eating and drinking places than ever before. [3]Parts of San Francisco look like an oriental bazaar, with hundreds of peddlers selling their goods. [4]The interest in plants and gardens is also growing in most cities. [5]None of the sentences is irrelevant.

3. 1 2 3 4 5

3. [1]Economic depression has some unexpected results. [2]The tourist industry, certainly a luxury business, flourishes in hard times. [3]Strangely enough, gambling profits also increase when money is

tight. [4]Furthermore, more people invest in expensive cars during economic depressions than in times of economic stability. [5]None of the sentences is irrelevant.

4. [1]Drinking too much gin destroys the liver. [2]Eating eggs raises the cholesterol level in men and older women. [3]A glass of wine with meals helps digestion. [4]Some foods certainly have harmful effects on the body. [5]None of the sentences is irrelevant. **4.** 1 2 3 4 5

5. [1]The tennis craze is still with us. [2]Programs that show televised tennis matches get high ratings. [3]Thousands of new tennis courts are built each week. [4]More young people play basketball, however. [5]None of the sentences is irrelevant. **5.** 1 2 3 4 5

Answers and explanations are on pages 246–247.

Unclear Sentence Relationships— *Sentences That Don't Logically Follow*

A paragraph must present ideas in a logical order. In all paragraphs, the sentences should relate to each other in a meaningful way so that the reader can follow the train of thought. In most paragraphs, each sentence grows out of the previous one. Clear connections among sentences, together with good organization, help the writer make his point. These connections can be made in a number of ways.

Transition Words—Bridges between Sentences

Transition words are used specifically to show the relationship between sentences. Special words can signal relationships such as contrast, result or effect, time, summary, comparison, illustration, and location. Examine the following examples of the use of transition words.

> The price of crude oil rose again. *As a result,* gasoline prices and electricity bills are higher.
>
> *As a result* expresses consequence or effect.
>
> The careers of most female movie stars end with their youth. *However,* some do succeed portraying older women when they can no longer play glamour roles.
>
> *However* shows a contrast.

The following chart lists transition words according to the type of relationship they express.

Relationship	*Transition Words*
summary	finally, in this way, on the whole, in conclusion
illustration	for example, for instance, such as, that is
comparison	similarly, likewise, in the same way, in like fashion, and
contrast	yet, but, on the other hand, however, at the same time
addition of an idea	besides, furthermore, also, in addition, again, moreover
consequence	thus, as a result, for this reason, consequently, therefore, it follows that
relationships of time	first, next, now, presently, meanwhile, eventually, later, then, finally
relationships of space	above, below, next to, at the right, at the left, beyond, before

Without transition words, a paragraph would be choppy and possibly confusing. Compare the two versions of these recipes.

Without transition words

Steam the chicken for about 30 minutes. Halve the tomatoes and remove the seeds. Put each half, cut side down, on a paper towel to drain. Cut the chicken off the bones and into pieces. Mix the chicken pieces with chopped celery, onions, and salt. Put the mixture into the tomato halves and serve.

With transition words

First, steam the chicken for about 30 minutes. *Meanwhile,* halve the tomatoes and remove the seeds. *Then,* put each half, cut side down, on a paper towel to drain. *When it is ready,* cut the chicken off the bones and into pieces. *Next,* mix the chicken pieces with chopped celery, onions, and salt. *Finally,* put the mixture into the tomato halves and serve.

Notice that the recipe that uses transition words is much easier to follow.

LOGIC AND ORGANIZATION: EXERCISE 4 (TRANSITION WORDS)

Directions: If one transition word in a group expresses the relationship between the two sentences and can connect them, blacken the space under the number corresponding to it. If none is appropriate, blacken the space numbered (5).

1. Most old cars are worth less than new ones
There are some that are incredibly expensive.

(1) Finally
(2) Similarly
(3) For example
(4) Above
(5) None is appropriate

1. 1 2 3 4 5

2. South American countries, generally speaking, have different types of land.
Ecuador consists of jungle, desert, highlands, and mountainous regions.

(1) Consequently
(2) For example
(3) Before
(4) Furthermore
(5) None is appropriate

2. 1 2 3 4 5

3. The sea sparkled with brightly colored lights.
The sky was cloudless.

(1) Therefore
(2) Above
(3) Next
(4) But
(5) None is appropriate

3. 1 2 3 4 5

4. Newspaper reporters have written about mail-order frauds.
Many consumers hesitate to buy through the mail.

(1) Moreover
(2) Besides
(3) As a result
(4) Eventually
(5) None is appropriate

4. 1 2 3 4 5

5. 1 2 3 4 5

5. First Johnson City was a mining town.
It became a bustling trade center.

(1) In conclusion
(2) Later
(3) In this way
(4) Likewise
(5) None is appropriate

Answers and explanations are on page 247.

Other Ways of Connecting Sentences

Repetition of Key Words. In addition to transition words and expressions, another way to connect sentences is to repeat key words or groups of words.

> The *Japanese* diet is considered to be one of the healthiest in the world. *Japanese* people eat mainly fish, rice, and vegetables.

If the word *Japanese* were not repeated, the relationship between the two sentences would not be absolutely clear.

Using Pronouns as Referants. Another method of sentence connection is the use of a pronoun to refer to the subject of a previous sentence.

> *Laughing gas* is an effective pain killer. *Its* side-effects are sometimes unpleasant, however.

The use of the possessive pronoun makes it absolutely clear that the side-effects of laughing gas are being discussed.

Repetition of Sentence Structure. If two sentences have the same structure, sentence connection results naturally.

> *In Israel, women are* drafted into the army. *In Australia, women are* expected to ride in the back seat of a car when the husband is driving.

By repeating the structure of the first sentence in the second sentence, the writer can establish a connection without using any additional words.

LOGIC AND ORGANIZATION: EXERCISE 5
(UNCLEAR SENTENCE RELATIONSHIPS)

Directions: If one sentence is not logically connected to the preceding one, blacken the space under the number corresponding to it. If the relationships among all sentences in a group are clear, blacken the space numbered (5).

1. [1]Whether or not war is an example of natural human behavior is a hotly debated question. [2]On one hand, entomologists, scientists who study insects, use the example of the ant as proof that aggression and destruction within a particular species can be found in nature. [3]On the other hand, some philosophers and sociologists blame society for teaching hostility to man, who would not be capable of killing if he were not exposed to these teachings. [4]Therefore, the entomologists are correct in their assertion that man is a born killer. [5]No change

   1. 1 2 3 4 5

2. [1]The reason for laughter at the beginning of the senator's speech in Norway recently became known. [2]The senator took great pains to memorize what he thought was the Norwegian phrase meaning "I too am Norwegian" so he could say it in his speech. [3]Unfortunately, he inserted an extra word. [4]As a result of the extra word, he said "I am a hot dog" instead. [5]No change

   2. 1 2 3 4 5

3. [1]In the deep part of an ocean a completely new universe exists. [2]Brightly colored fish flash by like neon lights, and green plants move with the current. [3]The underwater life found in the ocean is not always so pleasant to encounter, however. [4]Strange monsters appear there, too. [5]No change

   3. 1 2 3 4 5

4. [1]Most of the people in the hospital named Miss Rosewall as the nurse they admired most. [2]She was like a mother to all of them, and to all a friend. [3]As a result of this, Miss Rosewall had decided to become a nurse as a young woman. [4]In addition to her duties as a nurse, she acted as counselor, teacher, and social worker throughout her life. [5]No change

   4. 1 2 3 4 5

5. [1]A statue honoring the great engineer Schmidt was placed in the town square in 1815. [2]Years later, in 1940, it was moved into a corner of the museum. [3]An angry descendant of Schmidt demanded soon after that that it be put back in the square, where it stands today. [4]In 1832 a stray bullet knocked off the statue's nose. [5]No change

   5. 1 2 3 4 5

Answers and explanations are on page 247.

ANSWERS AND EXPLANATIONS—LOGIC AND ORGANIZATION: EXERCISES

EXERCISE 1 (THE TOPIC SENTENCE)

1. **(3)** All of the other sentences support the idea that babies do more than lie around all day.
2. **(2)** The main idea is the unexpected uses that sometimes can be found for an object. All the other sentences illustrate this idea.
3. **(5)** None is the topic sentence. All of the sentences give examples of how people behave on the bus; however, none of the sentences states a topic that would unify the group.
4. **(1)** The first sentence expresses the idea of farmers' close relationship to nature, which is illustrated in each of the other sentences.
5. **(3)** This sentence states the general idea that is illustrated in each of the other sentences.

EXERCISE 2 (METHODS OF PARAGRAPH DEVELOPMENT)

1. **(4)** This topic involves explaining why something is true; therefore, *cause and effect* would be the best method of paragraph development.
2. **(1)** This topic lends itself to pointing out the similarities and differences between two men; therefore, *comparison and contrast* would be the best method of paragraph development.
3. **(2)** Such a broad topic must be broken into component parts and examined. *Classification* would be the best way to accomplish this task.
4. **(2)** This involves explanation of a step-by-step process. *Sequence of events* is the only method that approaches a topic in this way.
5. **(5)** None is appropriate. The best method of attacking a description of something is *location,* but this is not given as an answer choice.

EXERCISE 3 (IRRELEVANCY)

1. **(2)** This sentence points out an advantage of zoos, information that is not related to the argument against zoos expressed in the others.
2. **(4)** An interest in plants is not related to the central idea of the growth of street life in America.

3. **(5)** None of the sentences is irrelevant. Sentence 1 states the main idea and the other sentences illustrate this idea.
4. **(3)** The fact stated in this sentence points out an advantage of drinking wine, information that is not related to the general topic of harmful effects of certain foods.
5. **(4)** All of the other sentences deal with some aspect of tennis.

EXERCISE 4 (TRANSITION WORDS)

1. **(5)** None is appropriate. A transition word that expresses contrast such as *however* is needed here.
2. **(2)** *For example* shows that the second sentence illustrates the first.
3. **(2)** *Above* expresses the location of the sky in relation to the sea.
4. **(3)** *As a result* would be appropriate since the second sentence is a consequence of the first.
5. **(2)** *Later* expresses the appropriate relationship of time.

EXERCISE 5 (UNCLEAR SENTENCE RELATIONSHIPS)

1. **(4)** This sentence is not a logical conclusion (the use of the transition word *therefore* indicates that the writer meant this sentence as a conclusion) based on the preceding sentences. There is no proof given that the entomologists are correct.
2. **(5)** No change. All of the sentences are logically related to one another in a *sequence of events* pattern.
3. **(5)** No change. All of the sentences in this group are logically related to one another. Sentence 1 states the main idea (it is the topic sentence), and the other sentences illustrate this idea.
4. **(3)** This sentence is not a result of the previous one. The transition words *as a result* signal a *cause and effect* relationship, but sentence 2 did not cause Miss Rosewall to make the decision stated in sentence 3; in fact, sentence 3 took place at an earlier time as indicated by the past perfect tense of the verb *had decided.*
5. **(4)** Because this sentence deals with an event that occurred in 1832, it would be correctly placed between the sentences dealing with the events occurring in 1815 and 1940 (sentences 1 and 2). As it stands, the sentence does not fall into the pattern of *sequence of events.*

LOGIC AND ORGANIZATION: REVIEW TEST 1

Directions: If the underlined sentence or part of a sentence is inappropriate, choose the best replacement for it and blacken the space under the number corresponding to it. If the underlined part is correct, blacken the space numbered (5).

1. 1 2 3 4 5

1. Vacations, it seems, can be a source of tension rather than a rest for some people. Because planning and arrangement of details require such a great effort, these people dread their time off. Even if they spend vacations at home, women might not want their husbands to sleep late.

(1) children could present problems.
(2) the interruption of their normal routines makes them feel tense and anxious.
(3) they would miss the mountains or the beach.
(4) they have to spend time reading to keep up with their work.
(5) No change

2. 1 2 3 4 5

2. A cold wind had started to whistle over the lonely mountainside. Far away, they heard an Indian playing his flute to forget his loneliness and the chill. Eventually, the rescue party arrived.

(1) They rolled the two climbers onto stretchers in preparation for the long trip back to the village.
(2) Flutes were invented by the Greeks.
(3) However, colder winds were common during that time of year.
(4) Unable to move, the pair of climbers listened to the sad music and prayed that help would come.
(5) No change

3. 1 2 3 4 5

3. No one will check to see if we have gone. On the other hand, the general gave us permission to leave.

(1) On the whole,
(2) Meanwhile,
(3) Furthermore,
(4) That is,
(5) No change

4. 1 2 3 4 5

4. In front of the pond pretty yellow flowers bloomed. To the left stood a group of squirrels.

(1) Eventually,
(2) At last,

(3) Yet,
(4) Moreover,
(5) No change

5. To contrast San Francisco with Chicago, one can see it as consisting of basically three parts, each with its own character. **5.** 1 2 3 4 5

(1) To compare San Francisco to Chicago,
(2) To break San Francisco into its component parts,
(3) To find the cause for San Francisco's uniqueness,
(4) To trace the history of San Francisco,
(5) No change

Answers and explanations are on page 254.

LOGIC AND ORGANIZATION: REVIEW TEST 2

Directions: Read each of the following passages carefully, and look for errors in paragraph logic and organization. Then, answer the questions, paying particular attention to the position and function of the sentence being examined. Note: Some of the questions will include material that you have already covered in the Sentence Structure and Style and Diction chapters.

[1]Sources of energy on which we are dependent are being rapidly depleted. [2]In addition, known pockets of crude oil can provide for the world's needs for only another twenty years. [3]One of these potential sources is the sun. [4]New sources of energy need to be developed. [5]The construction of solar houses in California and Arizona proves that it can be done but at a crazy cost. [6]People will have to help by using their cars less frequently.

1. 1 2 3 4 5

1. Sentence 2 should begin

   (1) the way it begins now
   (2) *For example, known pockets of crude oil*
   (3) *However, known pockets of crude oil*
   (4) *Nevertheless, known pockets of crude oil*
   (5) *As a result, known pockets of crude oil*

2. 1 2 3 4 5

2. What should be done with sentence 3?

   (1) It should be left as is.
   (2) It should be omitted.
   (3) It should be moved to the end.
   (4) It should follow sentence 4.
   (5) It should follow sentence 1.

3. 1 2 3 4 5

3. What should be done with sentence 5?

   (1) It should be left as is.
   (2) It should be lengthened to give more information about what was done.
   (3) It should be moved to the beginning.
   (4) It should be made into two separate sentences.
   (5) It should be shortened to *The successful construction of solar houses in California and Arizona proves it.*

4. 1 2 3 4 5

4. The word *crazy* in sentence 5 should be

   (1) left as is
   (2) changed to *insane*

(3) changed to *off the wall*
(4) changed to *very high*
(5) changed to *inconsequential*

5. What should be done with sentence 6? **5.** 1 2 3 4 5

(1) It should be left as is.
(2) It should be omitted.
(3) It should follow sentence 1.
(4) It should be joined to sentence 5 with *since.*
(5) It should follow sentence 4.

[1]The crew believed that the shark would bite off a piece of the boat, causing them to fall into the rough sea. [2]A giant white shark hurled it's huge body against the boat over and over again. [3]Submerging for a while only to emerge ready for battle. [4]Miraculously, in conclusion, they managed to sail safely into the harbor, arriving safe and sound at the dock.

6. What should be done with sentence 2? **6.** 1 2 3 4 5

(1) It should be left as is.
(2) It should be omitted.
(3) It should be moved to the end.
(4) It should begin the paragraph.
(5) It should be joined to sentence 1.

7. Sentence 3 should begin **7.** 1 2 3 4 5

(1) the way it begins now
(2) *Submerging for a while only emerging*
(3) *It would submerge for a while only to emerge*
(4) *For a while emerging, only to submerge*
(5) *Since it would submerge for a while only to emerge*

8. Sentence 3 is best placed **8.** 1 2 3 4 5

(1) where it is now
(2) after sentence 2 but before sentence 1
(3) after sentence 1 but before sentence 2
(4) at the beginning of a new paragraph
(5) at the beginning of this paragraph

9. Sentence 4 would be best if the beginning were **9.** 1 2 3 4 5

(1) left as is
(2) changed to *Miraculously, however*
(3) changed to *Miraculously, likewise*
(4) changed to *Miraculously, furthermore*
(5) changed to *Miraculously, generally*

10. 1 2 3 4 5

10. Sentence 4 would be improved if

(1) it were omitted entirely
(2) the entire sentence were joined to the end of sentence 3 with *but*
(3) a period were placed after *into the harbor*
(4) a period were placed after *safe and sound*
(5) a period were placed after *sail safely*

11. 1 2 3 4 5

11. The word *it's* in sentence 2 should be

(1) left as is
(2) changed to *his*
(3) changed to *her*
(4) changed to *its*
(5) changed to *a*

[1]If you didn't know in advance that they were twins, you wouldn't even think that they were from the same family. [2]There were more differences between them than there were similarities. [3]One was light-haired and one was dark-haired. [4]One was serious and one was never serious. [5]Another point of comparison between the two was physical appearance. [6]One was short and round; the other tall and thin. [7]Their personalities were completely different. [8]One was very outgoing; the other shy and quiet. [9]I liked them both for different reasons.

12. 1 2 3 4 5

12. What should be done with sentence 1?
(1) It should be left as is.
(2) It should follow sentence 2.
(3) It should be joined to sentence 2 with *however.*
(4) It should be moved to the end.
(5) It should be divided into two sentences by placing a period after *twins.*

13. 1 2 3 4 5

13. Sentence 5 would be improved if it began

(1) *Another point of argument*
(2) *Another point of contrast*
(3) *Another point of similarity*
(4) *Another point of confusion*
(5) *Another point of resemblance*

14. 1 2 3 4 5

14. The passage would be clearest if the sentence order were

(1) left as is
(2) 1, 2, 5, 6, 3, 7, 4, 8, 9
(3) 1, 2, 7, 8, 4, 5, 3, 6, 9
(4) 9, 1, 2, 3, 4, 5, 6, 7, 8
(5) 2, 1, 3, 5, 6, 8, 7, 4, 9

15. If the passage is to be divided into 3 paragraphs, the second paragraph should begin with **15.** 1 2 3 4 5

(1) sentence 7
(2) sentence 2
(3) sentence 9
(4) sentence 3
(5) sentence 8

Answers and explanations are on pages 254–255.

ANSWERS AND EXPLANATIONS—LOGIC AND ORGANIZATION: REVIEW TESTS

REVIEW TEST 1

1. **(2)** The underlined part of the last sentence does not refer to the central idea—that vacations can be a source of tension rather than a rest for some people. Only choice 2 refers back to this central idea.
2. **(4)** The underlined sentence is not logically related to the preceding ones. Only choice 4 could logically follow the preceding sentence. (Notice the reference to listening to the music.)
3. **(3)** The words *on the other hand* signal a *contrast;* however, a transition word indicating an *addition* should be used here to connect the two reasons why the subject *we* in the first sentence could leave.
4. **(5)** No change. The transition words *to the left* indicate *location.* These are the best transition words for connecting the physical description given in these two sentences.
5. **(2)** *Classification,* or breaking a subject into parts for analysis, is the development method being used here. There are no examples of contrast in the sentence.

REVIEW TEST 2

1. **(2)** *For example* would be the best transition phrase since the second sentence illustrates the first.
2. **(4)** Sentence 3 logically follows sentence 4 because sentence 3 gives an example of a new source of energy that could be developed.
3. **(2)** Sentence 5, as it now stands, is unclear. The phrase *proves that it can be done* needs to be expanded to tell the reader exactly what the construction of the solar houses proved about the use of solar energy.
4. **(4)** The word *crazy* is both inexact and too "slangy" to be used within the context of this passage. The words *very high* give a more specific description of the cost, and the language fits the tone of the passage.
5. **(2)** The passage does not discuss the measures that the average person will have to take to conserve energy. Sentence 6 does not logically follow any other sentence in the passage; therefore, it should be omitted.
6. **(4)** In order to follow a logical sequence of events, the writer of this passage should have put sentence 2 first. The shark's hurling itself against the boat is logically the first in the series of events in this story. Notice also that sentence 2 begins with the words *A*

giant white shark (general), and sentence 1 uses the words *the shark* (specific), implying a reference to a shark previously mentioned. This is another clue to the correct order of sentences in this passage.

7. **(3)** Sentence 3 is a sentence fragment. It does not have a subject. Choices (3) and (5) are the only ones that add a subject to this sentence fragment. Choice (5) can be eliminated because the word *since* makes it an incomplete thought and therefore not a sentence.

8. **(2)** Sentence 2 describes the movement of the shark in the water. This sentence along with sentence 2 should precede sentence 1 since both of these sentences provide a basis for the conclusion the crew draws in sentence 1.

9. **(2)** *However* is the appropriate transition word for this sentence. The sentences preceding sentence 4 lead the reader to believe that the shark will do some damage to either the boat or the crew. The outcome is in contrast to the expectations built up by these sentences; therefore, *however* is the best word for the sentence.

10. **(3)** The last words of sentence 4 *arriving safe and sound at the dock* are redundant; that is, they repeat the information given at the beginning of the sentence without adding anything new. It would therefore be best to eliminate this phrase to avoid unnecessary repetition.

11. **(4)** *It's* is the contraction that means *it is*. The possessive form *its* is needed in this sentence to refer to the shark.

12. **(1)** Sentence 1 is the main idea of the passage and is correct in the position it now occupies. The rest of the passage proves why *"If you didn't know in advance that they were twins, you wouldn't even think that they were from the same family."*

13. **(2)** The passage contrasts or points out the differences between the twins; therefore, the phrase *Another point of contrast* would be better than *Another point of comparison* since comparison implies similarities.

14. **(3)** For a logical order of ideas to be established, the passage should proceed from the main idea (the existence of differences between the twins) to an orderly presentation of those differences. An orderly presentation would involve first a presentation of all of the personality differences grouped together (7, 8, 4) and then a presentation of the physical differences grouped together (5, 3, 6) ending with the writer's conclusion (9).

15. **(1)** The only logical choice is sentence 7. Since a paragraph is defined as explaining one part of a topic, this sentence, which introduces the personality differences between the twins, is the only one out of the choices given that could reasonably begin a new paragraph.

SPELLING

GENERAL SPELLING HINTS

Spelling in English is difficult because there is little consistency in the sound-letter system. One sound can have many different spellings. For example, the *ay* sound in *hay* can also be heard in *freight, hate,* and *pain.* This lack of consistency is a result of the influence of many different language families on the English language.

To improve your spelling:

(1) Learn and apply the rules that provide hints to spelling. Even though all rules have exceptions, they apply to the great majority of cases. Put the law of averages on your side!

(2) Become aware of the spelling of words as you read. Also, read as much as possible. Exposure to more words will make you familiar with more spellings.

(3) Keep a special spelling notebook for problem words. As you come across a tricky word or one that you know you are not sure about, write it in your notebook with the difficult part of the word in a different color ink, or write the tricky part in capital letters.

EXAMPLES: sepArate
decEIve
cOUrse
cOArse

This emphasis will draw your attention to the problem area and help you to remember it.

(4) Pronunciation can help your spelling. Slowly pronounce words with many separate sounds to avoid putting in an extra sound or leaving one out. Check in the dictionary for the pronunciation if you are not sure about a word.

(5) Thinking of the derivation or root of a word will often help you to spell it correctly.

EXAMPLES: logi*cally* comes from logi*cal*
twel*fth* comes from twel*ve*
book • *keep* • *er* is a person who keeps books

(6) Familiarize yourself with common prefixes and suffixes. Knowing the special meanings of prefixes and suffixes will strengthen your vocabulary.

A **prefix** is a word part added to the front of a word, as in *un* • familiar

A **suffix** is a word part added to the end of a word, as in familiar • *ize*

Here is a list of common prefixes and suffixes:

Prefix	Meaning	Example
a-	without	apolitical; asymmetry
anti-	against	antidote; antithesis
aud-	hear	auditorium; audition
auto-	self	automatic; automobile
ante-	before	antecedent; antedate
bi-	twice; two	bicentennial; biweekly
bio-	life	biopsy; biology
cent-	hundred	century; centennial
co-, col-, com-, con-, cor-	together	cooperate; collaborate; communion; concurrent; correlate
contra-	against	contradictory
de-	away from, down	descend; deflate
dis-	not, away	disapprove; disappear
im-, in-	in, into	implant; inject
in-, il-, ir-	not	incapable; illegal; irreligious
inter-	between	interlace; intermediate
intra-, intro-	inside	intramural; introduce
non-	not	nonentity; nonexistent
post-	after	postpone; posterior
pre-	before	prehistoric; prejudge
pro-	for, forward	proponent; progressive
re-	again	reread; remission
semi-	half	semicircle; semiconscious
sub, sus-	under	subway; suspend
super-	above, over	superior; supersede
sym-, syn-	together, with	symbiosis; synonym
trans-	across	trans-Atlantic; transmit
un-	not	unhappy
uni-	one	universe; unicycle

Suffix	Meaning	Example
-able, -ible	able to	readable; terrible
-dom	state, condition	freedom

Suffix	Meaning	Example
-en	make, made of	lighten; flaxen
-er	unequal comparison; one who	faster; builder
-ful	full of	cheerful
-hood	state, condition	brotherhood
-ish	rather like	mannish; childish
-ism	state, belief	atheism; communism
-ist	one who	artist
-ize	make	mobilize
-ly	in the manner of	friendly
-ment	state, embodiment	government; treatment
-or	one who	sailor
-tude	state, quality	magnitude
-ure	condition	pleasure

GENERAL SPELLING RULES

(1) The i + e combination rule

i goes before *e* in combination

believe
sieve
niece

Except after the letter *c*

receive
perceive

Or when having the sound *ay*

neighbor
weigh

There are a few exceptions to the *c* rule

species	conscientious
ancient	financier
conscience	

And a few exceptions to the general combination rule

weird	forfeit
either	neither
foreign	leisure
height	seize
sovereign	

(2) The rule for word endings that sound like <u>seed</u>

Only one is spelled *sede*

supersede

Three are spelled *ceed*

exceed
succeed
proceed

All others are spelled *cede*

accede
precede
recede

(3) The <u>f</u> to <u>v</u> rule

Often, when *s* is added to a word ending in *f* or *fe*, the *f* changes to *v* (see page 32 for more examples).

elf, elves
wife, wives

SPELLING: EXERCISE 1 (RULES 1–3)

Directions: Pick out the misspelled word in each group and blacken the space in the answer grid under the number that corresponds to that word.

---

1. (1) achieve (2) beleive (3) grief (4) siege (5) receive — **1.** 1 2 3 4 5
2. (1) eight (2) ceiling (3) shield (4) relieve (5) wiegh — **2.** 1 2 3 4 5
3. (1) mischeif (2) priest (3) weird (4) ancient (5) pier — **3.** 1 2 3 4 5
4. (1) veil (2) deceit (3) heir (4) apiece (5) sieze — **4.** 1 2 3 4 5
5. (1) conceit (2) breif (3) belief (4) either (5) reign — **5.** 1 2 3 4 5
6. (1) accede (2) succeed (3) superceed (4) recede (5) proceed — **6.** 1 2 3 4 5
7. (1) precede (2) excede (3) secede (4) concede (5) cede — **7.** 1 2 3 4 5

8. 1 2 3 4 5 — 8. (1) intercede (2) supersede (3) succede (4) doves (5) wife

9. 1 2 3 4 5 — 9. (1) knives (2) staffs (3) shelves (4) wolfs (5) twelfth

10. 1 2 3 4 5 — 10. (1) drives (2) wharves (3) leaves (4) clefts (5) rooves

Answers and explanations are on page 271.

SPELLING RULES FOR THE ADDITION OF PREFIXES AND SUFFIXES

Before we study the next spelling rules, here are some definitions you should know:

---

vowel—*a, e, i, o, u,* and *y* (*y* is only a vowel if it is not in front of another vowel)

consonant—all the letters of the alphabet that are not vowels

syllable—a unit of a word that is pronounced as a separate sound (only one vowel sound)

EXAMPLES:

jump (one syllable)
free • dom (two syllables)
mys • ter • y (three syllables)

---

(1) Generally, a prefix or a suffix is added as an entire unit directly to a word, which keeps its original spelling.

un + necessary = unnecessary
dis + appear = disappear
exceptional + ly = exceptionally
open + ness = openness

There are some exceptions in which the word changes with the addition of a suffix:

argue + ment = argument
due + ly = duly
wonder + ous = wondrous
whole + ly = wholly
true + ly = truly

(2) The name of the vowel rule

The vowel *a* says its name in *bait, late,* and *stay.*
The vowel *e* says its name in *feet, neat,* and *mete.*
The vowel *i* says its name in *sigh, height,* and *mice.*
The vowel *o* says its name in *throw* and *hope.*
The vowel *u* says its name in *cute* and *suit.*

If the sound before the final consonant in a one-syllable word *says* the name of a vowel, the final consonant is not doubled when a suffix is added.

bait + ed = baited
hope + ed = hoped

When the sound before a final consonant does not *say* the name of a vowel, the final consonant is doubled.

bat + ed = batted
net + ed = netted
sit + ing = sitting
hop + ing = hopping

(3) The stress rule

In a word that has more than one syllable and ends in a consonant, double the final consonant when adding a suffix if the stress or emphasis is on the last syllable of the word.

The stress in the following words is on the last syllable; therefore, the consonant is doubled before a suffix.

transMIT + er = transmitter
reBEL + ious = rebellious
perMIT + ing = permitting

The stress in the next words is *not* on the final syllable. The consonant at the end is not doubled when a suffix is added.

OFFer + ed = offered
COUNsel + ed = counseled

The stress rule still operates even when the stress changes with the addition of a suffix. Ignore the pronunciation of the root word, and decide the question of whether or not to double the consonant based on the new stress.

METal + ic = meTALlic
preFER + ence = PREFerence
BUT: preFER + ed = preFERred

SPELLING: EXERCISE 2 (PREFIX AND SUFFIX RULES 1–3)

Directions: Find the misspelled word in each group and blacken the space in the answer grid under the number that corresponds to that word.

---

1. 1 2 3 4 5 — 1. (1) unatural (2) dictation (3) batting (4) conference (5) committed

2. 1 2 3 4 5 — 2. (1) murderer (2) stopped (3) occurence (4) comfortable (5) quizzes

3. 1 2 3 4 5 — 3. (1) government (2) foolish (3) skiing (4) planned (5) civillize

4. 1 2 3 4 5 — 4. (1) cancelled (2) developed (3) biggest (4) unhappy (5) goodness

5. 1 2 3 4 5 — 5. (1) controled (2) breakage (3) beginning (4) traveler (5) wonderful

6. 1 2 3 4 5 — 6. (1) appearance (2) opened (3) existence (4) metalic (5) getting

7. 1 2 3 4 5 — 7. (1) excellent (2) commitee (3) going (4) slandered (5) wistful

8. 1 2 3 4 5 — 8. (1) supersede (2) specialist (3) imaterial (4) succeed (5) professor

Answers and explanations are on page 271.

(4) The final y rule

Final *y* after a consonant changes to *i* before a suffix.

marry + ed = married
hurry + s = hurries

EXCEPTIONS:

Before a suffix beginning with *i*, the *y* is kept.

marry + ing = marrying
forty + ish = fortyish

Final *y* after a vowel is kept.

key + s = keys
coy + ly = coyly

(5) The unpronounced final e rule

Before a suffix beginning with a vowel, an unpronounced final *e* is dropped when it comes after a consonant or *u.*

revise + ion = revision
value + able = valuable

EXCEPTIONS:

When adding a suffix beginning with *a* or *o* the final *e* is kept after *c* and *g.*

trace + able = traceable
advantage + ous = advantageous

Final *ee* is considered a separate sound, so the last *e* is not dropped.

agree + able = agreeable

The unpronounced final *e* is kept before a suffix beginning with a consonant.

hate + ful = hateful
arrange + ment = arrangement

EXCEPTIONS: argument, truly, duly, wholly

(6) The es rule

Add *es* to a word ending in a *ch* combination that sounds like *church* or a final *sh* or *ss* combination.

bench + s = benches
wash + s = washes

However, when a final *ch* has the sound *k* as in *monarch,* add only *s.*

monarch + s = monarchs

SPELLING: EXERCISE 3 (PREFIX AND SUFFIX RULES 4–6)

Directions: Find the misspelled word in each group and blacken the space in the answer grid under the number that corresponds to that word.

1. (1) tried (2) noticable (3) argument (4) seeing (5) excitement — **1.** 1 2 3 4 5

2. (1) merciful (2) truest (3) roguish (4) continueance (5) migration — **2.** 1 2 3 4 5

3. 1 2 3 4 5 — 3. (1) acknowledgment (2) mischievous (3) marrage (4) courageous (5) sincerely

4. 1 2 3 4 5 — 4. (1) monarches (2) agreeable (3) truly (4) beautiful (5) accomplishment

5. 1 2 3 4 5 — 5. (1) hoped (2) happyness (3) trenches (4) allied (5) bookkeeper

6. 1 2 3 4 5 — 6. (1) valuable (2) traceable (3) wrenches (4) wholely (5) symphonies

7. 1 2 3 4 5 — 7. (1) easier (2) accommodation (3) monkies (4) twelfth (5) independent

8. 1 2 3 4 5 — 8. (1) desirable (2) pursueing (3) mysterious (4) adequately (5) precede

Answers and explanations are on page 272.

Here is a list of commonly misspelled words divided into syllables. You should study these words because they often appear on the GED and other tests.

A

absence—ab • sence
accessible—ac • ces • si • ble
accommodation—ac • com • mo • da • tion
acknowledge—ac • knowl • edge
acquire—ac • quire
actually—ac • tu • al • ly
advantage—ad • van • tage
advertised—ad • ver • tised
advice—ad • vice
agreeable—a • gree • a • ble
all right—all right
although—al • though
ambitious—am • bi • tious
annihilate—an • ni • hi • late
anonymous—a • non • y • mous
apologize—a • pol • o • gize
article—ar • ti • cle
associate—as • so • ci • ate
attendance—at • ten • dance
average—av • er • age
accept—ac • cept
accident—ac • ci • dent
accurate—ac • cu • rate
ache—ache
acquaintance—ac • quain • tance
activity—ac • tiv • i • ty
admission—ad • mis • sion
advantageous—ad • van • ta • geous
advise—ad • vise
aisle—aisle
already—al • read • y
altogether—al • to • geth • er
analyzc—an • a • lyzc
anxious—anx • ious
apartment—a • part • ment
arrangement—ar • range • ment
artificial—ar • ti • fi • cial
athlete—ath • lete
audience—au • di • ence

B

background—back • ground
banana—ba • nan • a
bathe—bathe
before—be • fore
believe—be • lieve
bicycle—bi • cycle
bookkeeper—book • keep • er
bouquet—bou • quet
breathe—breathe
bruise—bruise
burial—bur • i • al
busy—bus • y
buy—buy
baggage—bag • gage
bandage—band • age
beautiful—beau • ti • ful
beginning—be • gin • ning
benefited—ben • e • fit • ed
biscuit—bis • cuit
bought—bought
bracelet—brace • let
brochure—bro • chure
bureaucrat—bu • reau • crat
business—busi • ness
button—but • ton

C

calendar—cal • en • dar
carburetor—car • bu • re • tor
carriage—car • riage
ceiling—ceil • ing
certificate—cer • tif • i • cate
characteristic—
char • ac • ter • is • tic
chosen—cho • sen
circumstantial—
cir • cum • stan • tial
college—col • lege
community—com • mu • ni • ty
complexion—com • plex • ion
conceivable—con • ceiv • able
consciousness—
con • scious • ness
cooperative—
co • op • er • a • tive
correspond—cor • re • spond
courteous—cour • te • ous
culture—cul • ture
curious—cu • ri • ous
customer—cus • tom • er
campaign—cam • paign
caricature—car • i • ca • ture
caution—cau • tion
cemetery—cem • e • tery
changeable—change • a • ble
chimney—chim • ney
chocolate—choc • o • late
Christian—Chris • tian
cloth—cloth
clothes—clothes
committee—com • mit • tee
comparative—
com • par • a • tive
connoisseur—con • nois • seur
consent—con • sent
convenience—con • ve • nience
cordial—cor • dial
corporation—cor • po • ra • tion
country—coun • try
criticize—crit • i • cize
cupboard—cup • board
curriculum—cur • ric • u • lum

D

deceit—de • ceit
delicious—de • li • cious
dependent—de • pen • dent
desert—de • sert or des • ert
definite—def • i • nite
delivery—de • liv • ery
descendant—de • scen • dant
desirable—de • sir • able

desperate—des • per • ate
develop—de • vel • op
device—de • vice
dictionary—dic • tio • nary
diligent—dil • i • gent
disappear—dis • ap • pear
discipline—dis • ci • pline
diseased—dis • eased
distinguish—dis • tin • guish
dessert—des • sert
development—de • vel • op • ment
devise—de • vise
different—dif • fer • ent
dining—din • ing
disappoint—dis • ap • point
discourage—dis • cour • age
dissatisfied—dis • sat • is • fied
donor—do • nor

E

earnest—ear • nest
ecstatic—ec • stat • ic
efficient—ef • fi • cient
electricity—elec • tric • i • ty
enemies—en • e • mies
enough—enough
envelop—en • vel • op
equipment—equip • ment
European—Eu • ro • pe • an
exceptional—ex • cep • tion • al
exercise—ex • er • cise
exhibit—ex • hib • it
expensive—ex • pen • sive
explanation—ex • pla • na • tion
exuberant—ex • u • ber • ant
ecology—ecol • o • gy
education—ed • u • ca • tion
eighteen—eigh • teen
embarrass—em • bar • rass
engineer—en • gi • neer
enthusiasm—en • thu • si • asm
environment—en • vi • ron • ment
excellence—ex • cel • lence
executive—ex • ec • u • tive
exhaustion—ex • haus • tion
exhilaration—ex • hil • a • ra • tion
extremely—ex • treme • ly

F

familiar—fa • mil • iar
fascination—fas • ci • na • tion
fasten—fas • ten
February—Feb • ru • ary
financial—fi • nan • cial
fortunate—for • tu • nate
forum—fo • rum
freight—freight
fulfillment—ful • fill • ment
furniture—fur • ni • ture
further—fur • ther
famous—fa • mous
fascism—fas • cism
favorite—fa • vor • ite
fierce—fierce
foreign—for • eign
forty—for • ty
fourteen—four • teen
frequently—fre • quent • ly
fundamentally—fun • da • men • tal • ly

G

gaiety—gai • ety
gauge—gauge
genuine—gen • u • ine
government—gov • ern • ment
garage—ga • rage
generous—gen • er • ous
geometry—ge • om • e • try
gradually—grad • u • al • ly

grammar—gram • mar
guardian—guard • ian
guilty—guilt • y
great—great
guidance—guid • ance

H

handkerchief—hand • ker • chief
harassment—ha • rass • ment
height—height
hereditary—he • red • i • tary
honorable—hon • or • able
hypocrisy—hy • poc • ri • sy
happened—hap • pened
headache—head • ache
hereafter—here • af • ter
hero—he • ro
hygiene—hy • giene

I

illustrate—il • lus • trate
improvement—im • prove • ment
independence—in • de • pen • dence
inevitable—in • ev • i • ta • ble
inoculate—in • oc • u • late
insurance—in • sur • ance
intelligent—in • tel • li • gent
interrupt—in • ter • rupt
irrigate—ir • ri • gate
imagine—imag • ine
incidentally—in • ci • den • tal • ly
individual—in • di • vid • u • al
influential—in • flu •en • tial
instructor—in • struc • tor
intellectual—in • tel • lec • tu • al
interfere—in • ter • fere
irrelevant—ir • rel • e • vant

J

Japanese—Jap • a • nese
jewelry—jew • el • ry
junior—ju • nior
jealous—jeal • ous
judge—judge

K

kerosene—ker • o • sene
knives—knives
knowledge—knowl • edge
kindergarten—kin • der • gar • ten
known—known

L

language—lan • guage
league—league
lengthy—length • y
literature—lit • er • a • ture
luxury—lux • u • ry
laryngitis—lar • yn • gi • tis
leisure—lei • sure
liquor—li • quor
losing—los • ing

M

machinery—ma • chin • ery
management—man • age • ment
maintenance—main • te • nance
maneuver—ma • neu • ver

manufacture—man • u • fac • ture
mechanical—me • chan • i • cal
mineral—min • er • al
minute—min • ute or mi • nute
misspelling—mis • spell • ing
mysterious—mys • te • ri • ous
marriage—mar • riage
martyr—mar • tyr
message—mes • sage
miniature—min • ia • ture
mischievous—mis • chie • vous
mountain—moun • tain

N

national—na • tion • al
necessary—nec • es • sary
nephew—neph • ew
newspaper—news • pa • per
nineteen—nine • teen
noticeable—no • tice • able
naturally—nat • u • ral • ly
neither—nei • ther
neurosis—neu • ro • sis
niece—niece
ninth—ninth

O

obedience—obe • di • ence
occasional—oc • ca • sion • al
officially—of • fi • cial • ly
opportunity—op • por • tu • ni • ty
orphan—or • phan
obligation—ob • li • ga • tion
occurring—oc • cur • ring
omitted—o • mit • ted
orchestra—or • ches • tra
original—orig • i • nal
outrageous—out • ra • geous

P

pamphlet—pam • phlet
parliament—par • lia • ment
permanent—per • ma • nent
phenomenal—phe • nom • e • nal
picnicking—pic • nick • ing
pleasant—pleas • ant
politics—pol • i • tics
potatoes—po • ta • toes
prevalent—prev • a • lent
procedure—pro • ce • dure
psychology—psy • chol • o • gy
parallel—par • al • lel
particular—par • tic • u • lar
permission—per • mis • sion
physician—phy • si • cian
playwright—play • wright
pneumonia—pneu • mo • nia
possession—pos • ses • sion
precious—pre • cious
privilege—priv • i • lege
proceed—pro • ceed

Q

question—ques • tion
quite—quite
quietly—qui • et • ly
quotation—quo • ta • tion

R

rebel—reb • el or re • bel
receive—re • ceive
receipt—re • ceipt
referred—re • ferred

relieve—re • lieve
reminiscence—
rem • i • nis • cence
requested—re • quest • ed
resourceful—re • source • ful
restaurant—res • tau • rant
revolutionary—
rev • o • lu • tion • ary
remember—re • mem • ber
representative—
rep • re • sen • ta • tive
residence—res • i • dence
responsibility—
re • spon • si • bil • ity
rhyme—rhyme
rhythm—rhythm

S

sacrifice—sac • ri • fice
savage—sav • age
schedule—sched • ule
science—sci • ence
seize—seize
siege—siege
society—so • ci • ety
straight—straight
studying—study • ing
superintendent—
su • per • in • ten • dent
symmetry—sym • me • try
safety—safe • ty
scenery—scen • ery
school—school
secretary—sec • re • tary
separate—sep • a • rate
signature—sig • na • ture
standard—stan • dard
strength—strength
succeed—suc • ceed
supersede—su • per • sede
surgeon—sur • geon

T

temperature—tem • per • a • ture
territory—ter • ri • to • ry
theoretically—
the • o • ret • i • cal • ly
thousandth—thou • sandth
tongue—tongue
transcendent—tran • scen • dent
truth—truth
tendency—ten • den • cy
themselves—them • selves
therefore—there • fore
thorough—thor • ough
tomorrow—to • mor • row
tragedy—trag • e • dy
traveling—trav • el • ing
twelfth—twelfth

U

undoubtedly—
un • doubt • ed • ly
unfortunately—
un • for • tu • nate • ly
until—un • til
unforgettable—
un • for • get • ta • ble
universal—uni • ver • sal
unnatural—un • nat • u • ral
usually—usu • al • ly

V

vacuum—vac • u • um
varied—var • ied
vehicle—ve • hi • cle
valuable—val • u • able
vegetable—veg • e • ta • ble
versatile—ver • sa • tile

village—vil • lage
villain—vil • lain
volunteer—vol • un • teer

W

weather—weath • er
Wednesday—Wednes • day
whether—wheth • er
whisper—whis • per
whole—whole
withhold—with • hold
women—wom • en
worse—worse
wrist—wrist
written—writ • ten

Y

yacht—yacht
yesterday—yes • ter • day
young—young
yourselves—your • selves

ANSWERS AND EXPLANATIONS—SPELLING: EXERCISES

EXERCISE 1 (RULES 1–3)

1. **(2)** Unless the *i* and *e* combination follows the letter *c* or has the sound *ay* as in *day,* the order is *ie.*
2. **(5)** *Weigh* sounds like *way.*
3. **(1)** This combination does not have the *ay* sound. The correct spelling is *mischief.*
4. **(5)** *Seize* is an exception to the *i* and *e* combination rule.
5. **(2)** The *ie* combination here does not follow the letter *c* and does not sound like *ay*. Therefore, the spelling should be *brief.*
6. **(3)** *Supersede* is the only word in English that ends in *sede.*
7. **(2)** *Exceed* is one of a few words with the *ceed* ending.
8. **(3)** *Succeed* is one of the small group of words that end in *ceed.*
9. **(4)** *Wolf* is one of the words ending in *f* that changes to *ves* in the plural.
10. **(5)** The plural of *roof* is *roofs.* Not all words ending in *f* change to *ves* in the plural.

EXERCISE 2 (PREFIX AND SUFFIX RULES 1–3)

1. **(1)** A prefix is generally added to a whole word. Therefore, *un* + *natural* = *unnatural.*
2. **(3)** The final consonant *r* is doubled with the addition of the suffix *ence* when the stress is on the final syllable.
3. **(5)** The stress is on the first syllable, so the final consonant *l* should not be doubled with the addition of the suffix *ize.*
4. **(1)** The correct spelling is *canceled* because the stress is not on the last syllable before the suffix.
5. **(1)** Double the final consonant because the stress is on the last syllable before the suffix in con-TROL.
6. **(4)** Although the stress is on the first syllable in *metal,* with the addition of a suffix the stress changes, so the final consonant should be doubled.
7. **(2)** Following the *rule of stress,* the spelling should be *committee.*
8. **(3)** Add the prefix *im* to the whole word *material.*

EXERCISE 3 (PREFIX AND SUFFIX RULES 4–6)

1. **(2)** When adding a suffix that begins with *a* or *o*, the unpronounced final *e* is kept if the consonant before it is *c* or *g*.
2. **(4)** Generally, the unpronounced final *e* is dropped when a suffix that begins with a vowel is added.
3. **(3)** A final *y* changes to *i* when a suffix beginning with any vowel but *i* is added.
4. **(1)** Add only *s* when a final *ch* sounds like *k*.
5. **(2)** In adding a suffix, change a final *y* to *i* when there is a consonant before it.
6. **(4)** *Wholly* is an exception to the rule that a prefix or suffix is added to the complete word.
7. **(3)** Keep the final *y* in adding a suffix when there is a vowel before it.
8. **(2)** An unpronounced final *e* is usually dropped when a suffix beginning with a vowel is added.

SPELLING: REVIEW TEST

Directions: In each group there are four words spelled correctly and one word misspelled. Blacken the space in the answer grid under the number that corresponds to the number of the incorrectly spelled word.

1. (1) language (2) financal (3) cloth (4) buy (5) famous — **1.** 1 2 3 4 5

2. (1) fierce (2) liquor (3) unecessary (4) fulfillment (5) jealous — **2.** 1 2 3 4 5

3. (1) device (2) bruise (3) refered (4) sampled (5) dessert — **3.** 1 2 3 4 5

4. (1) league (2) minute (3) releive (4) mountain (5) acquire — **4.** 1 2 3 4 5

5. (1) martyr (2) paralel (3) imagine (4) sloping (5) parallel — **5.** 1 2 3 4 5

6. (1) junior (2) accepted (3) seperate (4) luxury (5) known — **6.** 1 2 3 4 5

7. (1) admission (2) safety (3) develop (4) territory (5) recept — **7.** 1 2 3 4 5

8. (1) tomorrow (2) straight (3) relieve (4) herditary (5) ninth — **8.** 1 2 3 4 5

9. (1) surgon (2) height (3) timidity (4) actual (5) pleasure — **9.** 1 2 3 4 5

10. (1) dissassociate (2) fibrous (3) abbreviate (4) bicycle (5) acknowledge — **10.** 1 2 3 4 5

11. (1) prevalent (2) privalege (3) principle (4) satisfactory (5) precious — **11.** 1 2 3 4 5

12. (1) obedience (2) eloquent (3) totaly (4) sagely (5) mortgage — **12.** 1 2 3 4 5

13. (1) reverent (2) spacious (3) wholly (4) gregarious (5) caracteristic — **13.** 1 2 3 4 5

14. 1 2 3 4 5 — 14. (1) upsetting (2) enviroment (3) exceptional (4) whisper (5) implacable

15. 1 2 3 4 5 — 15. (1) concious (2) regiment (3) bought (4) stationery (5) terrestial

16. 1 2 3 4 5 — 16. (1) equipment (2) savege (3) complexion (4) straight (5) instructor

17. 1 2 3 4 5 — 17. (1) beautiful (2) twelfth (3) maintainance (4) midwives (5) exhausted

18. 1 2 3 4 5 — 18. (1) apartment (2) requested (3) standerd (4) biscuit (5) caricature

19. 1 2 3 4 5 — 19. (1) bandage (2) individual (3) component (4) tonge (5) semblance

20. 1 2 3 4 5 — 20. (1) analyze (2) different (3) cordial (4) antisocial (5) acheivement

21. 1 2 3 4 5 — 21. (1) forty (2) anxious (3) hygiene (4) oportunity (5) argument

22. 1 2 3 4 5 — 22. (1) anxiety (2) business (3) abcent (4) kerosene (5) alphabetically

23. 1 2 3 4 5 — 23. (1) miserable (2) coordinate (3) European (4) safty (5) fission

24. 1 2 3 4 5 — 24. (1) vigilant (2) distress (3) comittee (4) stubbornness (5) national

25. 1 2 3 4 5 — 25. (1) preposition (2) paculiar (3) session (4) desperate (5) occurred

Answers and explanations are on pages 275–276.

ANSWERS AND EXPLANATIONS— SPELLING: REVIEW TEST

1. **(2)** The correct spelling is *financial.*
2. **(3)** Additions to either the beginning or end of a word are generally added to the whole word. The correct spelling is *unnecessary.*
3. **(3)** In adding to the end of a word, if the last syllable is stressed the consonant is doubled before the new ending. The correct spelling is *referred.*
4. **(3)** The rule for an *i* and *e* combination is as follows: except after *c* or when the sound is *ay* as in *weigh, i* goes before *e.* The correct spelling is *relieve.*
5. **(2)** The correct spelling is *parallel.*
6. **(3)** This commonly misspelled word is *separate.* To keep it in your mind, remember that there is *a rat* in this word.
7. **(5)** The correct spelling is *receipt.*
8. **(4)** The correct spelling is *hereditary.*
9. **(1)** The correct spelling is *surgeon.*
10. **(1)** See the explanation for question *2* above (*dis* + *associate* = *disassociate*).
11. **(2)** The correct spelling is *privilege.*
12. **(3)** The correct spelling is *totally* (*total* + *ly*).
13. **(5)** The correct spelling is *characteristic.*
14. **(2)** This commonly misspelled word is *environment.*
15. **(1)** The correct spelling is *conscious.*
16. **(2)** The correct spelling is *savage.*
17. **(3)** The correct spelling is *maintenance.*
18. **(3)** The correct spelling is *standard.*
19. **(4)** The correct spelling is *tongue.*
20. **(5)** See the explanation for question *4* above. The correct spelling is *achievement.*
21. **(4)** The correct spelling is *opportunity.*

22. **(3)** The correct spelling is *absent.*

23. **(4)** Unpronounced final *e*'s are kept when adding an ending that begins with a consonant (all letters except a, e, i, o, and u). The correct spelling is *safety.*

24. **(3)** The correct spelling is *committee.*

25. **(2)** The correct spelling is *peculiar.*

SPELLING EVALUATION CHART

Question Type	*Review Pages*	*Question Number*	*Amount of Question Type*	*Number of Wrong Answers*
A. Commonly Misspelled Words	264–270	1, 5, 6, 8, 9, 11, 13, 14, 15, 16, 17, 18, 19, 21, 22, 24, 25	17	______
B. Addition of Prefixes and Suffixes	260–261	2, 10, 12	3	______
C. The Stress Rule	261	3	1	______
D. i + e Combination	258	4, 7, 20	3	______
E. Unpronounced Final e	263	23	1	______

PASSING SCORE: 20 right out of 25 questions

YOUR SCORE: ______ right out of 25 questions

If you have more than three questions wrong in category A or any question wrong in any other category, you should reread the explanation of that type of problem in the review pages listed in the table.

FINAL WRITING SKILLS INVENTORY

The following one hundred questions are typical of the types of questions you will find on the GED test. Work through this section as though you were actually taking the test. Give yourself approximately one and one-half hours and do not take a break. The GED test requires a good amount of endurance.

The Final Writing Skills Inventory should give you an idea of what taking the actual GED test is like. Refer to the evaluation that follows the Answers and Explanations in order to determine which areas you need to review before you take the GED test.

SPELLING

Directions: In each of the following groups of words, one word is misspelled. Blacken the space in the answer grid under the number that corresponds to the misspelled word.

1. (1) receive (2) obliterate (3) measureing (4) sponsor (5) virtual — **1.** 1 2 3 4 5

2. (1) tripod (2) occurence (3) traveler (4) transparent (5) twelfth — **2.** 1 2 3 4 5

3. (1) supersede (2) elfs (3) illiterate (4) carnage (5) succulent — **3.** 1 2 3 4 5

4. (1) bicycle (2) severe (3) effect (4) criticle (5) moderation — **4.** 1 2 3 4 5

5. (1) resede (2) vocation (3) nonjudgmental (4) tardiness (5) dissolve — **5.** 1 2 3 4 5

6. (1) cushioned (2) baitted (3) neighbor (4) disappoint (5) costumes — **6.** 1 2 3 4 5

7. (1) hurricane (2) vanishes (3) fragrant (4) mischievous (5) reciepts — **7.** 1 2 3 4 5

8. (1) elusive (2) rhythm (3) mysticism (4) capible (5) prominent — **8.** 1 2 3 4 5

9\. 1 2 3 4 5

9\. (1) seperate (2) telescope (3) stadium (4) deficient (5) exercise

10\. 1 2 3 4 5

10\. (1) excellent (2) bacteria (3) spectater (4) photographer (5) lamb

CAPITALIZATION

Directions: In each of the following sentences, four letters have been underlined. If one of these letters represents a capitalization error, blacken the space in the answer grid under the number that corresponds to it. If there is no error, blacken the space numbered (5).

11\. 1 2 3 4 5

11\. The main character in the movie [1] entitled *Fiddler* [2] *on the* [3] *Roof* used to have conversations with god [4]. No error [5]

12\. 1 2 3 4 5

12\. Look for the highway signs on the edge of town [1] where Oak Avenue [2] runs into Twenty-Eighth [3] Street [4]. No error [5]

13\. 1 2 3 4 5

13\. Last Spring [1], the Jones [2] family [3] moved to South [4] America. No error [5]

14\. 1 2 3 4 5

14\. Dear sir [1]:

Please return Playtoy [2], Incorporated's [3] check.

Sincerely yours [4],

Tom True

No error [5]

15\. 1 2 3 4 5

15\. Her father [1], Dr. [2] Kimball, is the best Surgeon [3] in the East [4]. No error [5]

16\. 1 2 3 4 5

16\. Listen, mother [1], you buy that magazine [2], and I'll get *The* [3] *Daily Chronicle* [4]. No error [5]

PUNCTUATION

Directions: In each of the following sentences, four possible places for punctuation have been underlined. If there is an error in punctuation at this place in the sentence, blacken the space in the answer grid under the number that corresponds to it. If there is no error, blacken the space numbered (5).

17. Jack's father in-law wanted only three things: the money, the woman, and the glory. No error
(1: Jack's; 2: father_in-law; 3: things:; 4: woman,; 5: No error)
17. 1 2 3 4 5

18. Lt. Williams replied, "No way, son". No error
(1: Lt.; 2: replied,; 3: "; 4: ".; 5: No error)
18. 1 2 3 4 5

19. It seems, that knee-length skirts were "in" that year. No error
(1: seems,; 2: knee-length; 3: "in"; 4: year.; 5: No error)
19. 1 2 3 4 5

20. "Why, you don't say!" exclaimed Mrs. Johnson. No error
(1: don't; 2: !; 3: "; 4: Mrs.; 5: No error)
20. 1 2 3 4 5

21. In his latest book, Kingster wrote, ". . . [after his death] she mourned for years'." No error
(1: his_latest; 2: book,; 3: . . .; 4: years'."; 5: No error)
21. 1 2 3 4 5

22. Something about him seemed strange; in some way he had changed? Was Morris's romance over? No error
(1: strange;; 2: changed?; 3: Morris's; 4: over?; 5: No error)
22. 1 2 3 5

23. In a fit of anger, she threw down the map (maps always gave her so much trouble), and screamed into the telephone for a bottle of scotch to be sent to her room. No error
(1: anger,; 2: (maps always gave her so much trouble); 3:),; 4: telephone_for; 5: No error)
23. 1 2 3 4 5

24. If, as the old saying goes, Absence makes the heart grow fonder," try to explain this: Sarah's beloved Bill married Lisa when Sarah was away. No error
(1: If,; 2: _Absence; 3: fonder,"; 4: this:; 5: No error)
24. 1 2 3 4 5

25. 1 2 3 4 5

25. The following products arrived today: Lemonsweet, a new soap;
1
Wate-away, a weight reduction tablet; and Fostor, an anti-acne
2 3
cream. No error
4 5

GRAMMAR AND USAGE

Directions: In each of the following sentences, four words have been underlined. If one of these words represents an error in grammar or usage, blacken the space in the answer grid under the number that corresponds to it. If there is no error, blacken the space numbered (5).

26. 1 2 3 4 5

26 If you want to find there telephone number, you should look
1 2 3
in the directory. No error
4 5

27. 1 2 3 4 5

27. The dogs' toy and its bowl lay next to each other. No error
1 2 3 4 5

28. 1 2 3 4 5

28. Either this or that article is more longer than that one. No error
1 2 3 4 5

29. 1 2 3 4 5

29. The truck driver shouted that he would run over anyone that
1 2 3
got in his way. No error
4 5

30. 1 2 3 4 5

30. Medicine has a stronger effect on children then on adults.
1 2 3 4
No error
5

31. 1 2 3 4 5

31. John Duane, as well as Stan Davis, have a great deal of charm
1 2 3
and money. No error
4 5

32. 1 2 3 4 5

32. Many people prefer Sarah's cooking to Ross's. No error
1 2 3 4 5

33. Her doctor said that she had looked healthily on the day she
1 2 3 4
died. No error
5
33. 1 2 3 4 5

34. Raise the window besides the heater if it gets too hot. No error
1 2 3 4 5
34. 1 2 3 4 5

35. Neither this kind of man or that one is honestly trying to earn
1 2 3 4
a living. No error
5
35. 1 2 3 4 5

36. The bell would have rung early if the principal had went to
1 2 3 4
Washington. No error
5
36. 1 2 3 4 5

37. What occasion were their dresses bought for? No error
1 2 3 4 5
37. 1 2 3 4 5

38. Is you implying that policewomen consider themselves equal?
1 2 3 4
No error
5
38. 1 2 3 4 5

39. Each person is expected to take an interest in his schoolwork.
1 2 3 4
No error
5
39. 1 2 3 4 5

40. Deer have run here for twenty years'. No error
1 2 3 4 5
40. 1 2 3 4 5

41. After the movie, when you have set the table, see that the
1 2
curtains are hunged up. No error
3 4 5
41. 1 2 3 4 5

42. A friendly spider has woven a web for hisself. No error
1 2 3 4 5
42. 1 2 3 4 5

43. People do whatever they want and speak to whoever they please.
1 2 3 4
No error
5
43. 1 2 3 4 5

44. 1 2 3 4 5

44. The hostesses [1] made [2] sure that everyone [3] had had [4] enough to eat. No error [5]

45. 1 2 3 4 5

45. The car looks real [1] good [2], but it's [3] too [4] expensive. No error [5]

46. 1 2 3 4 5

46. These [1] species [2] belong [3] of [4] the same family. No error [5]

47. 1 2 3 4 5

47. When you go to [1] the party, why [2] don't you bring [3] a [4] camera? No error [5]

48. 1 2 3 4 5

48. The fish [1] is [2] in a tank under the stairs, so they can't be seen [3] easily [4]. No error [5]

49. 1 2 3 4 5

49. Although David was [1] not a lawyer, he can refer [2] you to [3] the proper [4] authority. No error [5]

50. 1 2 3 4 5

50. The reason for his constant headaches [1] are [2] the fumes from the gas with [3] which he works [4]. No error [5]

51. 1 2 3 4 5

51. The fastest [1] train takes five hours [2], but [3] the more comfortable [4] of all takes eight. No error [5]

52. 1 2 3 4 5

52. The man hid behind [1] a tree so that [2] the girl will [3] not see him [4]. No error [5]

53. 1 2 3 4 5

53. Jack, Bill, and me [1] are going to call Susan and him [2] as soon as we get [3] there [4]. No error [5]

54. Working (1) in that neighborhood is (2) dangerous (3) and had been (4) for some time. No error (5)

54. 1 2 3 4 5

55. She (1) was angry to (2) him (3) because he read (4) her mail. No error (5)

55. 1 2 3 4 5

STYLE AND DICTION

Directions: If one of the answers corrects or improves the style or word choice of the underlined segment, blacken the space under the number corresponding to it. If no answer improves the underlined part, blacken the space numbered (5).

56. When he saw the gun, the prisoner went into a panic.

56. 1 2 3 4 5

(1) goes into a panic
(2) got panicky
(3) panicked
(4) went into a terrible panic
(5) No change

57. In the interest of preserving my reputation, I hereby call it quits.

57. 1 2 3 4 5

(1) quit
(2) call the case quits
(3) endeavor to terminate services
(4) resign
(5) No change

58. The train traveled very slowly through the mountain pass.

58. 1 2 3 4 5

(1) crept
(2) went
(3) traveled extremely slowly
(4) zoomed
(5) No change

59. The beauty of the church's stained glass windows really knocked me out.

59. 1 2 3 4 5

(1) was like nothing I had ever seen before
(2) knocked me out
(3) was truly superb
(4) overwhelmed me
(5) No change

60. 1 2 3 4 5

60. Can I be of assistance with the boat, Sam?

(1) serve as assistant
(2) assist
(3) help
(4) render any necessary services
(5) No change

61. 1 2 3 4 5

61. The children rolled over and over in the snow.

(1) played
(2) frolicked
(3) fought
(4) tumbled
(5) No change

62. 1 2 3 4 5

62. He clawed his way to the top like a killer shark.

(1) like a shark
(2) as if he were a killer shark
(3) like a snake
(4) like a bear
(5) No change

63. 1 2 3 4 5

63. That guy in the drugstore with the stupid uniform on sure has an outgoing personality, doesn't he?

(1) outrageous
(2) ebullient
(3) awful
(4) interesting
(5) No change

64. 1 2 3 4 5

64. The story had a morale at the end.

(1) morass
(2) more
(3) moor
(4) moral
(5) No change

65. 1 2 3 4 5

65. As a person becomes older, he gains wisdom.

(1) A person knows more as he becomes older.
(2) The older a person becomes, the wiser he gets.
(3) It is oftentimes said that a person gains wisdom as he becomes older, or so I am told.
(4) When you get older, you will gain wisdom.
(5) No change

66. Jane wore a yellow dress to the office party. She looks good in yellow. **66.** 1 2 3 4 5

(1) Jane wore a yellow dress to the office party because she looks good in yellow.
(2) Jane, wearing a yellow dress to the office party, looks good in yellow.
(3) Jane looks good in yellow and wore a yellow dress to the office party.
(4) Jane wore a yellow dress (she looks good in yellow) to the office party.
(5) No change

67. Dr. Doe, a hard-working doctor, performed the operation. **67.** 1 2 3 4 5

(1) A hard-working doctor named Dr. Doe performed the operation.
(2) Because of Dr. Doe, a hard-working doctor, the operation was performed.
(3) The man performing the operation was Dr. Doe, a hard-working doctor.
(4) Dr. Doe, because he is a hard-working doctor, performed the operation.
(5) No change

68. Tom and his friends climbed hastily and somewhat clumsily over the fence. **68.** 1 2 3 4 5

(1) jumped
(2) scrambled
(3) burrowed
(4) stole
(5) No change

69. Professor, I was, unfortunately, unable to catch your final statement. **69.** 1 2 3 4 5

(1) make out
(2) dig
(3) distinguish
(4) hear
(5) No change

70. My friends think that I should find something to do with myself in my spare time. **70.** 1 2 3 4 5

(1) something to do in my spare time
(2) a spare-time activity
(3) a hobby
(4) something new to do
(5) No change

SENTENCE STRUCTURE

Directions: If a sentence has faulty structure, blacken the space under the number corresponding to the corrected version of it. If the sentence is correct, blacken the space numbered (5).

71. 1 2 3 4 5

71. Give it back.

(1) You should give it back.
(2) Give it here.
(3) I said to give it back.
(4) Give the money back.
(5) No change

72. 1 2 3 4 5

72. Whistling a happy tune.

(1) Whistling a happy tune and playing the guitar.
(2) They whistling a happy tune.
(3) They were whistling a happy tune.
(4) Whistling a happy tune?
(5) No change

73. 1 2 3 4 5

73. The saleswoman had tried to give up cigarettes and going on a diet.

(1) The saleswoman had tried giving up cigarettes and to go on a diet.
(2) There were two things the saleswoman tried to do: to give up cigarettes and going on a diet.
(3) The saleswoman was unsuccessful in going on a diet and to give up cigarettes.
(4) The saleswoman had tried to give up cigarettes and to go on a diet.
(5) No change

74. 1 2 3 4 5

74. Even though he bought the car in 1952.

(1) Although he bought the car in 1952.
(2) Even though he bought the car in 1952, it still runs.
(3) Even though he bought the car in 1952, still runs.
(4) Even though the car was bought in 1952.
(5) No change

75. 1 2 3 4 5

75. Experts can predict earthquakes now and they say that a big one will occur in California.

(1) Experts can predict earthquakes now, and say that a big one will occur in California.
(2) Experts can predict earthquakes now so they say that a big one will occur in California.
(3) Although experts can predict earthquakes now, they say that a big one will occur in California.

(4) Experts can predict earthquakes now, and they say that a big one will occur in California.
(5) No change

76. Latin music has a good beat, it makes people want to dance. **76.** 1 2 3 4 5

(1) Latin music has a good beat, so it makes people want to dance.
(2) Latin music has a good beat it makes people want to dance.
(3) Latin music, has a good beat, it makes people want to dance.
(4) Latin music has a good beat before it makes people want to dance.
(5) No change

77. Despite the fact that Frank works hard all day, he finds time for his family. **77.** 1 2 3 4 5

(1) Because Frank works hard all day, he finds time for his family.
(2) Until Frank works hard all day, he finds time for his family.
(3) Frank works hard all day, despite the fact that he finds time for his family.
(4) Despite the fact that Frank works hard all day he finds time for his family.
(5) No change

78. The mango, a tropical fruit can be eaten in a number of ways. **78.** 1 2 3 4 5

(1) The mango a tropical fruit can be eaten in a number of ways.
(2) The mango a tropical fruit, can be eaten in a number of ways.
(3) The mango, a tropical fruit can be eaten, in a number of ways.
(4) The mango, a tropical fruit, can be eaten in a number of ways.
(5) No change

79. Bluebeard was a pirate who had many wives, and Devil's Island is now a tourist attraction. **79.** 1 2 3 4 5

(1) Bluebeard, who had many wives, was a pirate, and Devil's Island is now a tourist attraction.
(2) Bluebeard was a pirate, who had many wives; Devil's Island is now a tourist attraction.
(3) Bluebeard had many wives and was a pirate, and Devil's Island is now a tourist attraction.
(4) Bluebeard was a pirate who had many wives. Devil's Island is now a tourist attraction.
(5) No change

80. 1 2 3 4 5

80. Trying to convince the ranchers to stay in Star City, the sheriff told them the railroad would pass through soon and bring wealth to the town.

(1) As he convinced the ranchers to stay in Star City, the sheriff told them the railroad would pass through soon and bring wealth to the town.
(2) He tried to convince the ranchers to stay in Star City, so the sheriff told them the railroad would pass through soon and bring wealth to the town.
(3) Telling them the railroad would pass through soon and bring wealth to the town, the sheriff tried to convince the ranchers to stay in Star City.
(4) The sheriff, who tried to convince the ranchers to stay in Star City, told them the railroad would pass through soon and bring wealth to the town.
(5) No change

81. 1 2 3 4 5

81. Elephants like peanuts, to eat popcorn, and to be fed cookies.

(1) Elephants like to eat peanuts, popcorn, and to be fed cookies.
(2) Elephants like peanuts, popcorn, and to eat cookies.
(3) Elephants like to eat peanuts, popcorn, and cookies.
(4) Elephants like peanuts, to eat popcorn, and cookies.
(5) No change

82. 1 2 3 4 5

82. Just a matter of time.

(1) It just a matter of time.
(2) It's just a matter of time.
(3) In just a matter of time.
(4) Just a matter of time, right?
(5) No change

83. 1 2 3 4 5

83. She went to the concert although she hated music.

(1) She went to the concert because she hated music.
(2) She went to the concert after she hated music.
(3) She went to the concert until she hated music.
(4) She went to the concert, so she hated music.
(5) No change

84. 1 2 3 4 5

84. Having waited for an hour, went home.

(1) We having waited for an hour, went home.
(2) Having waited, for a hour, went home.
(3) Having waited for an hour, we went home.
(4) Having waited for an hour went home.
(5) No change

85. The clown pulled out a rabbit in the funny suit. **85.** 1 2 3 4 5

(1) The clown in the funny suit pulled out a rabbit.
(2) The clown, in the funny suit pulled out a rabbit.
(3) The clown pulled out a rabbit, in the funny suit.
(4) In the funny suit the clown pulled out a rabbit.
(5) No change

LOGIC AND ORGANIZATION

Directions: Read each of the following paragraphs and then answer the questions about the paragraph's logic and organization. Blacken the space in the answer grid under the number that corresponds to the answer choice that will improve the logic and organization of the paragraph.

---

[1]Several astronomers now believe that life, in some form or other, exists or existed at one time on other planets. [2]The great number of stars in our galaxy alone, approximately 250 billion, makes it unlikely that the Earth is the only planet with conditions to support life. [3]Photographs of Mars, for example, reveal mountain ranges and river-formed canyons like those found on Earth. [4]Even planets in our solar system have been found to have Earth-like terrain. [5]UFO sightings all over the world can be cited as proof. [6]Many books have been written about the possibility of life on other planets. [7]Some evidence supports this theory; it is still a theory.

86. In sentence 1, *life, in some form or other, exists* is best **86.** 1 2 3 4 5

(1) left as it is.
(2) changed to *some form of life exists*
(3) changed to *some form or other of life exists*
(4) changed to *life, in some form, exists*
(5) changed to *life exists*

87. What should be done with sentence 3? **87.** 1 2 3 4 5

(1) It should be left as it is.
(2) It should be omitted.
(3) It should be joined to sentence 4 with *thus.*
(4) It should follow sentence 4.
(5) It should follow sentence 6.

88. 1 2 3 4 5

88. Sentence 5 would be improved if it were changed to read

(1) These life forms may have tried to contact us, and UFO sightings all over the world can be cited as proof.
(2) And, too, UFO sightings all over the world can be cited as proof.
(3) But you don't need to see photographs of Mars; UFO sightings all over the world can be cited as proof.
(4) UFO sightings all over the world tend to prove this theory.
(5) UFO sightings all over the world can be cited as further proof of the possibility of life on other planets.

89. 1 2 3 4 5

89. What should be done with sentence 6?

(1) It should be left as it is.
(2) It should be omitted.
(3) It should be moved to the end of the paragraph.
(4) It were lengthened to include some of the titles of these books.
(5) A period should be placed after *possibility,* and the rest of the sentence should be omitted.

90. 1 2 3 4 5

90. Sentence 7 would be improved if it were changed to read

(1) Although some evidence supports this theory, it is still a theory.
(2) Evidence supports this theory, but it is still a theory.
(3) Some evidence does support this theory.
(4) Nevertheless, all this is still a theory.
(5) This theory is still a theory.

[1]The beginning of anything new is always strangely upsetting. [2]Starting a new job always gives me the feeling that little men are running back and forth inside my stomach. [3]"Will I be liked by the people with whom I work?" is the first question that gnaws at me. [4]Then, "Will my boss like what I'm doing?" [5]That first night after working on a new job, I need at least three stiff drinks to calm my nerves. [6]Starting a new friendship has the same effect on me. [7]I never know if I've made a good impression. [8]I'm always sure that I've done or said precisely the wrong thing. [9]It's a wonder that I don't have an ulcer!

91. 1 2 3 4 5

91. In sentence 2, *gives me the feeling that little men are running back and forth inside my stomach* is best

(1) left as it is.
(2) changed to *gives me the feeling that something is wrong with my stomach*
(3) changed to *upsets my stomach*
(4) changed to *gives me an upset stomach*
(5) changed to *ruins my digestion*

92. Sentence 4 should begin **92.** 1 2 3 4 5

(1) *Then I wonder,*
(2) *My next question is*
(3) *Next,*
(4) *Even worse,*
(5) *In addition,*

93. If this paragraph is to be divided into two paragraphs, the second paragraph should begin with **93.** 1 2 3 4 5

(1) sentence 2.
(2) sentence 3.
(3) sentence 5.
(4) sentence 6.
(5) sentence 9.

94. What should be done with sentence 8? **94.** 1 2 3 4 5

(1) It should be left as it is.
(2) It should be omitted.
(3) It should be joined to sentence 7 with a semicolon.
(4) It should be joined to sentence 7 with *and.*
(5) It should begin with *Although.*

95. Sentence 9 would be improved if it began **95.** 1 2 3 4 5

(1) as it begins now.
(2) *With all of life's new experiences,*
(3) *In fact,*
(4) *With my upset stomach,*
(5) *The way I worry,*

Directions: In the following paragraphs, one part of the paragraph has been underlined. If the underlined section is improved or explained by one of the answer choices given, blacken the space in the answer grid under the number that corresponds to it. If no answer choice improves or explains it, blacken the space numbered (5).

---

96. Entertainers often lead very unhappy lives. The loneliness of the club and concert world, together with the pressure from competition and the lack of privacy, makes many people in show business feel depressed and unloved. Depression is not restricted to people in the performing arts. **96.** 1 2 3 4 5

(1) This sentence is the topic sentence.
(2) This sentence is a transition.
(3) This sentence should begin the paragraph.
(4) This sentence should begin a new paragraph.
(5) No change

97. 1 2 3 4 5

97. To break down the two games into component parts, it is logical to start with the similarities since they outnumber the differences.

(1) Change to: *To trace the history of the two games,*
(2) Change to: *To explain how the two games are played,*
(3) Change to: *To point out the cause and effect relationship between the two games,*
(4) Change to: *To compare and contrast the two games,*
(5) No change

98. 1 2 3 4 5

98. Children often ask where rain comes from. Science books tell them that rain is only one part of the earth's water cycle. All water on earth in the oceans, lakes, rivers, and containers evaporates slowly into the air. When conditions of pressure and temperature cause the evaporated water to fall to the surface of the earth, it is said to be raining.

(1) The paragraph lacks a topic sentence.
(2) The paragraph lacks supporting evidence.
(3) The order of the sentences is incorrect.
(4) The sentences are not logically connected.
(5) No change

99. 1 2 3 4 5

99. Many people are frightened at the sight of a black cat. Open ladders are generally walked around, not under. Few buildings have a floor numbered 13.

(1) This paragraph lacks a topic sentence.
(2) The paragraph lacks supporting evidence.
(3) The order of the sentences is incorrect.
(4) The sentences are not logically related.
(5) No change

100. 1 2 3 4 5

100. The apartment is not conveniently located. However, the rent is too high.

(1) Change to: *Generally,*
(2) Change to: *Besides,*
(3) Change to: *In summary,*
(4) Change to: *Regardless,*
(5) No change

ANSWERS AND EXPLANATIONS— FINAL WRITING SKILLS AND INVENTORY

SPELLING

1. **(3)** An unpronounced final *e* is dropped when an ending beginning with *i* is added; the correct spelling is *measuring.*
2. **(2)** When the stress is on the last syllable in a word ending with a consonant, the final consonant is doubled with the addition of a suffix if the vowel in the syllable does not say its name; the correct spelling is *occurrence.*
3. **(2)** Many words ending in *f* change to *ves* in the plural; the correct plural is *elves.*
4. **(4)** The correct spelling is *critical.*
5. **(1)** The correct spelling is *recede.*
6. **(2)** When a vowel or vowel combination says the name of a vowel, the final consonant is not doubled with the addition of a suffix; the correct spelling is *baited.*
7. **(5)** The *i* and *e* combination rule goes as follows: Only after *c* or when having the sound *ay* does *e* go before *i.* The correct spelling is *receipts.*
8. **(4)** The correct spelling is *capable.*
9. **(1)** The correct spelling is *separate.*
10. **(3)** The correct spelling is *spectator.*

CAPITALIZATION

11. **(4)** All words that name or refer to God are capitalized.
12. **(3)** The second number in names consisting of a hyphenated number is not capitalized.
13. **(1)** The names of the seasons are not capitalized.
14. **(1)** Important words in a letter greeting are capitalized.
15. **(3)** This is a general term, not a specific name.
16. **(1)** *Mother,* when replacing a name, should be capitalized.

PUNCTUATION

17. **(2)** Hyphens connect all parts of a compound noun.
18. **(4)** The period should be inside the closing quotation marks.

19. **(1)** The subject and the complete predicate should not be separated with a comma.

20. **(5)** No error

21. **(4)** Since there is no possession here, the apostrophe is incorrect.

22. **(2)** This is not a question, so the question mark should not be used.

23. **(3)** A comma should not split up a compound predicate; the parentheses already set off the words that only give additional information.

24. **(2)** Quotation marks should begin this quotation.

25. **(5)** No error

GRAMMAR AND USAGE

26. **(2)** The possessive pronoun *their* should be used in this sentence.

27. **(1)** The singular possessive *dog's* should be used because only one dog is being discussed. Notice that the singular possessive pronoun *its* is used, and all the other nouns are singular.

28. **(2)** In unequal comparisons between two things, the correct form is *longer than*. The use of *more* in this comparison is incorrect.

29. **(5)** No error

30. **(4)** The word *than* is used in a comparison.

31. **(2)** Words between the subject and verb do not affect agreement. The subject (*John Duane*) is singular; therefore, the singular verb *has* should be used.

32. **(5)** No error

33. **(3)** The adjective healthy should be used here. After verbs such as *appear, seem, look,* and *be,* an adjective is used if it describes the subject.

34. **(2)** The preposition *beside* meaning *next to* should be used in this sentence. *Besides* means *in addition to.*

35. **(2)** The second half of *neither* is *nor*.

36. **(4)** The past participle of *go* is *gone,* and the past participle is used after *has, have,* and *had.*

37. **(4)** The preposition *for* incorrectly falls at the end of this sentence. A sentence should never end with a preposition.

38. **(1)** The subject of this sentence is *you,* and the form of the verb that agrees with this subject is *are.*

39. **(5)** No error

40. **(4)** The possessive is incorrect here because there is no ownership or relationship that needs to be expressed.

41. **(3)** The past participle of *hang* is *hung*. *Hunged* is not a word.

42. **(4)** The correct form is *himself*.

43. **(4)** By mentally rearranging the second half of this sentence, putting the subject first, you get: "they please to speak to whomever." The object form is needed here, so it should be *whomever*.

44. **(5)** No error

45. **(1)** *Real* is an adjective. The adverb *really* is needed here because it modifies *good*, an adjective.

46. **(4)** The preposition that is correct after *belong* is *to*.

47. **(3)** *Take* would be correct here, since the sentence involves the action of carrying something *away* from the speaker.

48. **(2)** There are several fish, as indicated by the pronoun *they*, so the plural verb *are* should be used.

49. **(1)** The second verb is in the present tense, which indicates that this whole sentence is true in the present. The past tense *was* should be changed to the present tense *is*.

50. **(2)** The subject of this sentence is the singular noun *reason*, which requires the singular verb *is*.

51. **(4)** Because more than two trains are being compared, *most comfortable* is correct in this sentence.

52. **(3)** Because the main verb is in the past tense, the other verbs must be past also. Therefore, *would* is correct.

53. **(1)** The subject pronoun *I* is needed.

54. **(4)** Since this statement is still true, the present perfect tense, *has been*, should be used.

55. **(2)** *Angry* is followed by either *at* or *with*.

STYLE AND DICTION

56. **(3)** The active verb *panicked* makes the sentence stronger and saves words.

57. **(4)** Only *resign* is consistent with the formal, but direct tone of the sentence.

58. **(1)** *Crept* best expresses the meaning and saves words.

59. **(4)** This is the least "slangy" and the most direct way to state the idea.

60. **(3)** *Help* fits the informal situation and is direct.

61. **(4)** *Tumbled* best expresses the meaning and saves words.

62. **(4)** The simile involving *bear* is the only one that works because the word *clawed* was used.

63. **(5)** No change

64. **(4)** *Moral* is the correct word. *Morale* means *spirit.*

65. **(2)** The parallel structure of this sentence creates a pleasing rhythm and adds strength with the fewest possible words.

66. **(4)** Information not necessary to express the main idea is best inserted into the sentence and set off by parentheses.

67. **(5)** No change

68. **(2)** *Scrambled* best expresses the meaning and saves words.

69. **(4)** *Hear* is more formal than *catch* and therefore better in this sentence.

70. **(3)** *Hobby* expresses the same idea and saves words.

SENTENCE STRUCTURE

71. **(5)** No change. The subject of a command is understood.

72. **(3)** Only this sentence adds a subject (*they*) and completes the verb (*were* whistling).

73. **(4)** The verbs in the original sentence are not parallel. By changing *going* to *to go,* this error is corrected.

74. **(2)** The original version of this sentence is a sentence fragment The words *even though* express a contrast, but no contrast is made. By adding *it still runs,* the contrast is completed.

75. **(4)** This is a compound sentence, which requires both a conjunction (*and*) and a comma.

76. **(1)** To join two complete sentences, you must use more than a comma alone. The error is corrected by adding the conjunction *so.*

77. **(5)** No change

78. **(4)** The words *a tropical fruit* supply additional information that is not necessary for the meaning of the sentence; therefore, it should be set off with commas.

79. **(4)** Since there is no logical connection between these two complete thoughts, they should not be joined together.

80. **(5)** No change

81. **(3)** The original sentence lacks parallel structure. By eliminating the extra verbs, this error is corrected.

82. **(2)** The original sentence lacks both a subject and a verb. By adding *it's* (meaning *it is*), this error is corrected.

83. **(5)** No change

84. **(3)** The original sentence lacks a subject. By adding *we,* this error is corrected.

85. **(1)** The prepositional phrase *in the funny suit* should follow the word it modifies, *clown.* In the original sentence, the unintended meaning is that the rabbit was wearing a funny suit.

LOGIC AND ORGANIZATION

86. **(5)** The additional words do not help to make the meaning any clearer; they can easily be omitted to save words.

87. **(4)** Sentence 3 is an example of the statement made in sentence 4; therefore, it would logically follow sentence 4.

88. **(5)** The original sentence does not tie itself in with the main idea of the paragraph. By answering the reader's logical question, "They can be cited as proof *of what?*" by adding the words *further proof of the possibility of life on other planets,* the logical connection has been made.

89. **(2)** This paragraph is about the evidence that tends to support the astronomers' belief in life on other planets. Sentence 6 does not help support the main idea of the paragraph; therefore, it can safely be omitted.

90. **(1)** The use of the conjunction *although* makes the best transition from the statements of evidence to the statement that the possibility of life on other planets is only a theory.

91. **(3)** The words *upsets my stomach* express the same thought with fewer words and in the same style as the rest of the paragraph.

92. **(1)** The original sentence is not a complete sentence. By adding *I wonder* after *then,* the sentence is completed without repeating the word *question* as in choice (2).

93. **(4)** Since this sentence introduces a new situation, it would be logical to begin a new paragraph here.

94. **(3)** Since sentence 8 continues the thought stated in sentence 7, the two sentences should be connected. The use of a conjunction (*and*) is too weak to join these two thoughts; only a semicolon is strong enough to make the connection.

95. **(2)** Only this beginning ties the sentence to the main idea of the paragraph, beginning anything new.

96. **(4)** The paragraph gives some of the reasons for depression among entertainers. The last sentence introduces a discussion of depression among other types of people and should therefore begin a new paragraph.

97. **(4)** The underlined word group does not correctly introduce the comparison and contrast indicated by the rest of the sentence.

98. **(5)** No change. The paragraph includes a topic sentence and logically related supporting ideas.

99. **(1)** All the sentences provide support for a topic sentence that is missing. A general statement about superstition should either begin or conclude this paragraph.

100. **(2)** *Besides* would be correct because it adds an idea. *However* indicates a contrast.

WRITING SKILLS EVALUATION CHART

Below is a list of the general subject areas covered in the Final Writing Skills Inventory and the total number of questions in each area. The percentage of questions in each subject area reflects the format of the actual GED test.

Enter the number of questions you get right on the chart below.

Subject Area	*Question Total*	*Number Right*
Spelling	10	____
Capitalization	6	____
Punctuation	9	____
Grammar and Usage	30	____
Style and Diction	15	____
Sentence Structure	15	____
Logic and Organization	15	____

PASSING SCORE: 66 right out of 100.
YOUR SCORE: ____ right out of 100.

If you have less than a passing score on the Final Writing Skills Inventory, be sure to review the instructional and exercise material in the subject areas that gave you trouble before you take the GED test.

If you have a passing score on the Final Writing Skills Inventory, you can be confident that you will score high on the GED.